CW01572635

THE BIG BOOK OF
HOME CRAFTS:2

WITHERS, SKINNER, SAPSFORD, CAMPBELL, WILLAMS, BUCHANAN, JENKINS

APPLE

A QUINTET BOOK

Published by The Apple Press
6 Blundell Street
London N7 9BH

ISBN 1-85076-737-8

This book was designed and produced by
Quintet Publishing Limited
6 Blundell Street
London N7 9BH

Creative Director: Richard Dewing
Designers: Linda Henley, Ian Hunt, James Lawrence
Project Editor: Clare Hubbard
Photographers: Nick Bailey, Colin Bowling, Paul Forrester,
Laura Wickenden, Chas Wilder

Typeset in Great Britain by
Central Southern Typesetters, Eastbourne
Manufactured in China by
Regent Publishing Services Ltd
Printed in China by Leefung-Asco Printers Ltd

Material in this book previously appeared in:
Beadwork by Sara Withers, *Stencilling* by Jamie Sapsford
and Betsy Skinner, *Batik* by Joy Campbell, *Fabric Painting*
by Melanie Williams, *Tie-dyeing* by Celia Buchanan,
Christmas Crafts by Alison Jenkins (All *Start-a-Craft* titles)

CONTENTS

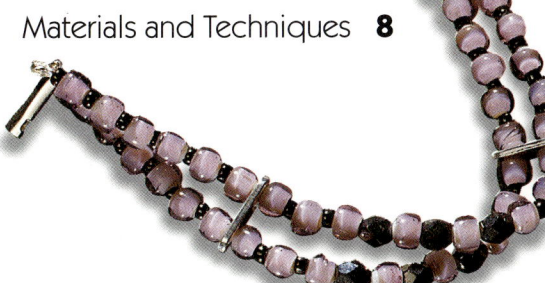

Bead work

Create unusual and attractive jewellery using
an endlessly fascinating variety of beads

INTRODUCTION

There are those who believe that beads can become an obsession - if so, it is one I can happily recommend. I have worked with beads on a full-time basis for nearly twenty years, and the pleasure I derive from their diversity and their history has increased over the years.

There are few crafts that offer such scope for creativity yet that require so few specialist tools and that do not need a special workshop. All you need are a table, good light, a few tools and some carefully selected beads and findings, and with these you can design and make really exciting pieces of jewellery. You can create something that will attract compliments every time it is worn – or even a piece that will become a family heirloom.

The projects are divided loosely between earrings, necklaces and bracelets, and within each overall group the projects become progressively more difficult. You do not, however, need to begin at the beginning and work through them. If you refer to the techniques section and the instructions for each piece you should be able to make any of them.

The projects use a wide range of techniques and materials in order to extend your skills and offer you opportunities to use your own creative talents. Even if the beads specified for each project are not available from your local supplier, you should be able to use other, similar kinds. All the findings listed for each project should be available in bead and most craft shops or by mail order.

Sizes and quantities are difficult to specify. If you are 1.6m (5ft 3in) tall and your friend is 1.7m (5ft 10in) tall, you will not both want to wear the same length of necklace. The quantities specified will allow you to lengthen the projects a little if necessary or to discard some of the smaller beads, if they become dropped or damaged, which will inevitably happen.

The important aspect of these projects is that you should use them to gain an understanding of the basic techniques and to learn how to use the different materials and then quickly begin to apply and adapt them to projects of your own.

If you do become obsessed with beads and want to know more about them, you will find several other books that outline their history and that show some of the potential. You might also want to join a local bead society so that you can share your ideas and experiences with fellow enthusiasts.

But that is for later.

Start with the projects and ideas here and remember, whatever happens, enjoy the beads you use.

MATERIALS AND TECHNIQUES

Before you start to make bead jewellery you need to learn a little about the beads that you can use. You also need to know about the tools, the findings – that is, the necklace fasteners and so on – and the different threads that are available. There is not a lot to learn, but understanding the basics will not only mean that your finished pieces look more professional but will also give you more scope for creativity.

BEADS

Beads are now easier to find and come in a wider range of materials than ever before. Most towns have a craft or haberdashery shop that sells beads, and some larger towns may even have specialist bead shops. You can also obtain a wide variety of beads by mail order, so you should easily be able to make the projects described in this book. Remember, too, that you can also use beads from old or broken necklaces, and, of course, one of the great advantages of bead jewellery is that if you are bored or dissatisfied with a piece, you can simply take it to pieces and use the components to make something quite different.

There are not many technical names for beads, but you should make a note of rocailles and bugles. Both are made of glass: rocailles are small and round, and they range in size from 11/0 (the tiniest) to 6/0 (the largest); bugles are small and tubular. They can usually be bought, by weight, in packets. Although they are often used in bead weaving, loom work and embroidery, they are useful in other designs. Most beads are sold by size, which is quoted in millimetres and which refers to the diameters, not the circumference, of the bead.

When you start to use beads you don't need to know much more about beads than whether you like the shape and colour, but as you become fascinated by them you will want to learn the names of the different kinds and understand the different materials. You will discover a world of Japanese lamp beads, Indian kiln glass beads, Ghanaian powder glass beads and many, many more. This book can introduce you to only a few of the dozens of kinds that are available.

When you buy beads in a shop, always check them for damage. Many beads are made quite roughly, so take care that the ones you are buying are perfect. Make sure that the holes are good and can be easily threaded and, of course, that the colours go well together.

FILE

SHARP SCISSORS

WIRE CUTTERS

ROUND-NOSED PLIERS

FLAT-NOSED PLIERS

TOOLS

You can do a lot with beads with only a few tools. The most essential tool is a pair of round-nosed pliers which you will use, among other things, for making loops for earrings. You need pliers with fairly short, fine points so that you can get close to your work. When you come to make necklaces and use crimps and calottes, you will need some flat-nosed pliers. Sprung round-nosed pliers are also available, and these are excellent for both earring and necklace making. Hold the pliers as shown in the photograph. If you work with beads a lot you should try out different kinds of pliers so that you know which kind you feel most comfortable with. In the projects round-nosed pliers have been specified when they are essential; otherwise the choice is yours.

You will need a pair of sharp scissors for most of the projects, and when you start to work with wire, you will need some wire cutters. The sprung wire (see page 11) responds better to heavier wire cutters, but you will be able to cut most wires with quite a light tool. When you work more extensively with wire – the Lapis and Silver Necklace on page 38, for example – you will need a file and a hammer. The file should be fine, and the hammer can be light. As you start to do knotting and beadwork you will need a selection of needles, and you will find a pair of fine-pointed, curved tweezers useful but not essential.

Finally, if you take up loom work you will need a loom. Although the metal looms are not as expensive as the wooden ones, they are not as easy to use. If you become enthusiastic about this technique it will be worth buying a wooden loom.

BEADING NEEDLES

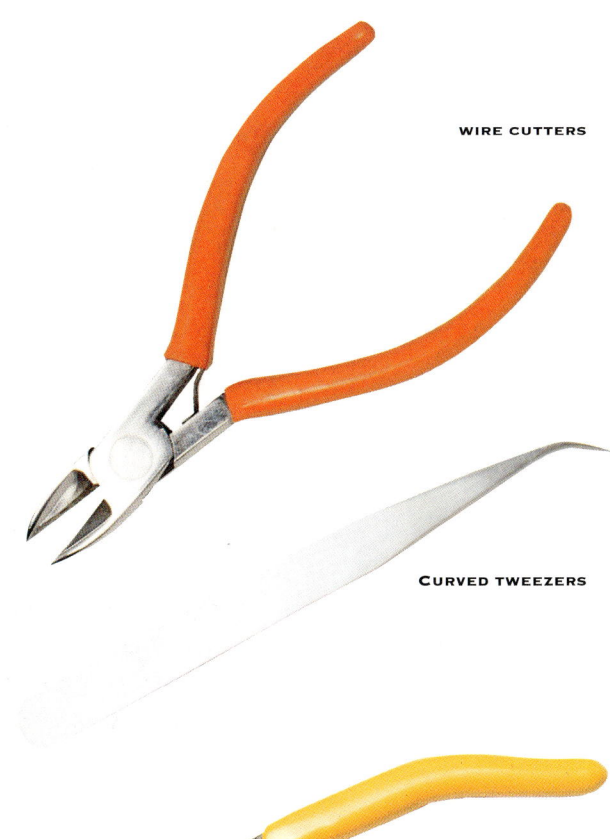

WIRE CUTTERS

CURVED TWEEZERS

SPRUNG ROUND-NOSED PLIERS

HAMMER

HOLD THE PLIERS LIKE THIS

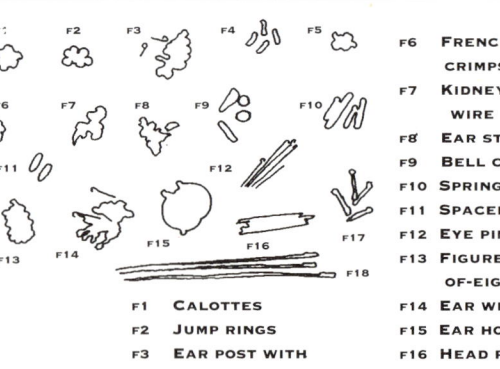

FINDINGS AND THREADS

This is an area in which you need to know some technical terms. All the findings mentioned here are available from many good craft stores, from specialist bead suppliers, and by mail order.

F1	CALOTTES
F2	JUMP RINGS
F3	EAR POST WITH HOOK
F4	BARREL CLASP
F5	LEATHER CRIMPS
F6	FRENCH CRIMPS
F7	KIDNEY EAR WIRE
F8	EAR STUDS
F9	BELL CAPS
F10	SPRING CLASP
F11	SPACER BAR
F12	EYE PIN
F13	FIGURES-OF-EIGHT
F14	EAR WIRES
F15	EAR HOOPS
F16	HEAD PINS
F17	SWIVELS
F18	HATPINS

MAKING EARRINGS

To make straight drop earrings, you will need to put the beads onto an eye pin or a head pin. Eye pins are more versatile than head pins because you can hang other beads from the loops and make longer earrings by adding two together. They are used with their own loop at the bottom of the earring to give a neat finish. If you have large, heavy beads, you can thread them onto 0.8mm or 1.2mm wire or you can use hat pin wires, but you need to clip the ends from the hat pin wires before you use them.

Hoop earrings can be made with 0.8mm wire, as shown on page 12, or from bought hoop findings.

If your ears are not pierced, you will need to use screws or clips, and it is now possible to obtain combined screw/clip findings. All of these are fitted in the same way that we have shown ear wires

being fitted. For pierced ears, you will need ear wires, and most of the earrings in the projects in this book have been made with hook or French ear wires. You can, however, also use a post with hook findings, and these are held in place with scrolls or butterflies. Another possibility is kidney wires. You will know from the earrings you have bought and worn in the past which kind of fastening you find most comfortable.

Always buy nickel-free ear wires to avoid allergic reactions. The wires used in the projects shown here are available in sterling silver, and it is well worth the additional expense. Some people can only wear gold, and you can still follow the instructions by simply using gold-colored eye pins, balls and so on, and by buying a few pairs of gold ear wires. You will soon be so adept at making your own jewelry that you will quickly be able to swap the wires from earring to earring.

MAKING NECKLACES AND BRACELETS

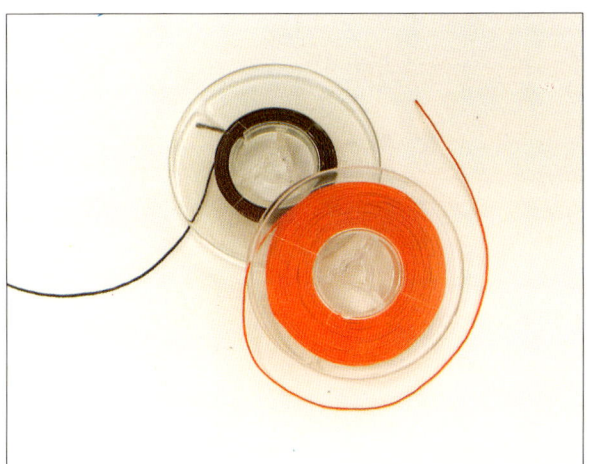

POLYESTER THREAD

When you make a necklace or bracelet you need to know about the different threads and findings that are available.

Simple necklaces and bracelets can be threaded on nylon monofilament, which is available from craft and bead shops and also from fishing equipment shops (you will need to ask for line with a breaking strain of about 6.75kg (15lb). This is best finished with French crimps because it doesn't knot well. Nylon line often shrinks eventually, which makes the necklace or bracelet rather rigid, so it is a good idea to leave about 5mm (¼in) between the last beads and the French crimps.

Tiger tail is nylon-covered steel cable, and it is, as you might expect, ideal for heavy beads. It does not

hang well with light beads, although it is suitable for short necklaces and bracelets. Use it with French crimps and take care that it does not kink as you work.

When you want a necklace that will hang beautifully or when you want to incorporate knotting (see page 31), use either polyester thread or silk thread. These can be finished with French crimps, calottes or knots. There are also some nylon threads on the market, but polyester or silk thread should meet most of your needs. Some colours of polyester thread are available in a waxed form, so you do not always need to use a needle. If you do decide to use this kind of thread with heavy beads, allow the threaded piece to hang for a few days before you finish it because the thread will stretch a little.

Silk thread is strong but delicate, and when you buy it on a card you will find a fine needle attached. The projects using silk thread have been planned to allow you to make the best possible use of your needles.

A fine, strong polyester thread is used with a beading loom.

You will also need a variety of fasteners, depending on the kind of thread you use, if you are sensitive to metals, buy clasps made of sterling silver or gold. The spring clasp, which is used in many of the projects in this book, is efficient and strong. More classic designs might call for screw clasps or bolt rings, which are used with jump rings. Multi-strand necklaces need cones or bell caps.

There are lots of other findings: little figures-of-eight for hanging; spacer bars with two, three or

NYLON MONOFILAMENT

TIGERTAIL

LEATHER THONGING

four holes, which can be used to make truly stunning chokers and bracelets; leather crimps, which are used with a hook to increase the potential of leather; various sizes of swivel, which are fun for earrings or chains; and hatpins, which are self-explanatory, but you may have to ask for the clutch on the end separately.

There are also several thicknesses of silver wire, which will be available from the best suppliers. Leather thonging can be bought on a roll or by the metre (yard). Finally, sprung wire is a new idea, which can be bought by weight.

SILK THREAD

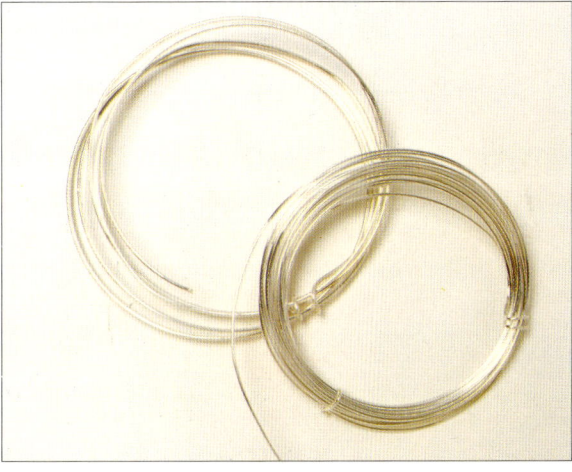

SILVER WIRES

SPRUNG WIRES

HOOP EARRINGS

You will need
◊ 0.8mm wire
◊ Black tubing (optional)
◊ 4 small glass beads
◊ 2 large glass beads
◊ 8 x 3mm silver plated balls
◊ 2 jump rings
◊ 2 ear wires

Other equipment
◊ Round former
◊ Wire cutters
◊ Round-nosed pliers

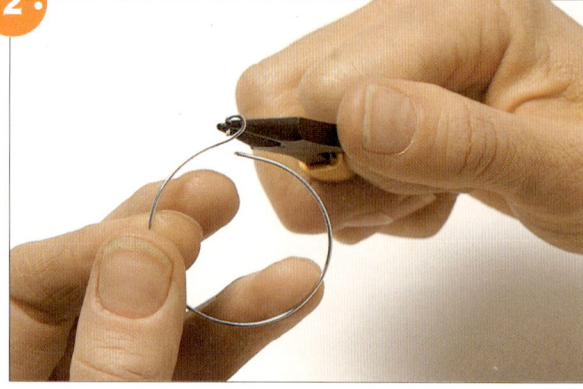

1 Form a loop around a round object, choosing a suitable size for the finished loop. We used a marker pen. Wind the wire around the former. Carefully slide the wire off the former and cut the loop so that the ends overlap by about 8mm (⅜in).

2 Roll one end of the wire around your pliers. Gently turn the loop so that it is at right angles to the hoop.

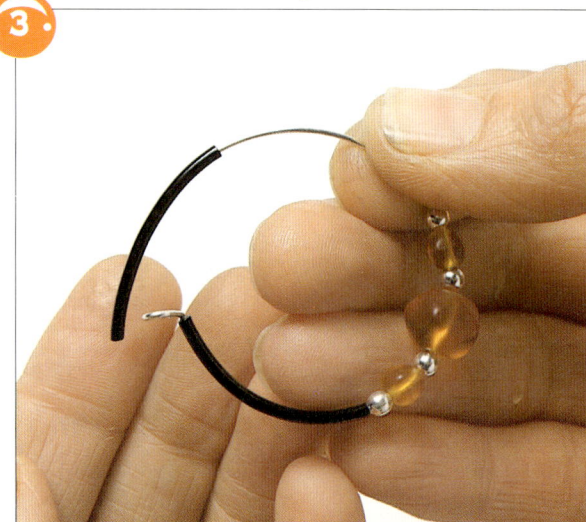

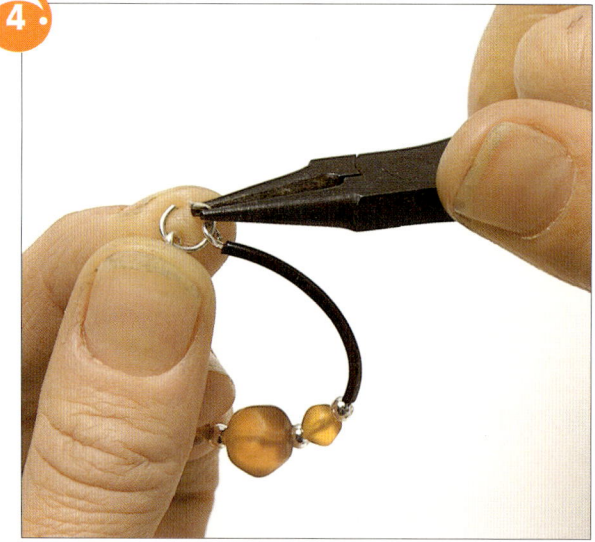

3 If you are using tubing cut it into four pieces to fit on either side of the beads; you will have to adjust the length of the tube to fit the size of the beads and the hoop. Thread on the beads. Add the second piece of tube and form another loop (see step 2).

4 Open a jump ring, slide it through the loop and close it.

5 Open the loop on an ear wire, hook it into the jump ring and close the loop.

STRAIGHT EARRINGS

You will need

◊ 2 x 50mm (2in) eyepins
◊ 2 round Peruvian beads
◊ 2 Peruvian tube beads
◊ 6 x 3mm silver plate balls
◊ 2 ear wires

Other equipment

◊ Round-nosed pliers

1 Thread the beads on the eyepins, leaving a gap of about 8mm (⅜in) at the top of the pin. Rest the eyepin on your third finger and hold the beads firmly in place with your thumb and first finger. Hold the top of the eyepin with your pliers, which should be close to the beads, and bend the eyepin towards you at an angle of 45 degrees.

2 Begin to make a loop by moving the pliers to the top of the eyepin and rolling the wire of the eyepin away from you, around the top of the pliers. If you do not complete the loop in a single movement, take out the pliers, reposition them and roll the wire again.

3 Take one of the ear wires and open the loop sideways.

4 Put the ear wire through the loop of your earring and close it again.

TIPS

• Remember that your first few loops are almost certain to be untidy, so have some spare eyepins and wire cutters to hand so that you can cut the loop off the drop and try again with a new pin.
• Always open the loops on eyepins or ear wires sideways.
• If the metal of an eyepin or ear wire feels weak, reject it and use another one.

BASIC TECHNIQUES

KNOTTING

If you are using precious or fragile beads you should put a knot between each bead to protect them – if a knotted necklace breaks, you will lose only one bead. When you rethread an old knotted necklace you will probably have to replace the knots so that your necklace does not become too short. You will need an additional 50 per cent more thread than the length of the finished necklace to make the knots. The Jasper Necklace on page 31 uses knots.

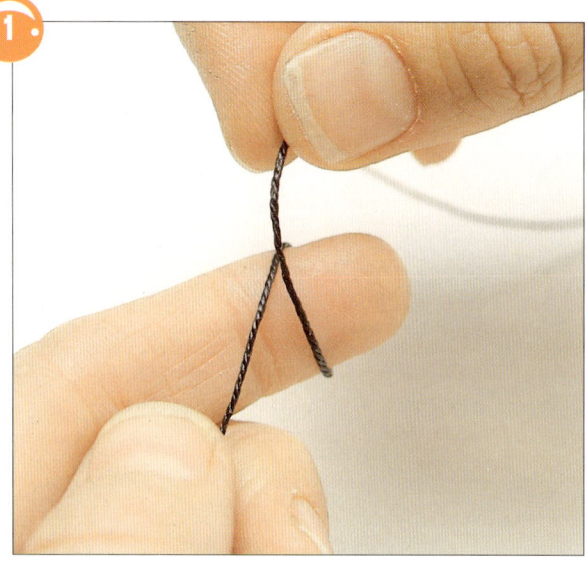

1 Start to make the knot around your finger.

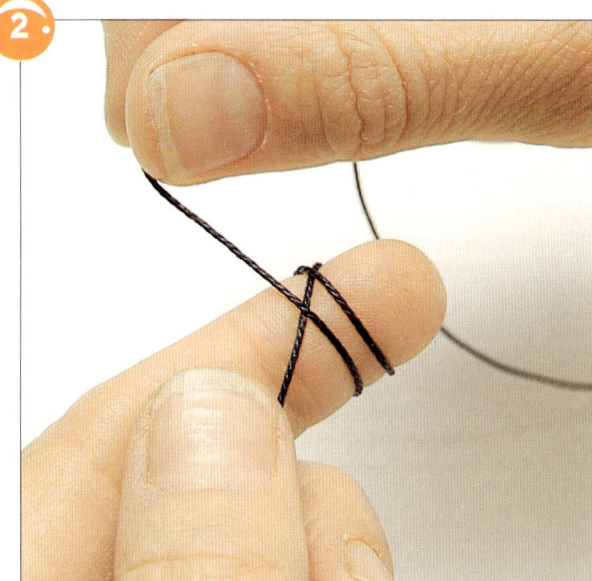

2 Make it a double knot and pull the thread through both loops.

3 Before you tighten the knot, place the needle in the knot so that you can control it.

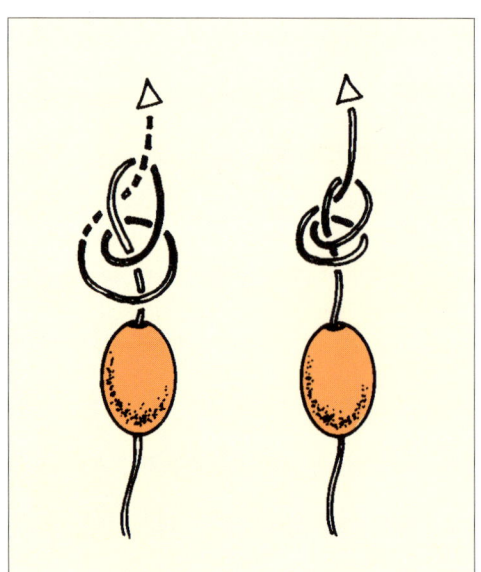

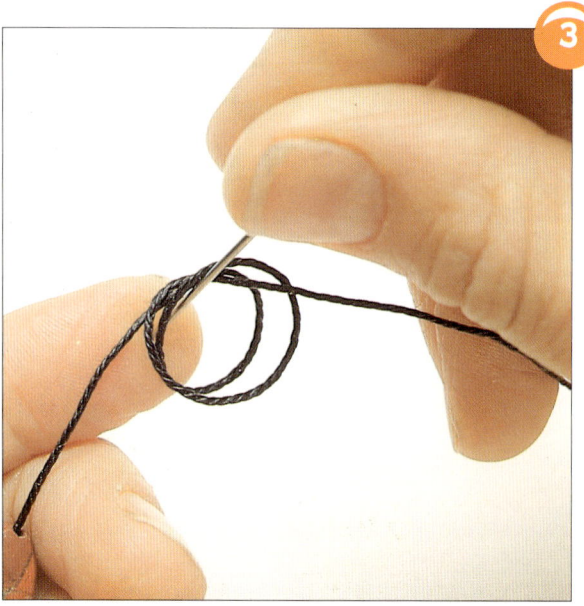

FROSTED NECKLACE

You will need
◊ Nylon monofilament or tiger tail
◊ 4 French crimps
◊ 1 fastener
◊ 8 x 18mm frosted pink beads
◊ 7 x 18mm frosted green beads
◊ 10 x 18mm frosted blue cones
◊ 6 x 15mm frosted blue cones
◊ 16 x 3mm silver plated balls

Other equipment
◊ Scissors
◊ Round- or flat-nosed pliers

4 Thread on the beads in your chosen pattern.

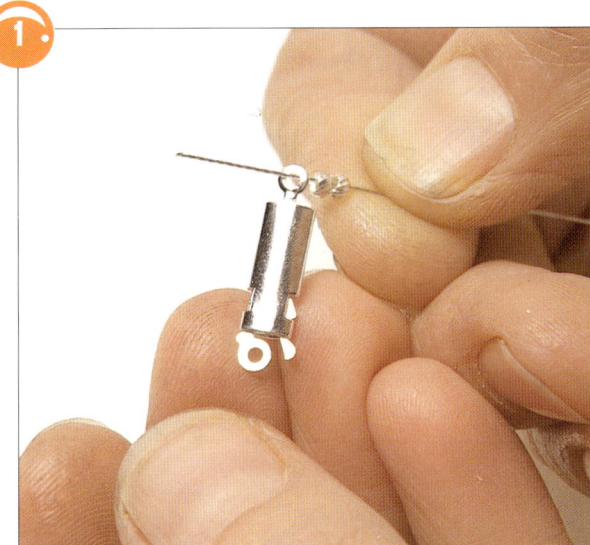

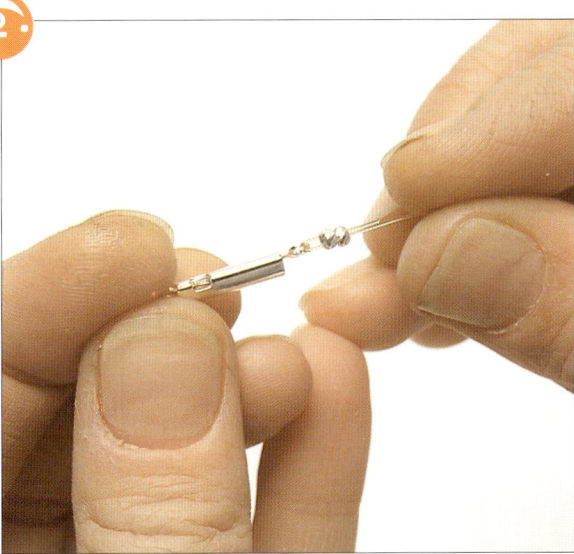

1 Cut a length of line about 55cm (21⅛in) long. Put two French crimps at one end of the line and thread through one end of the fastener.

2 Bring the line back through the crimps and make a neat loop, which should be small and tidy but not too tight against the fastener.

3 Squeeze the crimps with your pliers, making sure that they are tight but not so tight that they damage the line.

5 When you reach the other end, thread on the other two crimps. Thread the line through the fastener and loop it back through the crimps.

6 Squeeze the crimps firmly with your pliers and trim any loose ends with the scissors.

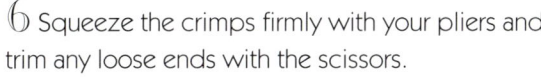

STARS AND MOONS

This delicate necklace and earring set uses crimps and gives an opportunity to practise your basic earring-making techniques and to do a little wirework.

You will need

◊ 2 x 38mm (1⅛in) eyepins
◊ 4 x 25mm (1in) eyepins
◊ 7 stars
◊ 6 moons
◊ 30 small black glass beads
◊ 50 x 3mm silver plated balls
◊ 2 earring hoops of 0.8mm silver plated wire and jump rings or hoop findings
◊ 2 ear wires
◊ 70 silver plated 6mm Heishi tubing
◊ French crimps
◊ Fastener
◊ 7 figure-of-eight findings
◊ Tiger tail

Other equipment

◊ Round- or flat-nosed pliers
◊ Wire cutters
◊ Scissors

TIP

• Have some spare eyepins close to hand in case you overwork the metal as you open and close the loops. You will be able to feel with your pliers if the metal becomes weak.

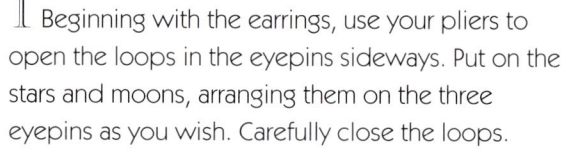

1 Beginning with the earrings, use your pliers to open the loops in the eyepins sideways. Put on the stars and moons, arranging them on the three eyepins as you wish. Carefully close the loops.

2 Thread the silver balls and black beads on the eyepins and roll the top by bending the top 8mm (⅜in) of the pin towards you to an angle of about 45 degrees. Move your pliers to the top and roll the wire around your pliers, away from you. If the loop is not quite closed, use your pliers to adjust it until there is no gap.

3 If you are using a ready-made hoop finding check that one side is firmly closed and open the other side, which will slide out from the hanger at the top of the hoop. Thread the beads and eyepins on to the hoop, beginning with a silver ball and a black bead. Remember that the loops in the tops of the eyepins should face in the same direction and there should be a black bead between each one.

4 Slide the end of the hoop back into the hanger and use your pliers to press the metal of the hanger together to trap the end of the hoop. You will need to press quite hard to secure the hoop firmly.

5 Use your pliers to open the loop on the ear wire sideways. Insert it in the top of the hanger and close the ear wire, making sure that the point of the ear wire and rough side of the hanger face in the same direction.

6 Begin the necklace by attaching the moon and stars to the figure-of-eight findings so that they hang flat. Open one loop of the figure-of-eight sideways, put on a moon or a star and close the loop again with pliers.

7 Cut a piece of tiger tail to the length you want your necklace, adding an extra 2cm (about ¾in) at each end for the crimping. Put two crimps on one end of the tiger tail, taking care not to kink the tiger tail as you work. Thread the tiger tail through the fastener and back through the crimps. Squeeze the crimps tightly with the base of round-nosed pliers or with the tip of flat-nosed pliers. Begin to thread on the silver tubing and work to the centre of the design. Thread on the stars and moons on their findings. When you have finished the central pattern, finish off with silver tubing to match the first half.

8 Check that the pattern is symmetrical, then put on two more crimps and thread the tiger tail through the other end of the fastener. Take the tiger tail back through the crimps, check the spacing to make sure that the beads are not too tight but that there are no gaps. Squeeze the crimps and trim off the loose ends.

TIP

• If you cannot obtain hoop findings, make a hoop as shown in the techniques section (page 12).

VENETIAN-STYLE GLASS NECKLACE

This dramatic necklace and glamorous matching hatpin are made from lovely Indian beads, which are made in the same way as old Venetian beads, and Thai silver beads. These are simple pieces to make but will give you some ideas for designs of your own.

You will need
◊ Tiger tail
◊ 40 tiny blue beads size 7/0
◊ 12 ornate drop beads
◊ 8 ornate round beads
◊ 4 small Thai silver beads
◊ 1 large Thai silver bead
◊ 50 x 5mm blue glass beads
◊ 50 x 6mm turquoise beads
◊ French crimps
◊ Fastener
◊ Hatpin with clutch

Other equipment
◊ Scissors
◊ Round- or flat-nosed pliers
◊ Clear, all-purpose adhesive

1 Cut a length of tiger tail, allowing an extra 3cm (1¼in) at each end. Thread on a tiny blue bead and slide it to the centre of the tiger tail. With both ends together, thread on a drop bead. Still using two threads together, thread the hanging group of beads, ending with the large Thai silver bead.

2 Separate the two threads and work on one side at a time. Thread on a tiny blue bead and continue as follows: turquoise round bead, tiny blue bead, ornate drop, 5mm blue, turquoise round bead, 5mm blue, ornate round, 5mm blue, turquoise round bead, 5mm blue bead, ornate drop (upside down), tiny blue bead, turquoise round bead, tiny blue bead, small Thai silver bead.

3 This pattern is used one and a half times on each side of the necklace. Take care to push the beads down towards the centre as you thread them on. Make sure that both sides are symmetrical.

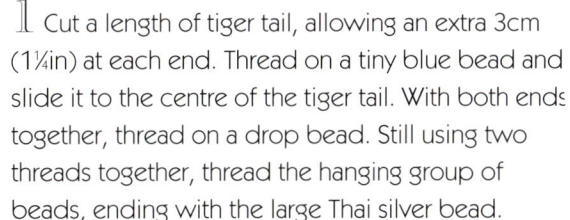

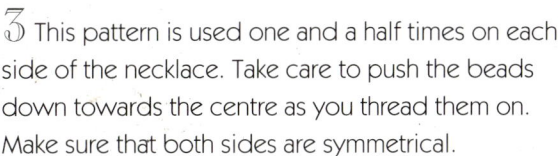

TIP
• Cut a good length of tiger tail but take care that it does not kink as you work.

4 Thread on small blue and turquoise beads, which will sit comfortably at the back of your neck, and thread on two crimps and one side of the fastener. Loop the tiger tail back through the crimps and squeeze them tightly with your pliers.

5 Check again that the design is symmetrical and finish off at the end. Neatly trim off the tails of thread.

6 Take the clutch off the end of the hatpin and thread on a tiny bead, making sure that the head of the pin cannot go through it. Thread on the pattern of beads. When you are happy with the arrangement, put a crimp beneath them and squeeze it firmly.

7 For extra security, put a spot of glue at the end. Try to get it on the end bead only because the adhesive will spoil the beads.

A CHAIN OF FISHES

Ceramic fish and painted fish beads from Peru swim along on a chain of swivels. Simple earring-making techniques have been built up to make this chain and matching earrings.

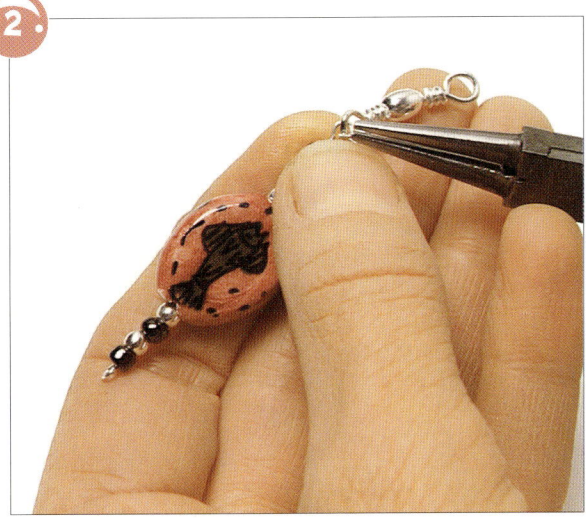

1 Start with a fish bead, an eyepin and some tiny beads and balls. Thread on the main bead with the small beads on either side. Roll the top of the eyepin by bending the wire towards you until it is at an angle of 45 degrees. Move the pliers to the top and roll the wire around the pliers to make a neat loop.

2 Carefully open the loop to the side, insert a swivel and close the loop.

You will need
◊ 6 fish beads
◊ 25 x 50mm (2in) eyepins
◊ 70 tiny grey beads, size 8/0
◊ 70 x 3mm silver plated balls
◊ 17 x 18mm (¾in) swivels
◊ 8 striped ceramic beads
◊ 4 ceramic fish
◊ 2 ear wires
◊ Fastener or extra swivel

Other equipment
◊ Round-nosed pliers

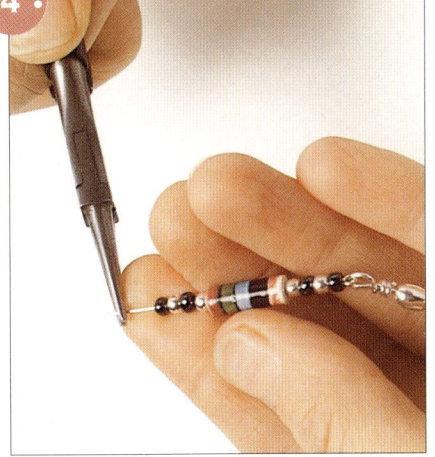

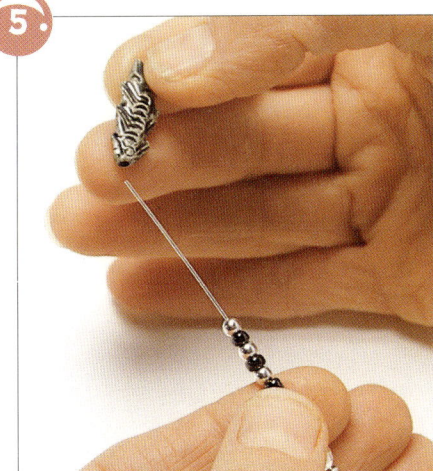

TIP
• If any of the eyepins feel weak, reject them and use a new one.

3 Add another eyepin to the swivel by opening the bottom loop of the eyepin and hooking it through the swivel. Close the loop neatly.

4 Thread a striped bead onto the eyepin with some small beads on either side and roll the top.

5 Continue to build up the chain in the same way, working alternately at each side of the first fish bead to make sure the design is symmetrical.

6 The chain is long enough to go over your head, but if you want to use a fastener, add it instead to one of the swivels between one of the fish bead and striped bead sections. Hook it between two loops in the same way as the other pieces.

7 Make the earrings in the same way as the chain, using a painted fish bead and a swivel. Open the loops of the ear wires and hang the swivels from them. Close the ear wires neatly.

CHINA BLUE NECKLACE

This project demonstrates how very simple techniques can produce very sumptuous results. By threading a variety of Chinese porcelain beads and different glass beads and by using basic crimping techniques, you can make a really stunning necklace.

You will need

◊ Black or blue polyester thread
◊ 10 round Chinese beads
◊ 1 triangle bead
◊ 10 oblong Chinese beads
◊ 16 enamelled bead caps
◊ 8 x 8mm round beads
◊ 80 blue glass beads
◊ 100 green frosted beads
◊ 200 small black beads
◊ 20 French crimps
◊ 2 cones
◊ Fastener

Other equipment

◊ Scissors
◊ Round- or flat-nosed pliers

1 Cut four lengths of thread, each about 50cm (20in) long, and lay them out. Thread beads on to each one at the same time, working to achieve a pleasing balance among the different strands. Aim to have the smaller beads towards the outside of the pattern and leave about 8cm (3¼in) of thread at each side of all the threads. The enamelled bead caps should be threaded either side of the plain 8mm round beads to give the extra richness.

2 When you are happy with the pattern of the strands, hold each strand carefully at each end to check that it hangs well. Take this opportunity to reposition any beads that do not look right. At this stage you should still have some of each of the beads left.

3 Make a small loop at one end of a strand, slide a crimp on it and squeeze the crimp with your pliers. Move the beads towards this end, make a loop, add a crimp at the other end and squeeze the crimp. Repeat with the other strands and trim off all loose ends.

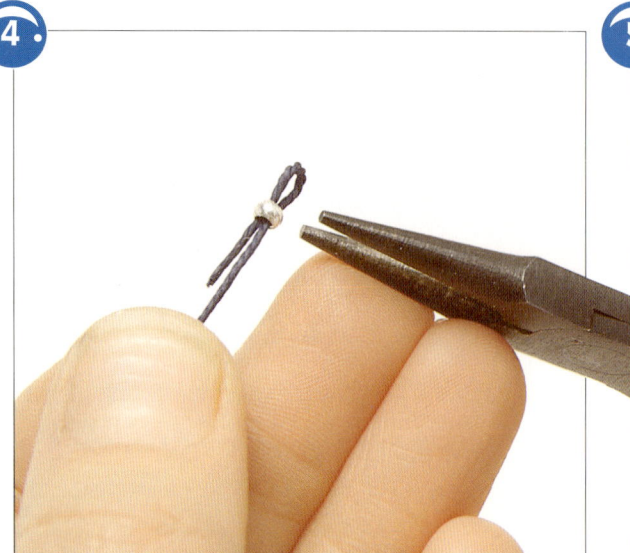

4 Cut two more lengths of thread, each about 20cm (8in) long, and make a loop at one end of each.

5 Take the short pieces of thread through the loops at the end of the beaded strands. Pass the threads back into their own end loops.

6 Thread a cone onto each short piece so that the ends of the beaded strands are neatly hidden.

7 Thread beads onto the two short ends; you can make these symmetrical or work a slightly random pattern. When you are happy with the length of the necklace, put two crimps on one end of one of the threads and take the end through a loop in the fastener and then back through the crimps.

8 Squeeze the crimps with your pliers and check that they are tight. Repeat this at the other side with the other end of the fastener before trimming off all loose ends.

CLAY AND TILE BEAD NECKLACE

This necklace is more complicated to make, but if you work through the steps carefully, you will make a lovely thick cluster of rope and tassels.

You will need
◊ White polyester thread
◊ 300 white tile beads
◊ 400 tiny brown beads
◊ 1 clay ring
◊ 2 large round clay beads
◊ 10 clay discs
◊ French crimps
◊ Wire
◊ 2 bell caps
◊ Fastener

Other equipment
◊ Glue
◊ Round- or flat-nosed pliers
◊ Wire cutters
◊ Clear, all-purpose adhesive

1 Cut four lengths of thread, each about 80cm (32in) long, and thread 10 white tiles and 11 small brown beads alternately on the centre of each. Thread two of these into each side of the clay ring so that four lengths emerge from both sides.

2 Put these four threads through a large clay bead on either side of the central ring.

3 Working on one side, thread on five white tiles and six small brown beads alternately on each of the threads and put all four threads through a clay disc.

4 Work four more sections and push all the beads back towards the central ring. Pick up five small brown beads on each thread and push them back.

5 Make a small, neat loop at the end of each thread and put a crimp on it. When the loops are neat and even on each thread, squeeze the crimps.

6 Repeat the pattern on the other side, making the patterns symmetrical and pushing the beads back towards the centre before crimping the loops at the ends of each thread.

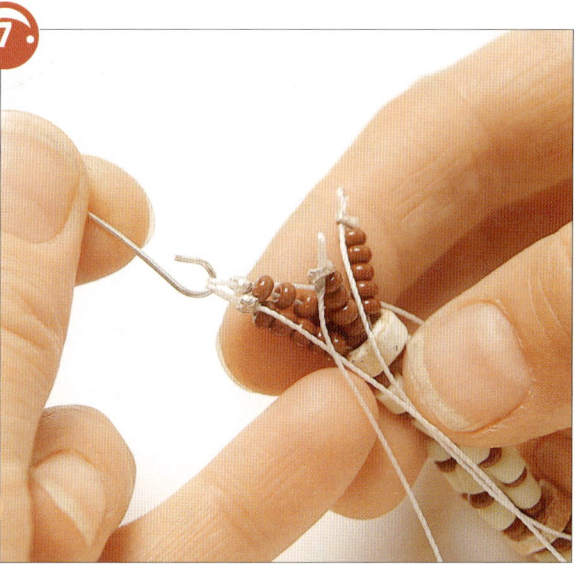

7 Use wire cutters to cut a small length of wire. Roll the wire around the round-nosed pliers to make a loop. Put the loops on the ends of the threads through this and close it neatly.

8 Trim all the ends of thread.

9 Put the bell cap on the wire. Clip the wire, leaving just sufficient to make a neat loop.

10 Make the loop with your pliers, open it sideways to hook on the fastener and close the loop neatly. Repeat to match at the other side.

11 Cut three pieces of thread, each about 18cm (7in) long, and make a firm knot at one end of each length, adding a spot of adhesive to the knot. Leave the glue to dry and thread on some small brown beads and white tile beads. You can make the threads the same or slightly different lengths if you prefer.

12 As each short length is half-threaded, work it through the clay ring, then add the beads to the other end of the thread.

13 Make a knot at the loose end of each length, placing a needle in the knot so that you can slide it back towards the beads. Make sure the beads are close together but not so tight that they are rigid. When you are happy with the knot, put a spot of adhesive on the knot, avoiding the beads if possible, and trim the ends of the tassels.

MONOCHROME CHOKER

Beads similar to those in the centre of this choker have been made for over a century for pilgrims to Mecca.

This project combines them with black and white beads to introduce one of the first stages of bead weaving.

1 Unwrap a reasonable amount of black silk from both cards and straighten the needles so that they are ready for use.

2 Take both threads through a white bead, separate the threads and pick up a black bead on each. Take both threads through another white bead before picking up a black bead on each thread. Repeat this pattern.

You will need
◊ 2 cards of black silk with attached needles
◊ 35 white glass beads
◊ 70 black glass beads
◊ 5 mosque beads
◊ White silk
◊ 2 black beads with large holes

Other equipment
◊ Scissors
◊ Masking tape (optional)

3 Keep pulling the beads back towards the cards and release more silk as you work.

4 As you reach the centre of the choker, replace alternate white beads with the mosque beads, taking the thread through from each side of the bead in the same way. Continue to pull the choker back towards the cards. You should aim to have about 30cm (12in) of thread at each end of the choker.

5 When the beads are threaded and you are sure they are firmly and correctly placed, cut a 120cm (4ft) length of white silk for each end. Using it double, tie one onto one end of the choker with the black silks.

6 Working with the black threads together, plait the three double strands together. You might find it easier to plait the threads if you use masking tape to hold the choker to your working surface.

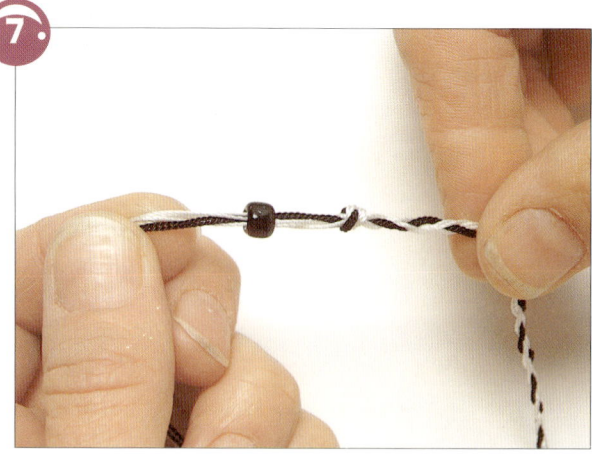

7 About 8cm (3¼in) from the end of the silk threads, knot them with a simple knot. Thread on one of the beads with a large hole.

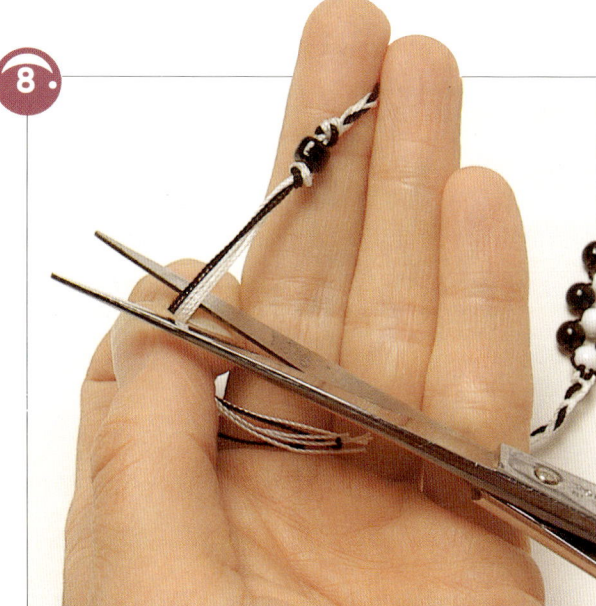

8 Make another simple knot close to this bead and trim the ends of the silks neatly. Finish the other end of the choker in the same way and wear it tied around your neck, with the ends hanging attractively down the back.

JASPER NECKLACE

These chunky semi-precious beads are knotted onto thick thread to create an ethnic look.
Making this necklace will allow you to master the knotting technique that can be used with
different kinds of beads to give different effects.

1 Cut a length of thread that is almost double the length that you want the necklace to be. You need extra thread to knot between the beads, plus some extra for knotting near the fastener. Make a single knot about 10cm (4in) from one end and place your needle through it. Tighten the knot but leave the needle in place.

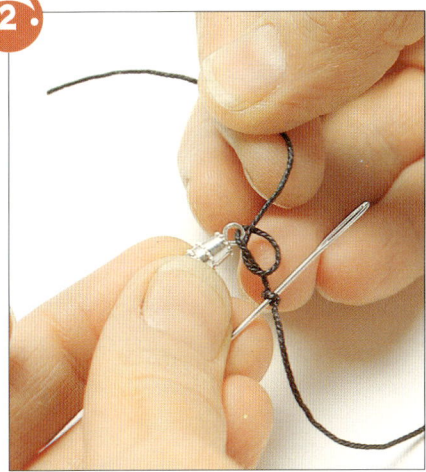

2 Put the fastener on, tying it with a single knot about 2cm (¾in) from the first knot.

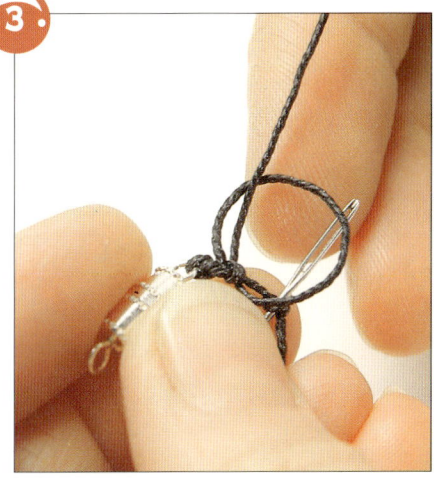

3 Make a series of neat single knots to fill the gap between the two original knots. Make a loop around the main thread, bring the short end through and tighten it.

You will need
◊ Polyester thread, silk or similar thread
◊ About 20 20mm jasper beads
◊ Fastener

Other equipment
◊ Scissors
◊ Needle
◊ Clear, all-purpose adhesive
◊ Curved, fine-pointed tweezers (optional)

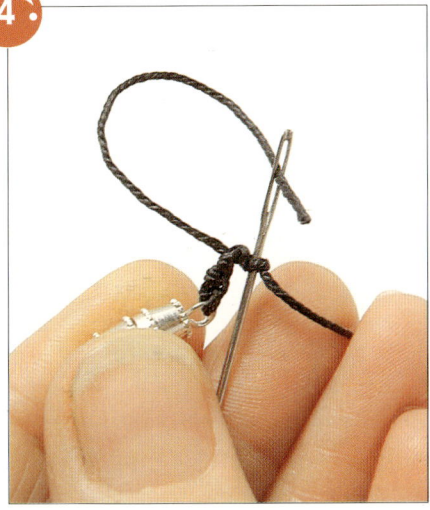

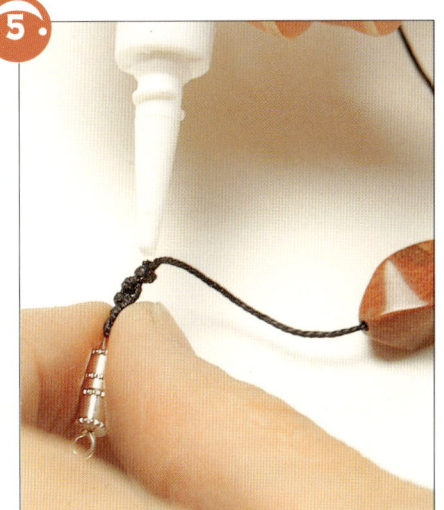

4 When you reach the first knot and needle, thread the short end through the needle and draw it through the original knot. This will make the end secure.

5 Thread on the first bead. If you can, push the short end through it to neaten the end. If you cannot, trim the short end and put a spot of adhesive on the short end to hold it. Wait until the adhesive is dry before pushing the bead against the knot.

6 Make a double knot after the bead when it is in place and put the point of a needle into the knot. Use the needle to guide the knot, pulling the thread gently and carefully so that the knot lies close to the bead. Pull the thread as you remove the needle so that the knot continues to tighten against the bead.

7 Keep on adding beads, making a double knot between each one. You are certain to make some knots that do not lie as neatly against the beads as you would like, but you can unpick the knots with fine tweezers, although you must take care not to damage the thread.

8 When the necklace is the correct length, make a simple knot close to the last bead and leave a needle through it. Take the end of the thread through the fastener, again leaving a gap of about 2cm (¾in). Make single knots next to the fastener to match the first side.

9 Take the short end through the needle and draw it through the knot that is next to the last bead. When the knots are neat and tight, take the short end of thread through the last bead if you can. Alternatively, cut it neatly and add a spot of adhesive, taking care not to get glue on the beads.

AFRICAN CHOKER

This choker uses powder glass beads from Ghana and old Czech beads, which were made mainly for the African market. The project involves a macramé technique, which is an attractive and useful way to use threads to finish necklaces and chokers.

1 Cut the thread in five lengths, four about 1m (3ft 3in) long and one 50cm (20in) long. Use the four longer threads to make the central patterns.

You will need
◊ 31 powder glass beads
◊ 120 brown Czech beads
◊ 2 four-hole spacer bars
◊ 4.5m (15ft) black polyester thread

Other equipment
◊ Scissors
◊ Needle
◊ Clear, all-purpose adhesive

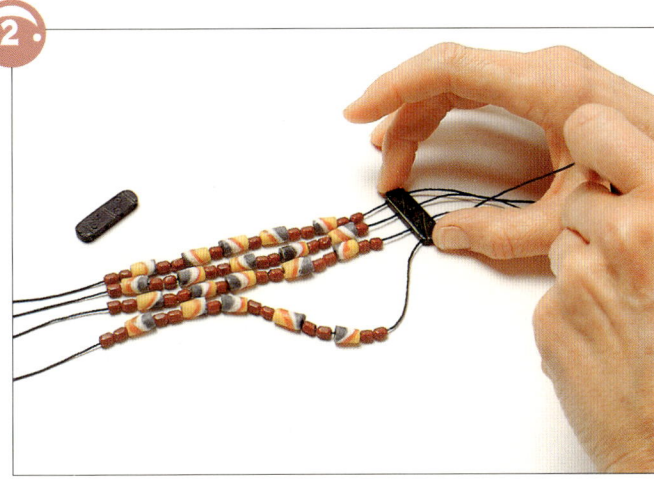

2 Thread a spacer bar on each side, then continue to pick up the beads on the four threads in pattern.

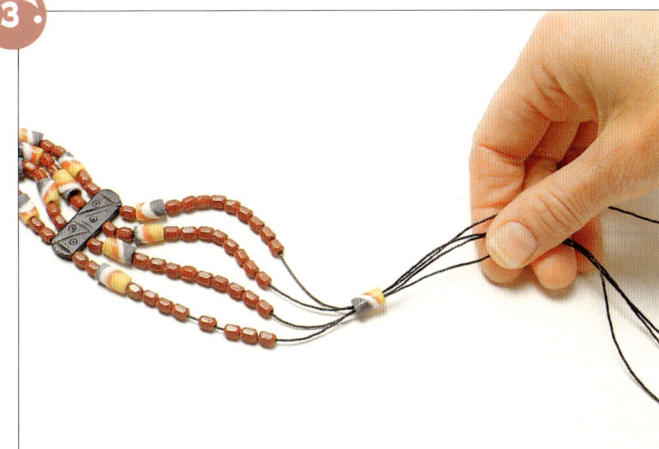

3 Use all the beads but one, which is used as a fastener, and finish off by working the four threads through a powder glass bead at each end. Loosely knot one side and trim the ends level but do not cut them short.

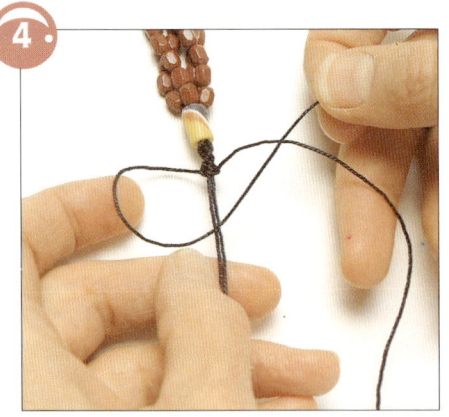

4 Make a macramé braid with the lengths of thread by keeping two threads straight in the centre and by bringing the left-hand thread under these centre threads and over the right-hand thread.

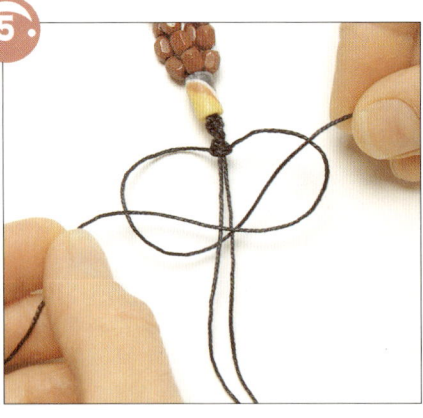

5 Take the right-hand thread over the centre threads and under the original left-hand thread.

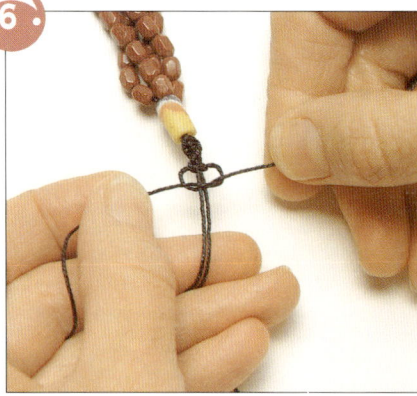

6 Pull the ends evenly from both sides and, at the same time, pull down the centre threads to create a firm, even braid. Continue to braid the threads in this way until the choker is about 3cm (1¼in) shorter than the length you want.

7 Attach the short length of thread cut in step 1 to the centre threads.

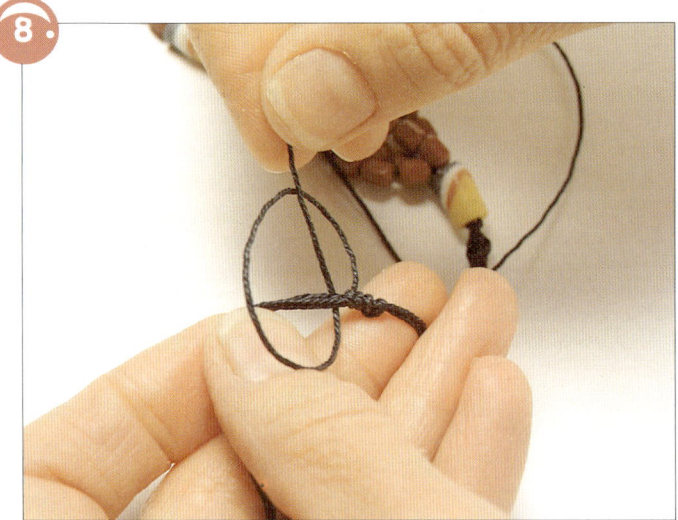

8 Use the thread to bind the centre threads to form a button loop. Take the thread over the centre threads, bring it back through its own loop and pull tightly. Continue until you have bound 2cm (¾in) of the centre threads.

9 Form the bound length into a loop and arrange all the loose ends so that they lie towards the choker. There should be a gap between the button loop and the macramé work. Return to the macramé threads and continue to work over all the loose ends by the original braiding method (steps 4, 5 and 6). Pull the threads tight as you work towards the button loop to keep the braid even and secure.

10 Check that the powder glass bead will go sideways through the loop, and pull the braid tight. Trim all loose ends close to the braid.

11 Thread the macramé ends on a needle and weave them into the braid to finish securely.

12.

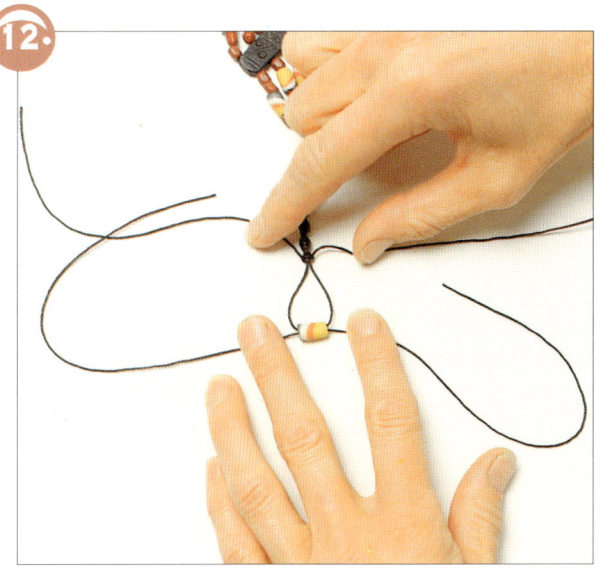

13.

14.

12 Undo the loose knot at the other end and push all the beads towards the other end before you start to make a braid. Use the macramé technique with the four lengths of thread, stopping about 2cm (¾in) from the finished length. Pick up the powder glass bead by threading the two central threads through the bead from opposite sides.

13 Turn these ends back towards the choker and continue with the macramé technique working firmly over these ends. When you reach the powder glass bead, pull the threads tightly together.

14 Finish off in the same way as at the other end, trimming the loose ends neatly and running the working threads back through the braid with a needle.

SPECIAL BEADS AND LEATHER

This is a good way of using "collectable" beads — some beads you might have picked up when you were on holiday abroad, for example, or from an antique shop or bead fair. If you cannot find beads exactly like the ones listed here, look out for something similar.

You will need
◊ 1 Pumtek bead from Mizoram
◊ 2 Venetian millefiori beads
◊ 2 old Turkish beads
◊ 2 brass beads from Mali
◊ 6 Indian matt glass beads
◊ Leather thonging
◊ Leather crimps
◊ 1.2mm silver plated wire

Other equipment
◊ Round-nosed pliers
◊ Wire cutters
◊ File

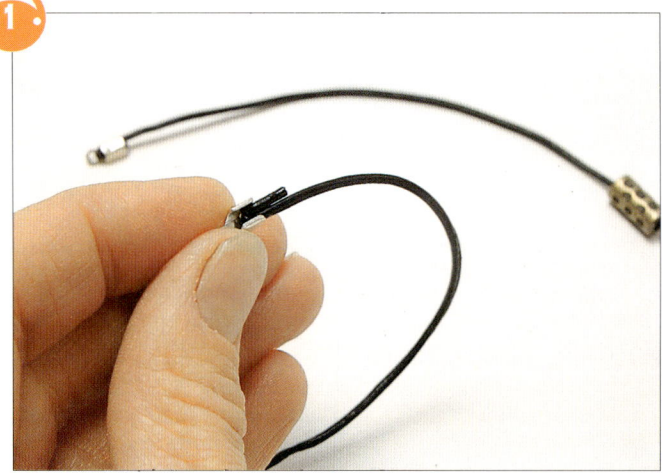

1 Arrange the beads on a length of thonging. Fold one end, and put the leather in a leather crimp. If you are using fairly thick leather, you will not need to fold it.

2 Use pliers to press down one side of the crimp. Then press down the other side over the first so that the leather is held firmly in the crimp.

3 If you cannot buy a hook for the crimps, make one by cutting about 3cm (1¼in) of wire.

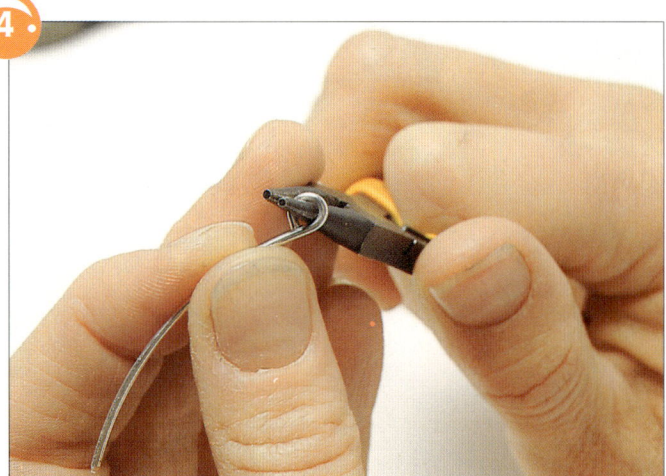

4 Hold the end of the wire with your pliers and use your thumb and first finger to roll the wire into a small loop.

5 Use the curve in the wire and bend it around the wider part of the pliers.

6 When you have made a neat hook, bend the point a little and clip the remaining wire with wire cutters.

7 File the end smooth.

8 Open the loop on the hook sideways and insert one of the leather crimps. Close the loop. The hook will go through the leather crimp on the other end when you wear the necklace.

LAPIS AND SILVER NECKLACE

This is a stylized, somewhat abstract piece, which will develop your wire working skills and encourage you to use more tools.

You will need

◊ 6 coral glass beads
◊ 6 black glass beads
◊ 6 old silver beads
◊ 1 antique spotted bead
◊ 1 large lapis bead
◊ 4 lapis shapes
◊ 0.8mm silver plated wire
◊ 1.2mm silver plated wire
◊ Leather thonging
◊ Leather crimps

Other equipment

◊ Round-nosed pliers
◊ Wire cutters
◊ File
◊ Hammer

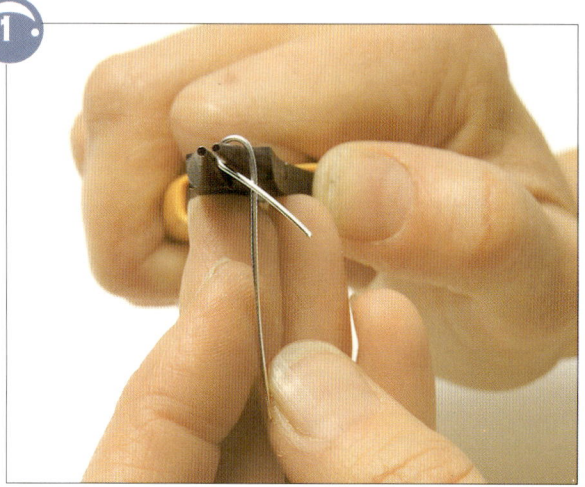

1 Wire the lapis shapes so that they will hang from the necklace. Some of the shapes that are available have holes running from top to bottom, and if you have this kind, cut a piece of 0.8mm wire and make a loop with a long end.

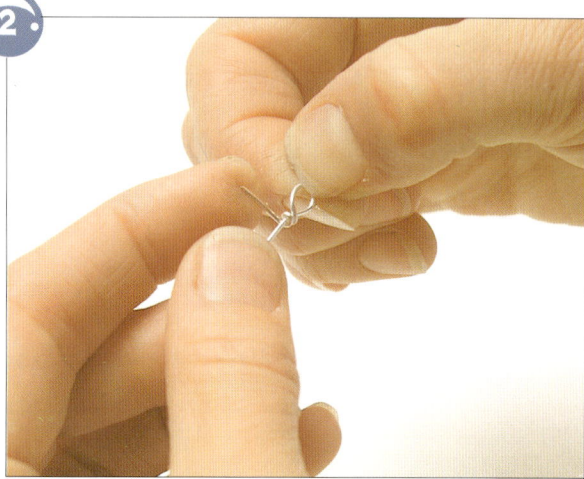

2 Use your fingers to wrap this end around the bottom of the loop.

3 Make some neat coils beneath the loop, clip the end of the wire and use pliers to flatten the end of the wire under the bottom of the coils.

4 Pick up the lapis, trim the wire and use pliers to make a neat loop under the shape to hold it securely.

5 If the lapis shapes you have are those with a hole running from side to side, make a loop in the wire and thread it through the shape, curving the wire as you do so. Leave a gap between the loop and the lapis shape.

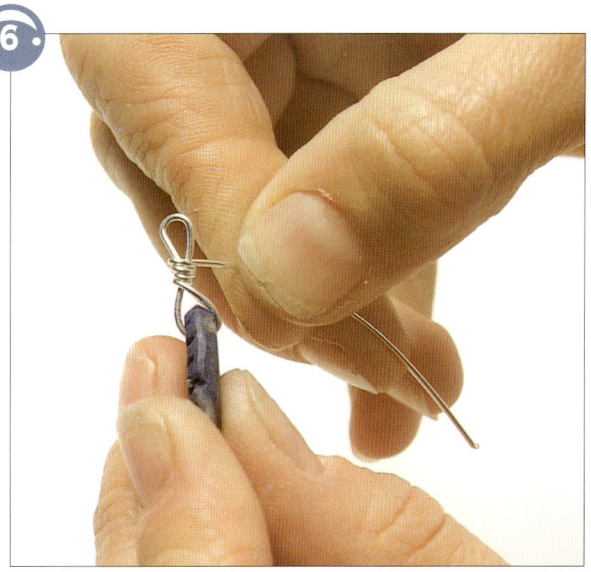

6 Use your finger and thumb to bend the wire firmly around the base of the loop a few times. Clip off the end of the wire and use pliers to flatten it under the coils.

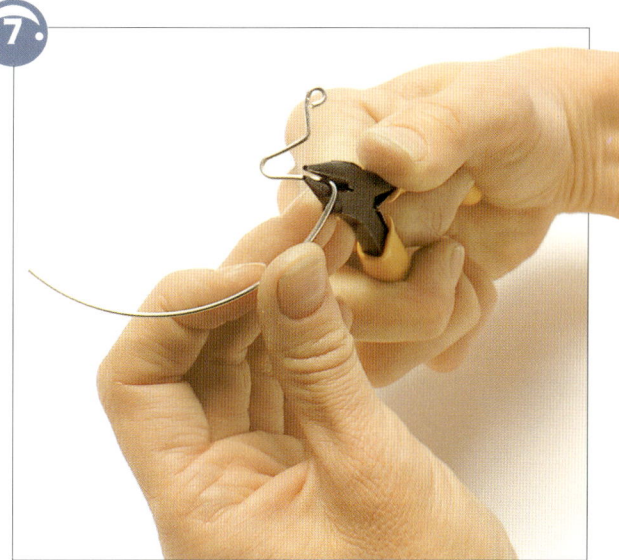

7 Make the abstract wire pieces from pieces of thicker gauge wire about 20cm (8in) long. Roll the bottom end of the wire then form it into interesting shapes by curving it from side to side against your pliers.

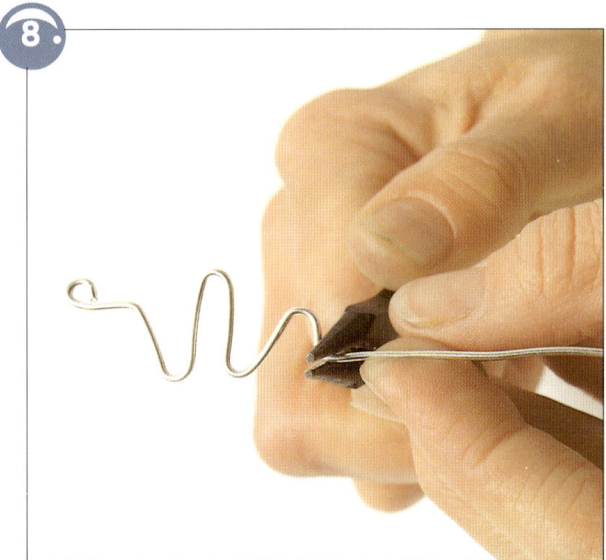

8 Continue to work until you are happy with the zigzag shape. You will need three of these shapes in all, but they need not be identical.

9 To make the necklace even more interesting, you can hammer the silver wire flat. This roughens the surface and allows you to glimpse the brass beneath the silver plating.

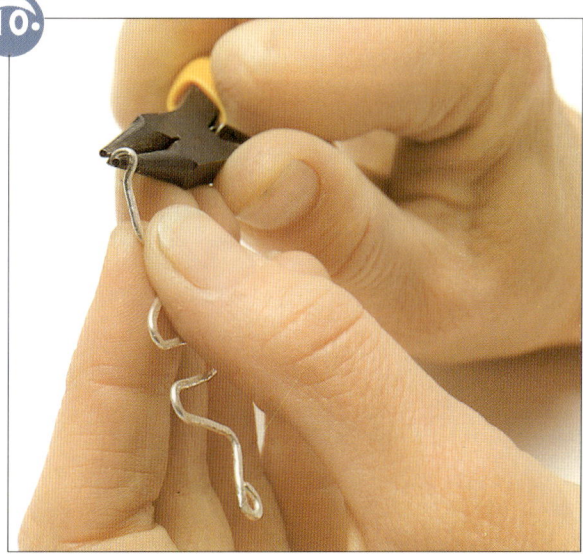

10 Roll the tops of the finished zigzag shapes so that they can be threaded.

11 Thread the pieces onto the leather. These pieces look most effective if the arrangement is asymmetric.

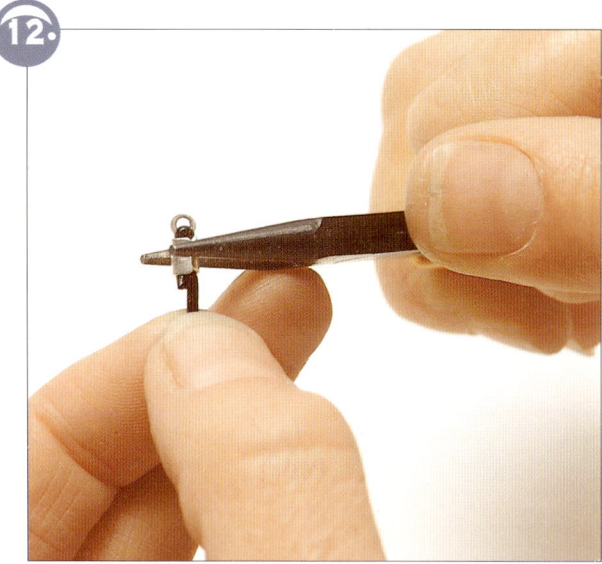

12 Put leather crimps on the ends and make a hook to fasten the necklace as described in steps 3–8 of the previous project.

SPRUNG WIRE BRACELET

This and the following project illustrate two different ideas for bracelets.

Sprung wire is easy to use, but you do need strong hands.

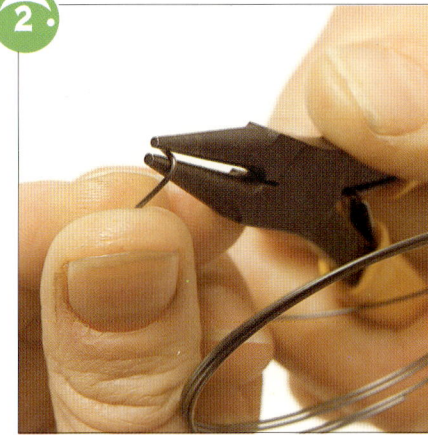

1 You can sometimes buy cut lengths of sprung wire or you can cut the necessary amount from a longer roll. You will need to press hard to do this.

2 Use pliers to roll a loop at one end. This is quite hard to do, and you should keep moving your wire and making little turns while you hold the wire with your other hand.

3 Thread on the beads. The pattern can be random, but distribute the larger beads evenly among the smaller ones. You will need to unroll the wire from time to time so that the beads can slide down.

You will need
◊ 3 loops of sprung wire, approximately 60cm (24in)
◊ 6 small Peruvian beads
◊ 33 frosted green beads
◊ 15 turquoise and green round glass beads
◊ 65 tiny black glass beads

Other equipment
◊ Wire cutters
◊ Strong round-nosed pliers

4 Leave about 1cm (⅛in) at the end of the wire and roll the end with your pliers.

TWO-STRAND BRACELET

Although it requires patience to make, the finished bracelet is extremely pretty.

You will need

◊ Tiger tail or nylon monofilament
◊ French crimps
◊ 50 pink glass beads
◊ 50 tiny grey glass beads
◊ 6 grey faceted beads
◊ 2 two-hole spacer bars
◊ 2 split rings or jump rings
◊ Fastener

Other equipment

◊ Scissors
◊ Round- or flat-nosed pliers

1 Cut two lengths of tiger tail or monofilament to fit around your wrist, but be generous or the work will become fiddly and time consuming. Allow an extra 6cm (2⅜in) on each strand. Put two crimps near the end of one strand and loop the tiger tail back through them. Squeeze the crimps with your pliers. Pick up the first beads and take the thread through the top of the spacer bar.

2 Continue working on this strand, picking up the beads in pattern for the central section before threading on the second spacer bar. When the strand is symmetrical, put on two more crimps, make another neat loop to match the first and squeeze the crimps firmly.

3 Make another matching loop on the second strand and repeat the pattern of beads, threading through the lower hole in the spacer bars in the appropriate places.

4 Carefully open a jump ring or split ring and thread on both loops and a fastener. Repeat this at the other end.

TIP

• Split rings will make the bracelet stronger than jump rings, but they are more difficult to use. Try working a strong needle between the rings to hold them open.

LOOM-MADE BRACELET

This is an easy project to work on a beading loom. When you have mastered this bracelet you will be ready to try some more ambitious pieces.

You will need
◊ 160 white rocailles, size 8/0
◊ 60 black rocailles, size 8/0
◊ 30 blue rocailles, size 8/0
◊ White polyester loom thread
◊ Button

Other equipment
◊ Loom
◊ Scissors

1 Cut seven warp threads, each 80cm (about 32in) long, and knot them together at one end.

2 Tighten the bars on the loom, then hook the warp threads on one end of it and bring them over the bar. Use a needle to separate the threads until they lie side by side in the grooves of the loom.

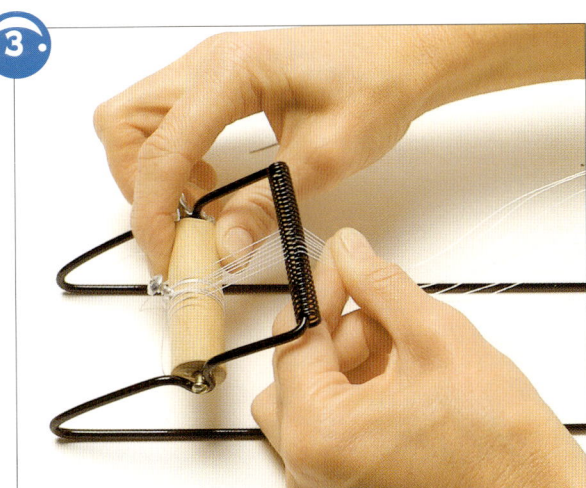

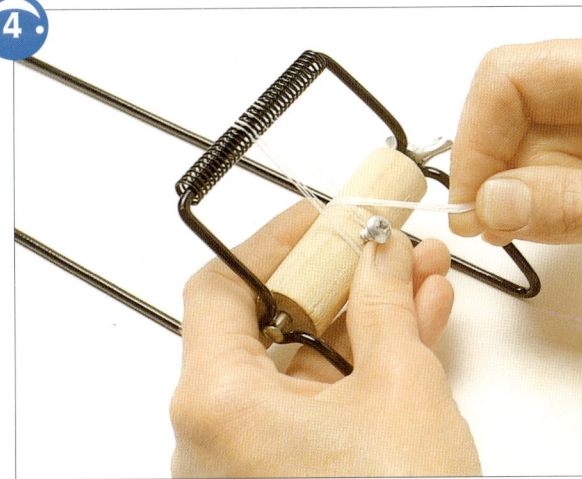

3 Turn the roller a few times to make sure that the warp threads are taut.

4 Take the threads down the loom and separate them over the opposite grooves at the other end. Secure the warp threads around this roller, keeping the threads as taut as you can.

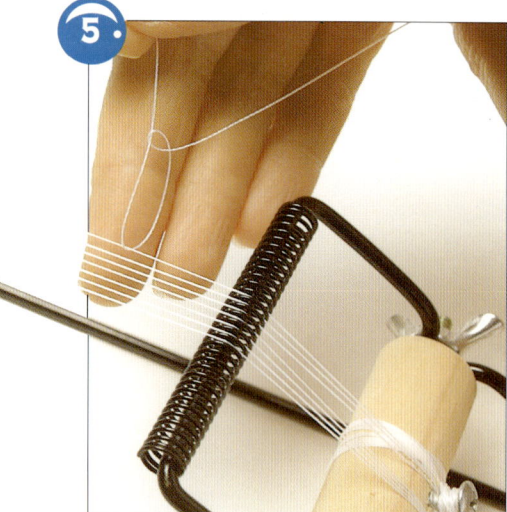

5 Cut a beading thread about 1.5m (5ft) long and tie it to an outside warp thread. Thread it on a needle.

6 Keeping the beading thread below the warp threads, position two rocailles in the centre two spaces. Bring up your needle before the two outside warp threads.

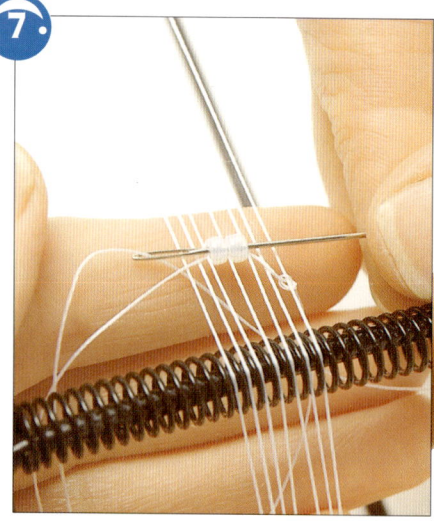

7 Thread the needle back through the two rocailles, working over the warp threads. Repeat this step with two beads four more times and then take the beading thread down between the first and second warp threads. Use four rocailles for two rows.

8 Start to work over the full width of the warp threads so that six rocailles fit into the spaces. Work the pattern with black and blue rocailles.

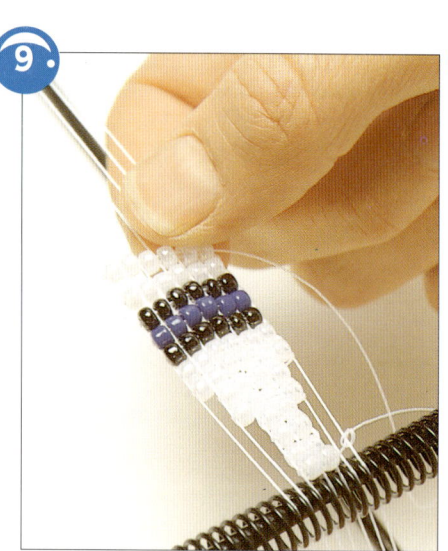

9 As you work along the loom, keep moving the rocailles back against the previous row to keep the work firm.

10 When you have completed the pattern and reduced the number of rocailles at the other end of the bracelet, loosen the rollers at both ends and take the bracelet off the loom.

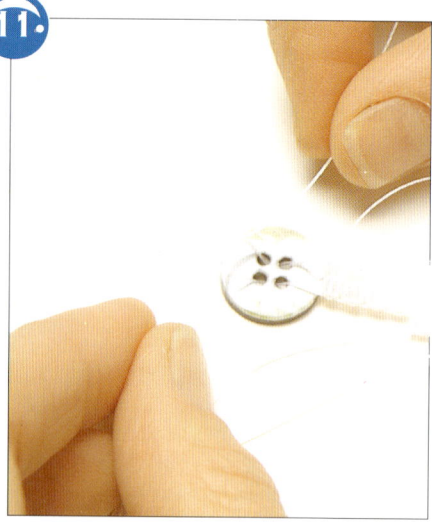

11 Put the button on one end by threading four of the warp threads through the buttonholes, knotting them neatly behind and working the warp threads back into the bracelet.

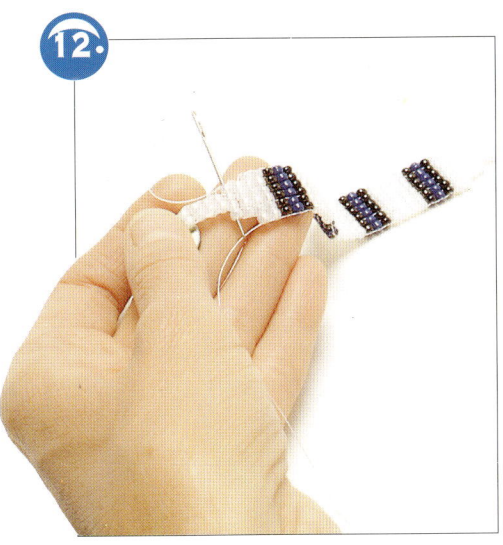

12 Work the other warp threads at this end back into the rocailles and trim them neatly once they are securely finished off.

13 At the other end, use a needle to thread about eight additional rocailles (depending on the size of the button) onto each of the centre two warp threads.

14 Work each thread back down the opposite row of rocailles to form a loop with the two threads running through it in opposite directions. Tighten the threads and use a needle to weave the ends back into the bracelet. Finish this end by weaving the warp threads back into the bracelet and trimming off the loose ends once they are securely finished off.

SUPPLIERS

UK

Bead Shop
43 Neal Street
Covent Garden
London WC2H 9PJ

Hobby Horse
15–17 Langton Street
London SW10 0JL

London Bead Company
25 Chalk Farm Road
London NW1 8AG

Beads
259 Portobello Road
London W11 1LR

Rocking Rabbit Trading Company
Market Street
Newmarket
Suffolk CB8 8EE

MAIL ORDER ONLY

Bojangles
Old Cottage
Appleton
Oxon OX13 5JH

Ahenzi
91 High Street
Winslow
Bucks MK18 3DG

USA

Beadworks
For catalogue:
139 Washington Street
Norwalk
CT 06854

Peruvian Bead Company
1601 Callens Road
Ventura
CA 93003

AUSTRALIA

Creative Bead Imports
255 South Terrace
South Fremantle
Western Australia

WORKSHOPS WITH SARA WITHERS

Available through
Oxford Arts & Crafts
Gable End
Hatford
Near Faringdon
Oxon SN7 8JF

Bead Society of Great Britain
Carole Morris
1 Casburn Lane
Burwell
Cambs CB5 0ED

Stencilling

Use this versatile craft to decorate a whole range of objects from a simple gift tag to reviving an old piece of furniture

Introduction

Welcome to the joys of stencilling!

Stencilling will take you on a simple, step-by-step guided tour of 11 imaginative projects, and by the time you reach the end of this section you will have experienced the wonderful and creative world of stencilling and all it offers.

A stencil is simply a design shape cut out of a piece of wax card, thin metal or plastic film. When paint is applied through the cut-out, the shape is reproduced on the surface below.

Stencilling is not a modern craft. It has been used for centuries as a means of decorating fabrics, books, pottery and of course, the home itself. Early examples can still be seen in homes and museums all over the world, especially in the USA. When expensive European wallpapers were imported to the USA in the 19th century, most people could not afford to buy them. The designs provided stencil artists with new inspiration, and the art

of stencilling meant that the effects of the wallpaper could be imitated at a fraction of the cost of the real thing.

Eventually, mass-production meant that even the expensive wallpapers were within the reach of most people, and stencilling lost its popularity. However, in recent years, as people have looked for new ways to bring individuality to their homes, stencilling has come back into fashion.

The projects in this book explore the versatility of the craft. They range from a very simple yet effective gift tag, through more complicated items to the challenge of designing your own stencil. The projects have been planned to allow you to develop your knowledge and skills of stencilling in a gradual way, so that when you have mastered one technique you will have the confidence to move on to more creative,

demanding things. Each project includes extra ideas to inspire you and helpful tips to enable you to produce professional-looking stencils.

The materials you will need can usually be found at your local art shop or do-it-yourself store, and you can also buy a wide variety of ready-made stencils. If you want to make your own stencils, see Designer's Delight (see page 78), which covers designing and cutting. A selection of our designs can be found in the pattern library at the back of the book.

So, let's go! All you have to do is gather your tools and materials together, follow the projects in this book, and you can take part in the revival of this appealing and rewarding craft.

Happy stencilling!

Jamie Sapsford and Betsy Skinner
The Bermuda Collection

Materials and Equipment

PAINTING KIT

You will need some or all of these materials:

Ready-made Stencils

There is a wide choice available, but do consider the size, shape and intricacy of a design when you are deciding what would be most appropriate for a particular project.

Stencil Brushes

Thick bristled brushes are used to apply paint through the stencil, and they are available in a variety of sizes. A good range to start would be sizes 4, 8, 12 and 16.

Low-tack Masking Tape

You must make sure that the stencil lies flat in place for painting, and low-tack tape reduces the risk of damaging your work surface, such as a wall. Spray adhesive is an alternative for fixing your stencil temporarily in place.

Stencil Paints

Artist's acrylics can be applied to most surfaces. Fabric paints should be used for fabrics, and special paints are available for use on ceramics and glass. Use fast-drying paints to avoid smudging problems during layering. Water-based paints are easier to clean up.

Bowls

Old, small china bowls are useful for mixing colours, and they are easy to clean.

Paper Kitchen Towel

This is essential for general cleaning up and for removing excess paint from your brush.

Scrap Paper

Have plenty of scrap paper handy so that you can practise.

Ruler

Always have a ruler for measuring and placing your stencils.

RIGHT
Painting materials.

Scissors

Apart from trimming some of the papery projects, you will need a pair of scissors for dozens of other uses.

Pencil, Sharpener and Rubber Eraser

Finally, make sure your pencil is sharp so that you always cut along a clean line.

> After every project, clean up when you have finished and wash out your brushes and stencils made of polyester with soap and warm water.

CUTTING KIT

Polyester Drafting Film

This is excellent material for making your own stencils. The frosted transparent film is easy to draw on and perfect for lining up extra layers. It is also hard wearing and can be used repeatedly. Thick, waxed paper is an alternative.

Cutting Knife

You will need a scalpel knife with extra blades to cut your own stencil designs because a very sharp blade is necessary. A blade set at an angle is ideal for cutting arcs and circles.

Cutting Mat

A "self-healing" mat, obtainable from most artist's materials suppliers, is best for cutting out your stencil designs because it will not disintegrate or blunt your blade as quickly as a cutting board would.

Tracing Paper and Graph Paper

You will find that both of these items are extremely useful for copying and reproducing balanced designs.

Now that you have all the materials and equipment you will need, let's start with the first project.

LEFT Cutting materials.

Fun Gift Tag

This is a great project to introduce you to the art of stencilling because it is simple yet effective. Enhance your gifts with a specially stencilled gift tag and delight everyone.

You will need
◊ Painting kit with acrylics
◊ Pad of coloured paper
◊ Hole punch
◊ Curling ribbon

1 We have chosen to stencil a white heart on red paper. Choose an appropriate stencil and paper colour. Measure and cut your paper to approximately 3 × 4in/7.5 × 10cm, and fold it in half along the 2in/5cm line. Decide whether your tag will be horizontal or vertical and punch a hole in the top left-hand corner, leaving enough room for your design.

2 For our practice session we chose to stencil a red heart onto white scrap paper. Put a small amount of paint into a bowl. Dip the bristles of a medium sized brush into the paint and rub off any excess paint on kitchen towel. Your brush should be very dry.

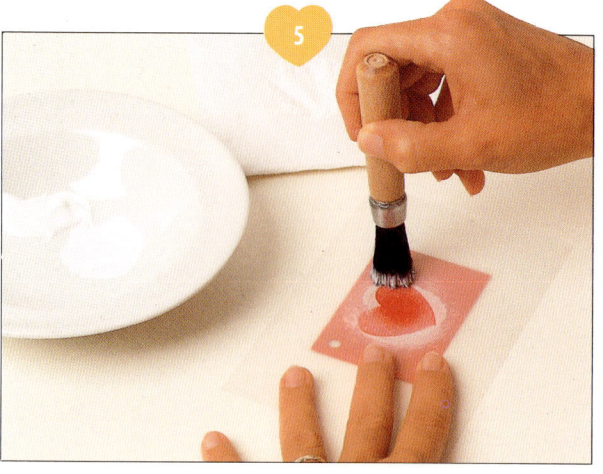

3 Place your stencil design over your scrap paper and hold it with one hand. Hold your stencil brush upright and press it through the stencil cut-out, moving it in a circular motion around the inside edge of the stencil. Continue to build up the colour by moving the brush around the edges. You can do this quite quickly. Try approximately 10 turns but do not let the colour build up in the middle of the cut-out.

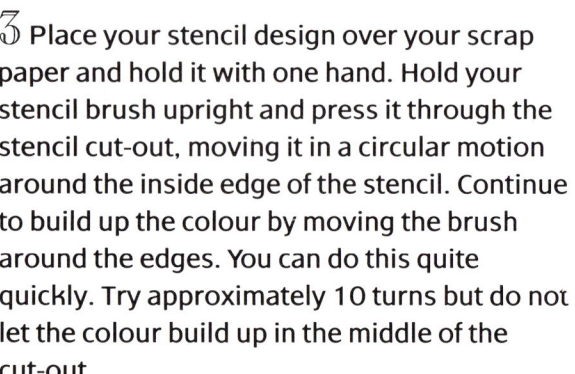

4 Practise, practise, practise! If your brush is too wet with paint it may result in a flat, filled-in stencil shape that bleeds around the edges; see the top heart. The brush really does need to be very dry — drier than you would imagine — although the very faint heart has taken this

to the extreme. The heart at the bottom of the photograph, with the shaded edges and light area in the middle, is perfect.

5 Once you are confident with your practice session you can apply exactly the same principle to your pre-cut tag. Use a clean, dry brush. Choose your paint colour and put a little into a clean, dry bowl. Dip the brush in the paint and wipe off the excess. Position the stencil over the tag, hold both firmly in place and build up the colour in a circular motion around the edge of the cut-out.

HANDY HINTS

When you are cutting out your tag, placing your cutting knife along the edge of a ruler offers a more accurate line than cutting with scissors. Use a metal ruler and hold the ruler and paper firmly in place, taking care to keep your fingers out of the way!

Finally, twirl a good length of ribbon and feed it through the hole. Just look at the wonderful gift tags you can easily make yourself. If you want to impress your friends by stencilling the wrapping paper to match too, read on!

All Wrapped Up

Let's take the gift tag project a stage further and decorate some wrapping paper, too. Learn how to repeat your design over a large area.

You will need
◊ Painting kit with acrylics
◊ 1 large sheet of coloured paper

1 We chose to use the same tag stencil as the previous project to make some matching wrapping paper. First, plot some evenly spaced points on a few sheets of scrap paper. Now try some different design layouts.

2 Put some paint in a clean bowl. Dip a clean brush in the paint and wipe off the excess on some kitchen towel. Position your stencil where you want to start on the scrap paper and hold both down firmly. Move your upright brush in a circular motion around the inside edges of the stencil.

3 There are endless ways of building up your own layouts with any stencil. Move the stencil along the grid to see. Try stencilling several different layouts before you decide which you prefer.

4 Sometimes simplest is best. This design is easy to plot, and you don't have to remember to skip any gaps.

6 Position the stencil on the grid. Trace the points of the paper grid on to the stencil using a pencil or permanent ink. This will make it easy for you to position the stencil every time by simply matching the dots so that your alignment will always be perfect.

7 Now stencil your wrapping paper. Get a fresh bowl, brush, paint, and kitchen towel. Place your stencil on the paper and match up the alignment points of the stencil and paper. Hold the stencil and paper firmly and begin.

8 Continue stencilling the whole sheet, remembering to line up the stencil points and paper grid. Compare the stencilled images with each other so that they are roughly the same intensity, but don't try to match them perfectly because their differences add to the appeal of this craft.

The finished wrapping paper with its own matching tag from the first project. A beautiful job, well done!

5 Having chosen your layout, plot the same grid on the real paper. Use very light pencil dots – dark enough for you to be able to use them as a guide to line up your stencil, but not so dark that they detract from your creative efforts.

HANDY HINTS

◊ Do not worry if your stencil images do not fit perfectly within the edges of the paper – when you wrap your gift you may end up cutting off some of the design.

Great Greetings Cards

You can make greetings cards to suit any occasion, but we chose a Christmas card. This project shows you how to use two colours in your design as well as being able to produce several cards at once.

You will need

◊ Painting kit with acrylics
◊ Set of matching cards and envelopes

1 Have at least five plain cards with matching envelopes ready. Make sure that your chosen stencil design is a suitable size for your cards.

2 A two-part stencil gives you an opportunity to use two colours within different parts of the design. Our wreath stencil has separated the green leaves from the red bow and berries. Have ready two bowls, two brushes, two different colours, some kitchen towel and pieces of scrap paper.

3 Try out your first stencil on scrap paper. On a good two-part stencil the first image is cut out and the second image, intact, is drawn in with dotted lines. These dotted lines indicate the rest of the design and are invaluable when you come to line up your second image correctly. Move your brush confidently around the cut-out several times in one direction.

4 Hold the first stencil in place and lift off one corner to peek at your efforts so far. If the image is not strong enough replace the stencil and continue to build up the colour.

5 Now take your second bowl, brush, colour and stencil. Lay the second stencil over the first image. The wreath now shows the bow and berries cut out. The leaves are intact and shown as dotted lines, allowing easy alignment. Stencil your second image.

6 Once you are happy with your practice efforts, have everything to hand to stencil your set of five matching cards.

7 Place your stencil in the appropriate position on the card and hold both firmly. Stencil all five cards in succession with your first image and first colour. Remember to peek at your progress.

8 Carefully position your second image, using the dotted lines for alignment. Hold it down securely to stop it moving.

9 Stencil all five cards with the second image in the second colour. Remember to move your brush in a circular motion in one direction.

You could add a detail of the design to the envelopes for a wonderful finishing touch. Congratulations! You have just completed a production line of hand-decorated cards.

HANDY HINTS
◊ Always use a clean, dry brush for each colour.
◊ Transparent stencils make it easy to line up two or more colours.
◊ You may find a ruler helpful if you cannot easily position your stencil by eye.
◊ When you have very small cut-outs do not try to stencil the edges of each one. You will achieve effective results by simply moving the brush over the cut-outs repeatedly but in only one direction.

Magical Mirror

Have fun with a mirror. This project introduces you to stencilling on a glass surface, which involves a new technique and requires different paints.

You will need
◊ Painting kit with ceramic paints
◊ Mirror to decorate
◊ Practice mirror

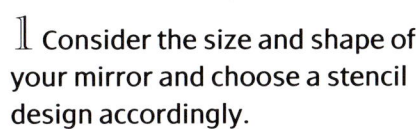

1 Consider the size and shape of your mirror and choose a stencil design accordingly.

2 Practise some design layouts on scrap paper. Note, too, that our shell design has been given some red shading to give it more definition. You will see how to achieve both a highlighting technique (light paint on dark) and a shading technique (dark on light) later on in this project.

3 Practise your stencilling technique on a spare mirror. Glass is not absorbent, so take care not to use too much paint, or it will smudge.

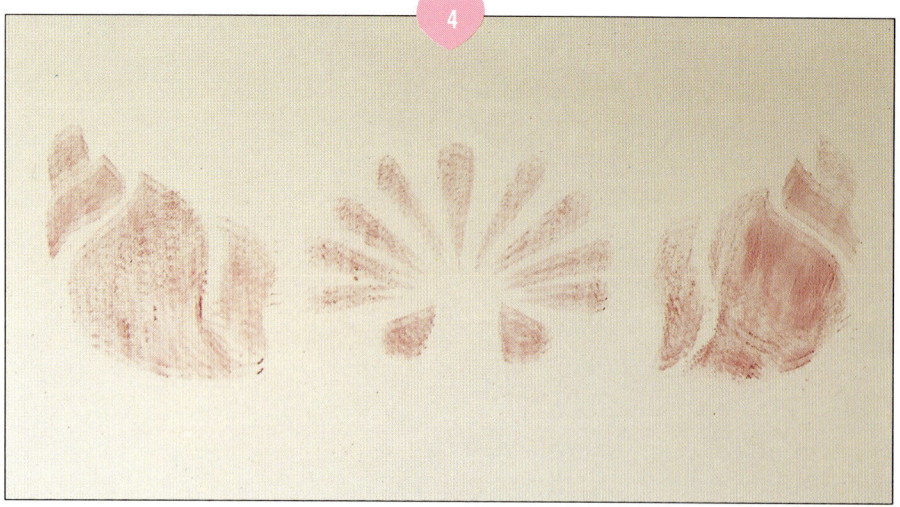

4 Do not use too little paint either. Here the outline of the image is barely distinguishable.

5 This is what you need to aim for. The combination of the properties of this type of paint and this slippery surface means you will need to use more paint and allow it to build up.

6 Now practise stencilling with your first colour.

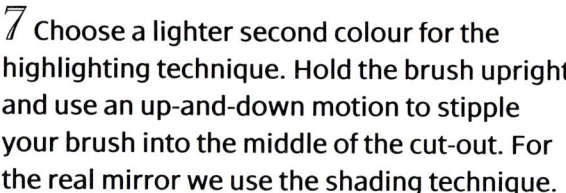

7 Choose a lighter second colour for the highlighting technique. Hold the brush upright and use an up-and-down motion to stipple your brush into the middle of the cut-out. For the real mirror we use the shading technique.

8 When you are ready to move on to the real mirror offer up your stencil to judge the best position. Use your sketches for inspiration. Fix your stencil in place with masking tape to stop it moving about on the slippery surface.

9 Continue your layout with the first colour.

10 For the shaded technique use a darker colour and stipple the edges of the cut-outs with an up and down motion.

A plain mirror has been transformed into a highly individual and decorative piece.

HANDY HINTS

◊ If you need to section off part of your design use masking tape as shown on pages 75–77, or simply hold some spare pieces of paper in place.
◊ Check the drying times of your ceramic paint on the manufacturer's instructions.

Merry Mugs

Stencilled mugs will brighten any kitchen and they also make great gifts. In this project we made a set of three.

You will need
◊ Painting kit with ceramic paints
◊ 3 matching mugs in a plain colour

1 Decide on a design that will suit the shape and size of your mugs. We chose stars.

2 Experiment with colours on a scrap piece of coloured paper. Silver and gold are ideal for stars, and they work well on a blue background.

3 Holding your stencil with masking tape on the curved surface will make stencilling easier.

4 Stencil your first image in the usual way. You may need to stipple the edges to deepen the colour on this dark, non-absorbent surface.

7 As a finishing touch, spatter some silver paint over the mugs. Put more paint on your brush, then pull back the bristles so that they are a little way from the mug and let them flick onto the mug so that small flecks of paint are deposited on the mugs — and everywhere else too! Before you do this, protect anything you do not wish to spatter, including the insides of the mug.

8 Finish off the other mugs also using the spattering technique. It works especially well with the star stencil design, giving the impression of distant galaxies!

Here is your new set of mugs. Treat a friend or yourself!

5 Continue to apply the first image to all three mugs. By the time you have stencilled the third mug, the first mug should be dry enough for you to apply the next image.

6 We have chosen smaller silver stars for the next image. Use a freer and less regimented approach here and build up the small stars into an attractive pattern.

HANDY HINTS
Personalize a mug with a stencilled name to make the perfect gift.

Pots of Gardener's Delight

Stencilling is a wonderful way of transforming plain terracotta flowerpots into a gardener's dream.

You will need
◊ Painting kit with ceramic paints
◊ Any number and size of terracotta pots

1 Select your stencil design according to the size and shape of the pots. You might like to coordinate the colours of the stencil with the plants that are to go into them.

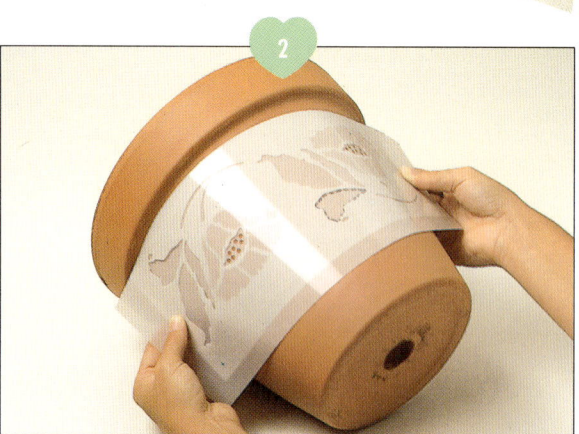

2 Calculate the position of the image by offering up the stencil to the pot. You may need to stretch or squeeze in a repeat pattern.

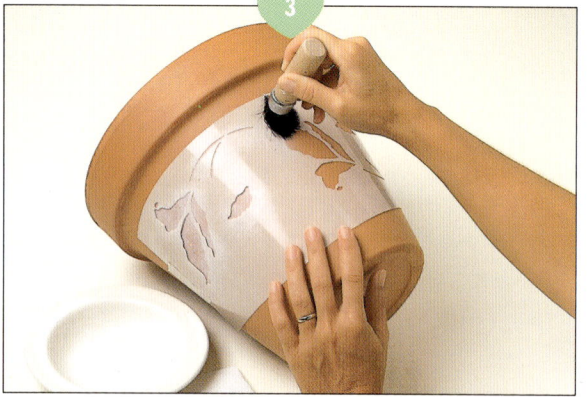

3 Use masking tape to secure the stencil to the pot, then stencil on your first colour.

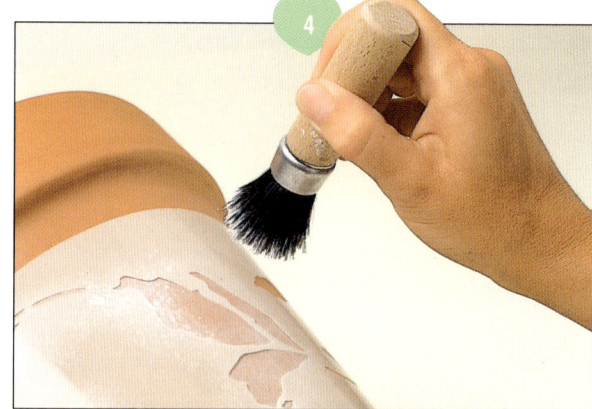

4 Stipple the design to add depth before moving the stencil along to continue the first colour.

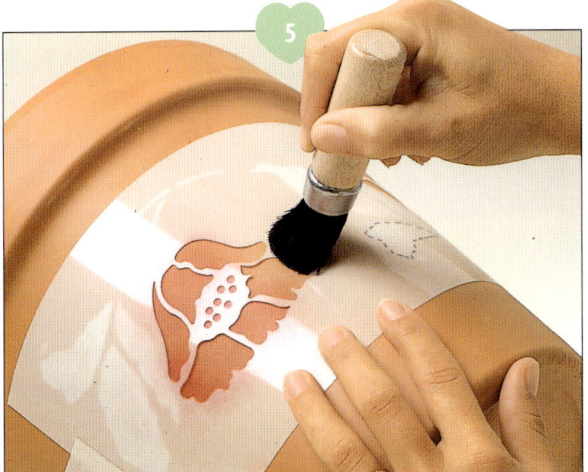

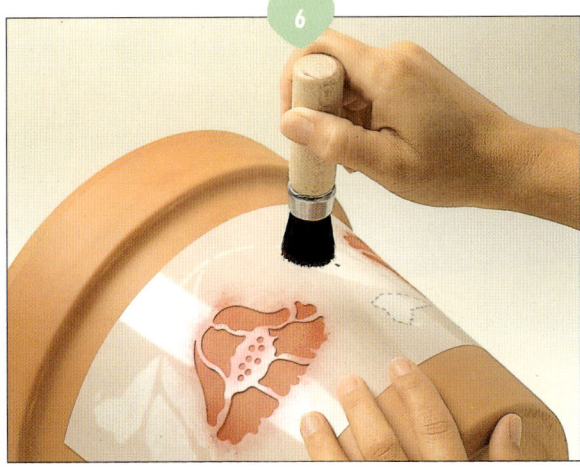

7 The finished design on a large pot shows the effect achieved by the stippling technique.

8 Just look at what you can do. Rather than continuing the design around this pot, we felt that it would work better as a central feature.

A selection of different sizes of pots and designs.

5 Align your second stencil and apply your second colour.

6 Use the stippling technique again to deepen the edges of the design. Move the stencil around the pot to complete your design.

HANDY HINTS

◊ You may find your stencil more manageable if you trim it to follow the curve of the pot.

◊ This porous surface may require more paint than usual to build up the colour.

Friendly Floor Covering

Let's move your stencilling talents to the floor. A scatter rug can be decorated to suit any room, and this is a good introduction to working on a larger scale. Remember to apply a varnish to protect the design against inevitable foot traffic.

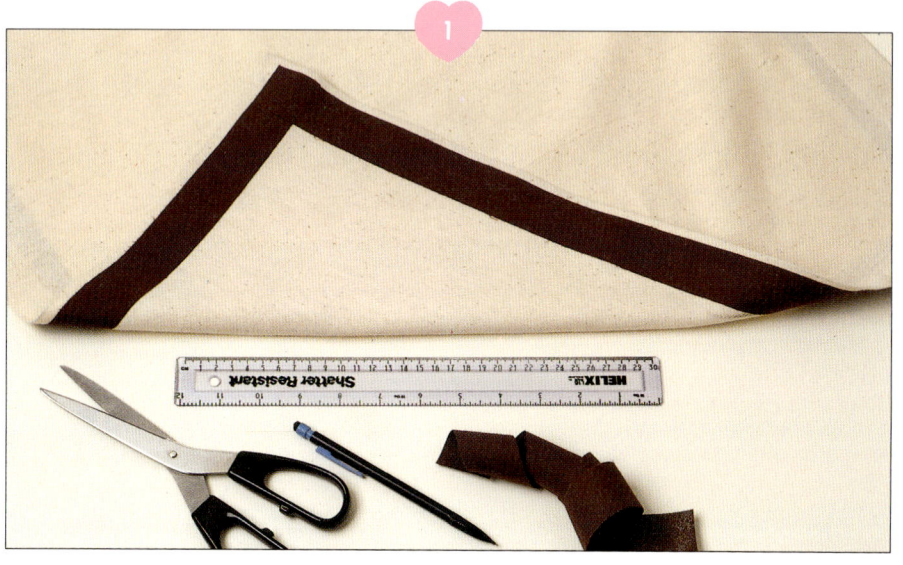

You will need
◊ Painting kit with acrylic paints
◊ Decorator's heavy twill dust sheet or canvas
◊ Iron-on hemming tape or sewing machine
◊ Small tin of matt emulsion paint
◊ Small tin of varnish
◊ Decorator's paint brush

1 Measure and cut your fabric to a manageable size – ours is 2 × 3ft/60 × 90cm. Fold down and seal your edges with hemming tape or use a sewing machine to turn down a hem.

2 Apply a coat of matt emulsion paint to the rug to seal the fabric. Leave to dry. Wash out your brush.

3 Choose a stencil and sketch some possible layouts on scrap paper, remembering to allow for a border line. There are so many ways you can build up designs with your stencil.

4 Once the paint is dry, measure and mark the border line on your rug. We have marked our pencil lines approximately 2½in/7cm and 4in/10cm from the edge.

5 Apply the masking tape to the pencil lines, leaving a 1½in/3cm gap between.

6 Allow the masking tape to overlap at the corners to create an interesting break in the border.

7 Use a large brush to stencil the 1¼in/3cm gap all around the rug.

8 Remove the masking tape to reveal your border. Refer to your sketches for inspiration and offer up your stencil design to calculate the best spacing. Mark key points.

9 Use your key points to place the stencil and apply your first image over the whole rug. Hold or tape your stencil in place.

10 Line up and apply the second image and continue over the whole rug.

11 On the other side of your border line build up another border with a detail from the stencil. We cut two triangles as a separate stencil for ease of application.

12 Once all the yellow triangles are complete, flip over the stencil and place some upside-down triangles in the design using another colour.

13 Apply at least two coats of varnish to the whole rug.

A truly friendly floor covering to brighten any room!

HANDY HINTS
◊ Choose a background emulsion colour that will suit the room in which you will place the rug.
◊ When you apply the emulsion and varnish, place some newspaper under the rug to protect your work surface.

Child's Cheerful Chair

This is your first attempt at decorating a piece of furniture. A plain child's stool can be made to look extra special with a stencilled seat and is certain to be a hit!

You will need
◊ Painting kit with acrylics
◊ A new, wooden child's stool, untreated (i.e. not varnished or waxed)
◊ Pair of compasses
◊ Fine-grade sandpaper
◊ Tin of polishing wax

1 Select an appropriate stencil design and a suitable colour scheme. Give the stool a light rub down with fine sandpaper.

2 We decided to stencil our floral design in a circular layout. Start by drawing your circle with the compass on rough paper. Placing an edge of your image on the pencil mark and following the line of the circle will enable you to calculate how close the repeats should be to complete the circle.

3 Apply your first colour. Because you are being creative with this approach, you will be unable to rely on your stencil for the exact spacing of the images, so line them up by eye as well.

4 Apply your second colour, following the line of the circle. Again you will need to line up the stencil by eye as you work around the circumference.

5 Use your compass to mark a light circle on the seat of the stool. Allow enough room between the line and the edge of the stool for your design.

6 Roughly calculate the position of the design and apply your first colour, following the line of the circle.

7 When you have completed the circle with the first colour apply your second image and second colour.

8 Add any finishing touches to suit the piece.

9 Seal your design by applying a coat of wax polish. Buff it up to obtain a deep lustre.

This chair will cheer up any child's day!

A New Lease of Life

You can give any old piece of furniture a new lease of life by adding a stencilled decoration. Resurrect something from your attic and bring it back into your home. We have given an old school desk a pretty, rustic feel.

You will need
◊ Painting kit with acrylics
◊ Paint and varnish stripper
◊ Fine-grade sandpaper
◊ Small tin of emulsion paint
◊ Old piece of furniture
◊ Small tin of varnish

1 Almost any old piece of furniture can be used as long as it is in good repair and is well prepared. You will need to remove old paint and varnish.

2 Consider your stencil design and colour scheme and gather the materials you will need.

3 The old varnish on this desk must be removed. Apply the varnish remover and scrape it off. Take care with these materials; always follow the manufacturer's instructions and wear protective clothing.

4 When it is dry, rub down the surface with fine sandpaper to give a smooth, clean surface. Dust off with a brush or cloth.

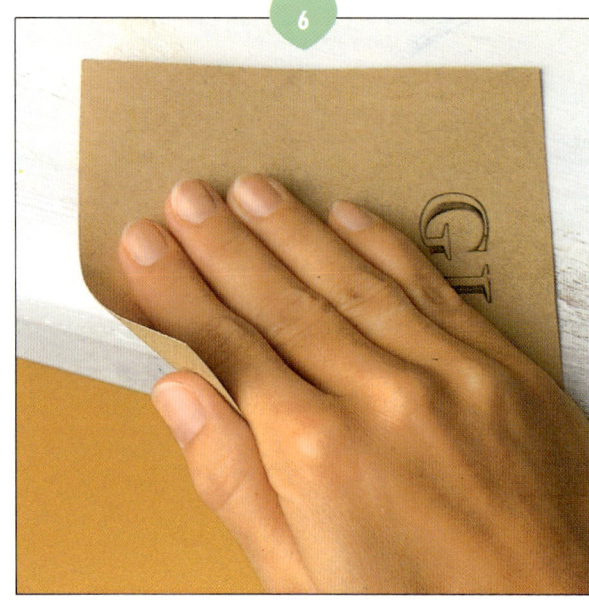

5 Apply a coat of slightly thinned emulsion paint in your chosen background colour. Allow to dry.

6 Rub down the emulsion coat with fine sandpaper to highlight the grain.

7 The combination of the beech wood grain and emulsion give the desired rustic effect.

8 We have chosen a border design for the desk lid. Measure and mark a light guideline so that you can position the stencil correctly.

9 Make sure that the stencil is applied in the correct place and fix it with masking tape.

10 Apply the first colour over the whole area.

11 Line up your second stencil and apply all of the second colour.

12 Continue with a third colour.

13 A close-up of the completed design reveals that the yellow and green are a little bright for the overall rustic feel of the desk.

14 We stencilled the edges of the design with a little burnt sienna to tone down and add depth to the flowers and leaves.

HANDY HINTS

◊ If your piece of furniture needs only a good clean, use sugar soap.

◊ When you apply the coat of emulsion, paint your strokes in the same direction as the grain.

◊ To give an even more rustic look, lightly sand over your finished design.

15 The result is an "older" and much more interesting design.

16 Add some finishing touches to suit the piece.

17 Seal in the effect and design with two coats of varnish.

A total transformation — the desk is worthy of pride of place!

Finishing Touches

Stencilling on a wall can bring a room to life. A design above a picture or a plain window can provide the perfect finishing touch, and this project provides an opportunity to coordinate colours with the rest of the room.

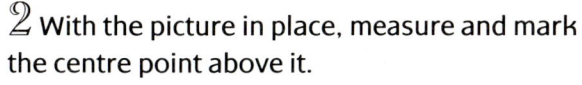

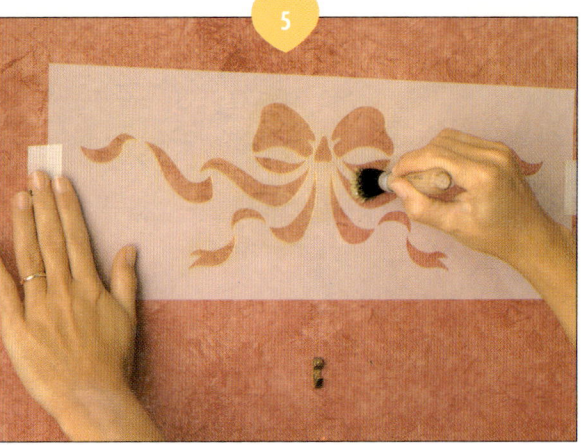

You will need
◊ Painting kit with acrylics
◊ Clean, dry wall
◊ Tape measure
◊ Step ladder

1 The space above this picture is the perfect place for a ribbon stencil.

2 With the picture in place, measure and mark the centre point above it.

3 Centre the stencil above the picture, making certain it is straight, and mark the key points.

4 Remove the picture. Line up your stencil on the key points and fix it in place on the wall with masking tape.

5 We have chosen iridescent gold for this project to complement the gold highlights in the picture frame. Stencil in the usual way.

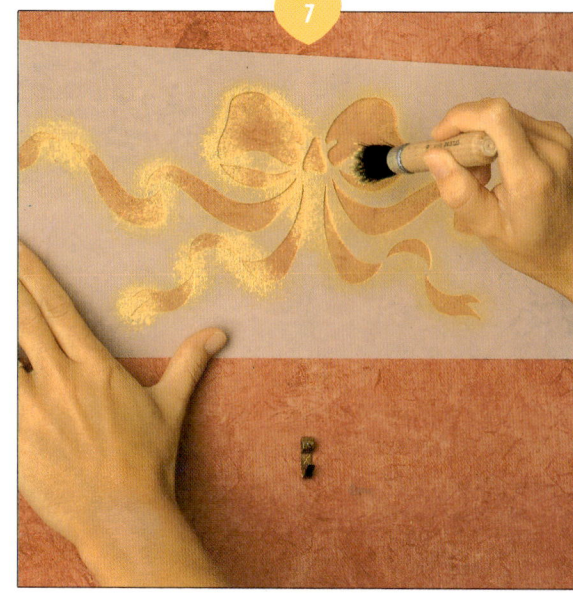

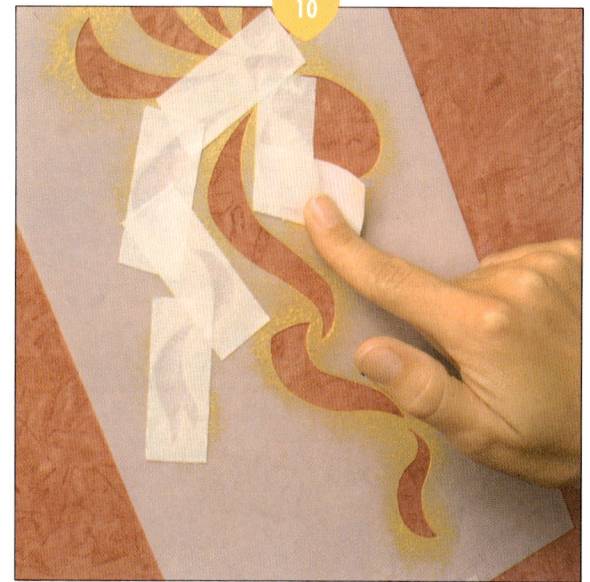

6 A peek at our efforts shows that we need to build up this transparent medium on such a dark background.

7 Heavy stippling is required on key edges of the design.

8 Now that's more like it!

9 Hang your picture back up and admire your handiwork. Does it need anything else?

10 Add a finishing touch by selecting a bit of the design. Tape off the specific areas you want to use.

11 Measure and mark the centre and key points again. Stencil as before.

The stencil has provided an elegant finishing touch for this study.

Designer's Delight

The aim of this project is to design, cut and apply your own border stencil. Your inspiration should come from your own surroundings. We have chosen some lobelia flowers and used them to create a glorious border for a living room.

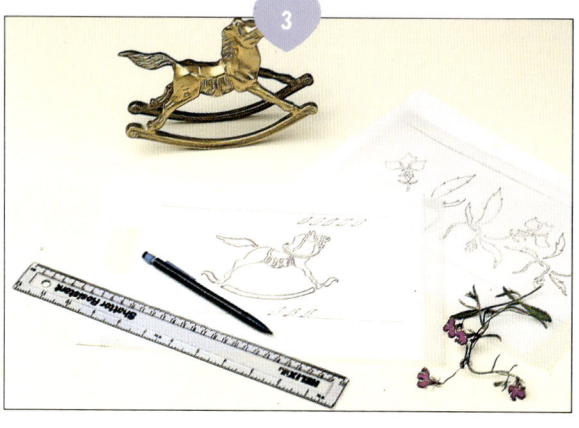

You will need
◊ Cutting kit
◊ Painting kit with acrylics
◊ Appropriate wall space to decorate
◊ Reference material
◊ Coloured pencils
◊ Permanent felt-tip pen

1 Look around for inspiration for a design for your own border stencil.

2 Choose simple objects and practise simplifying the shapes. Look at your chosen object and break it down into sections.

3 Trace the design you like best and hold it in place over graph paper with masking tape. The graph paper will be invaluable in building a straight border. Choose a simple shape from your design to build the outside border.

4 Experiment with different ways of developing your design and also with colours, bearing in mind the room in which you will be stencilling. Make sure that your design is straight by using masking tape to attach your tracing paper to graph paper.

5 Once you have decided on your design and colour scheme, transfer your design to clear polyester drafting film. Use one piece of film for each colour. Fasten your graph and tracing paper to your work surface with masking tape. Place your first piece of film with the frosted side up and hold it in place. Trace a straight line from the graph paper. Now trace all the design shapes of the first colour only. Ensure that the straight line tracing is always aligned with the graph paper.

9 Continue in the same way with all three pieces of film. Each piece should have its own shapes cut out to correspond to your planned colour design.

10 Now you can do a trial run with your new stencil on a piece of rough paper. Stencil your first colour, align and stencil your second image and continue with your third.

11 Now you are ready to move to your chosen wall.

6 When you have traced all the shapes for your first colour on to the first piece of film, trace the rest of your design in dotted lines with a permanent felt-tip pen. These dotted lines are essential if you are to align the stencil accurately.

7 On the second piece of film trace all the second colour shapes in a continuous line. Then trace the rest of the design in dotted lines. Continue in the same way for your third colour image.

8 Now you can begin cutting your own stencil, but practise on a spare piece of film first. Use your cutting mat and a sharp blade. Turn the stencil when you come to a corner rather than trying to turn your blade. Cut out the shapes of the continuous line from each piece of film. Do not cut any dotted lines.

12 This pretty room needs a little something to finish it off.

13 Start your first stencil in a relatively inconspicuous place because you will become more confident as you proceed and your technique will improve. This way your best efforts are most visible. After using your first stencil once, move it along and position the repeat by laying your first cut-out over the last image.

14 Once you have completed all of the chosen area with the first colour, proceed with the second colour. Your dotted lines will make alignment simple.

15 Complete the design with the third colour.

16 Put your room back together

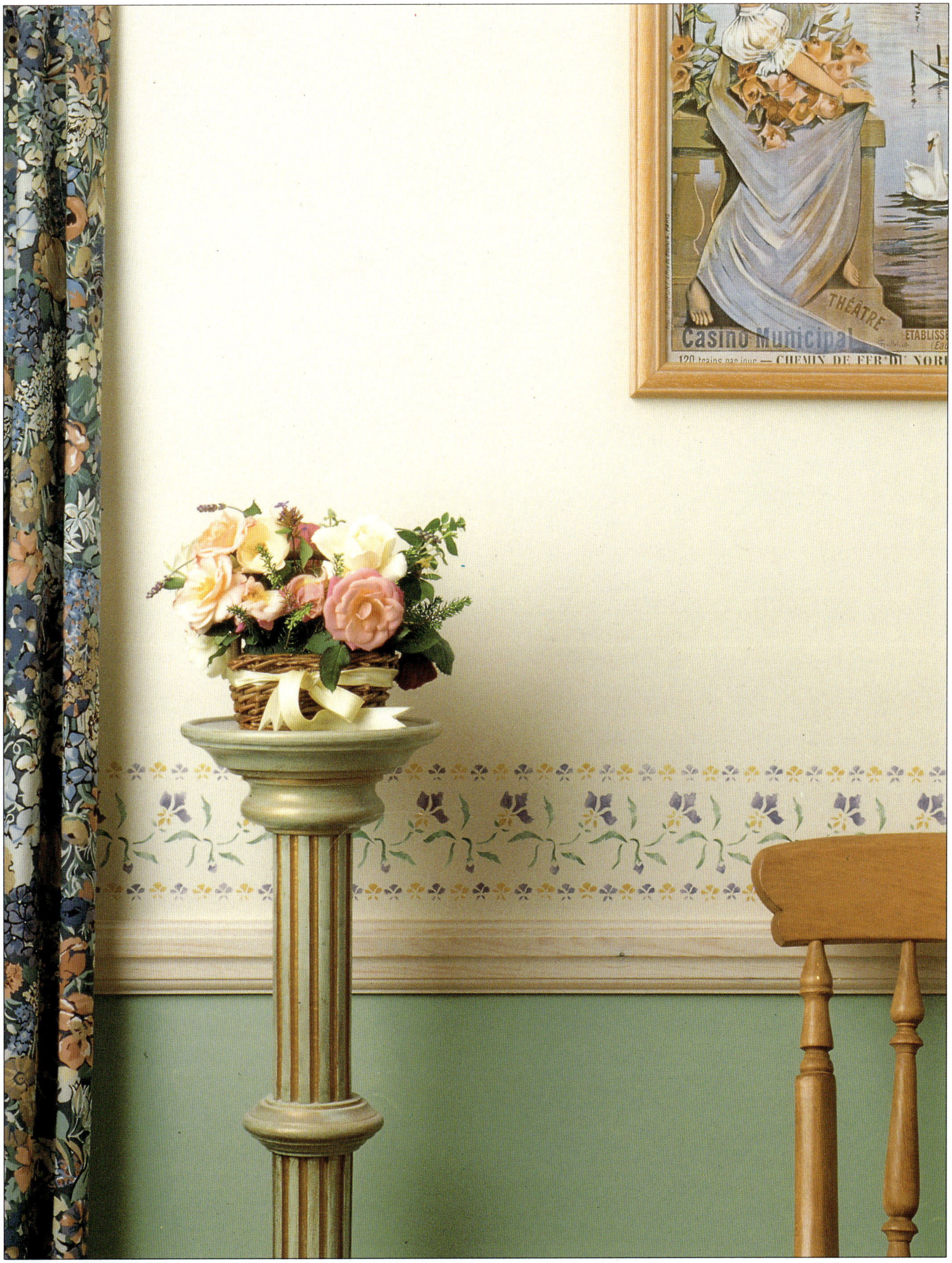

Congratulations! A work of art and a cause for celebration.

HANDY HINTS

◊ The more of your repeat you can fit on to your stencil, the more images you will be able to colour in one go. Remember, though, that the cutting time will be increased.

◊ When you align your repeat by laying a cut-out over a stencilled image, as in Step 13, do not worry if alignment is not exact. You have cut this by hand, so it is bound to be a little different.

◊ Do not use more than three colours.

◊ If your design cuts or tears, it can be easily mended; apply tape on both sides of the tear and trim the excess tape with a blade.

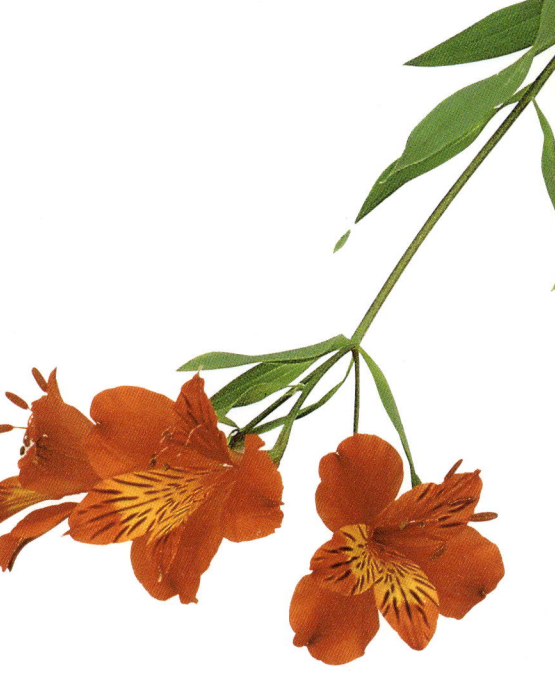

Pattern Library

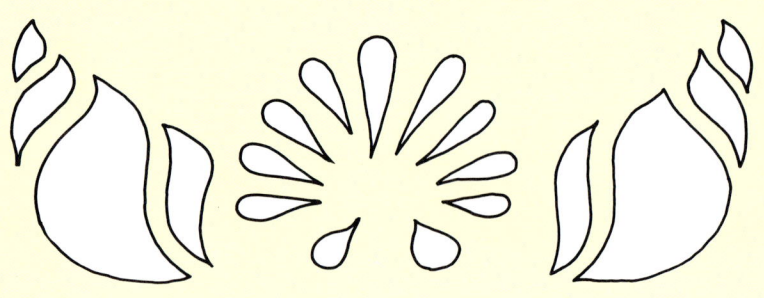

◊ Magical Mirror

◊ Pots of Gardener's Delight
(Use the shell template from Magical
Mirrors for the small pot) Add pollen
dots by hand

◊ Pots of Gardener's Delight

◊ Gift Tag *and* All Wrapped Up

◊ Gift Tags *and* Merry Mugs

◊ Designer's Delight

◊ A New Lease of Life

◊ Great Greetings Cards

◊ Gift Tag

◊ Finishing Touches

◊ Child's Cheerful Chair

◊ Friendly Floor Covering

Batik

This beautiful craft, based on one simple principle, enables you to produce stunning pictures, cushions, bags and fabric

INTRODUCTION

◆

Batik is an ancient method of applying coloured designs to fabric. It is called a "resist" method because traditionally hot wax is used to penetrate the cloth to prevent or "resist" the dye spreading to areas so protected. Rice paste or mud is sometimes used instead of wax. Designs may be of one colour or of many colours, depending on the number of times the resists are applied and the fabric is dipped into baths of different dyes. Modern, simple-to-use dyes allow the technique of "pool" batik to be practised. In this process wax is applied to surround complete areas of fabric and to prevent the dye spreading from one area to another, which means that colours can be used next to each other to give results that would be more difficult to achieve by the traditional immersion method.

The precise origins of batik are disputed. There is early evidence of batik in the form of garments depicted in Indian wall paintings; linen cloth dating to the 5th century has been excavated in Egypt; in Japan batik was made into silk screens from the 8th century, the work probably being carried out by Chinese artists; and in Java 13th-century temples show figures possibly wearing batik cloth. It is more certain that as early as AD 581 batik was being produced in China and probably being exported to Japan, central Asia, the Middle East and India via the Silk Route.

Wherever it originated, however, the batik method was adopted more enthusiastically in Indonesia, especially Java, than anywhere else. It was the Javanese who developed the canting (pronounced "chanting" and originally spelled *tjanting*) to facilitate and refine the application of wax. It is basically a metal bowl to hold the hot wax, with a spout through which the wax flows out, attached to a wooden handle. The invention of the canting opened up the possibility of producing the wonderfully intricate array of designs seen in Javanese batiks.

The word batik derives from the Javanese word, *tik*, meaning spots or dots. Early batiks were executed by means of tiny dots of wax, which were applied to the fabric to form the design. By the 13th century it had become a highly developed art, a fitting leisure pastime for women of noble birth. They often took months to complete a piece of fabric, just as an aristocratic European lady might have worked at her fine needlework.

Early batik designs were believed to have magical powers which would protect the person who wore them, and individual designs were reserved for particular noble families. The Garuda symbol, which was associated with prosperity and success in life, for example, could be used only by members of the royal courts. Today, this creature, half-man, half-eagle, who carried the god Vishnu, has become the national symbol of Indonesia, just as batik fabric has become the national dress of Java.

The production of batik fabric became the main industry and export of Java, from which it spread throughout the world. It was brought to Europe via Holland after the colonization of

Java by the Dutch in the early 17th century. By the 1830s several factories had been established in Europe, and these used Indonesian techniques, taught by Indonesians, who were brought to Holland specifically for that purpose.

By the 1840s the Javanese were using caps (pronounced "chaps" and originally spelled *tjaps*), a form of block to print the wax on with. These were adapted from an Indian technique, and they made the process faster, an advance that made the imitation batik sarongs produced in Switzerland uneconomic to make.

A group of Eurasian women, called collectively the Indische School of Batik, produced fabric for Dutch colonial officials and their families. Their designs, which were a combination of the traditional forms of Java and the colour and simplicity of Chinese paintings, became fashionable in the early years of the 20th century. Also around the late 1800s the British African print trade began, and more styles were incorporated into batik fabric designs. Africans had produced resist-dyed fabrics for centuries — the Yoruba of west Africa used cassava paste as a resist, while the

people of Senegal used rice paste. In India, where cotton rather than silk was used, the batik industry reached its zenith in the 17th and 18th centuries.

Western production of batik on a large scale collapsed with the general economic decline after World War I and it reverted to being the domain of the individual craftsman in Indonesia. In Europe artists and craftsmen continued to work in batik, developing and experimenting with its possibilities. In the 1920s modern dyestuffs started to replace traditional vegetable dyes, changing the

appearance of batik fabric by bringing deeper, darker and more varied shades to the range of possible colours.

Batik is undergoing a revival in appreciation and interest in the West. In addition to the traditional uses of batik fabric for clothes and soft furnishings, the medium's potential is being explored and applied as a fine art, with artists seeking expression through dye instead of paint. However, it is still to Indonesia, especially to Java, that the batik enthusiast goes to learn about the process and the art at first-hand.

BELOW Traditional batiked material from Indonesia.

EQUIPMENT AND MATERIALS

—— ◇ ——

In the projects described in this book you will gradually gain the knowledge you need to accomplish a wide variety of batik pieces. The basic methods, equipment and materials you will need are discussed in the projects and I have introduced new techniques in this gradual way so that newcomers to the craft are not overwhelmed and discouraged before they have even begun. You do not need to be able to draw in the first few projects, and motifs are printed for your use where necessary until you gain confidence to find or make up your own.
All of the projects do, however, use a number of basic pieces of equipment and materials, and I have listed these below, together with the quantities you will need. The only exception is the first project, the greetings cards, for which you need only the first 11 items.

You will need

◊ Plastic sheet to protect your work surface. Large bin liners, cut open, can be used. Choose white rather than black so that you can see any dye.

◊ Cotton wool.

◊ Sponge, 1in (2.5cm) thick by 12in (30cm) square.

◊ Rubber gloves — the thin ones like hairdressers' gloves are best.

◊ Iron — preferably use an old one in case you get some wax on it.

◊ Newspaper.

◊ Measuring spoons. You will need to be able to measure 1 tablespoon, 1 teaspoon, ½ teaspoon and ¼ teaspoon.

◊ Dyes — 1oz (25gm) pots of MX 4G (brilliant yellow), MX G (turquoise), MX G (peacock blue), MX 5B (cerise) and Kenactive Black 2647. Apart from the black, these are Procion fibre-reactive dyes; there is not a ready-made Procion black.

◊ 2 pt (1 litre) measuring jug.

◊ 1lb (500gm) sodium carbonate (washing soda) or soda ash.

◊ 1lb (500gm) sodium bicarbonate (baking soda).

◊ 1lb (500gm) urea — this is obtainable from specialist shops.

◊ 2lb (1kg) batik wax — this quantity should be sufficient for all of the projects, although you could start off with a 1lb (500gm) packet. This is available from specialist shops.

◊ Wax pot — some cheaper alternatives are discussed on page 96, but if you are going to do a lot of batik, you should buy a wax pot from a specialist. shop. I have used a wax pot set on mark 5 for all the projects in this book.

◊ Natural bristle brushes, small and medium sizes and both flat and round for making different marks.

◊ Cantings — small, medium and large spouts should be sufficient, with

perhaps one novelty multi-spout. Indonesian cantings are the best if you can get them.

◊ Soft, absorbent cloths (rags will do).

◊ Scouring kit — a large saucepan, detergent and wooden tongs (see page 98).

◊ Fabric — 6yd (5.5m) of 36in (90cm) wide fine cotton should be ample for all the projects in the book and allow for some mistakes too. It must be 100 per cent cotton, not polycotton. You will also need 1yd (1m) silk, although 18in (46cm) would be sufficient. All fabric has to be prepared — that is, scoured and ironed — before you start a piece of work. If you buy 6yd (5.5m) cotton and want to scour it all at once you can put it into the boil wash of your machine with half your normal amount of ordinary washing liquid, although this will vary according to the softness of your water. Do **not** boil silk.

LEFT A wax pot, caps, cantings and wax brushes.

BELOW The five basic dye colours you will need.

Chemicals, dyes, hot wax should all be treated with respect. Follow the safety tips throughout the book and you will have fun and peace of mind.

GREETINGS CARDS

◆

The simplest kind of batik you can do is on paper using ordinary white household candles to apply the wax resist. You can use almost any kind of paper as long as it is not coated with a shiny finish and it is not too flimsy — photocopying paper, which is usually about 80gsm, is suitable. Making these greetings cards introduces you to working with the soda solutions, mixing and applying dyes, ironing out and the "halo" that results from wax seeping when you iron your work.

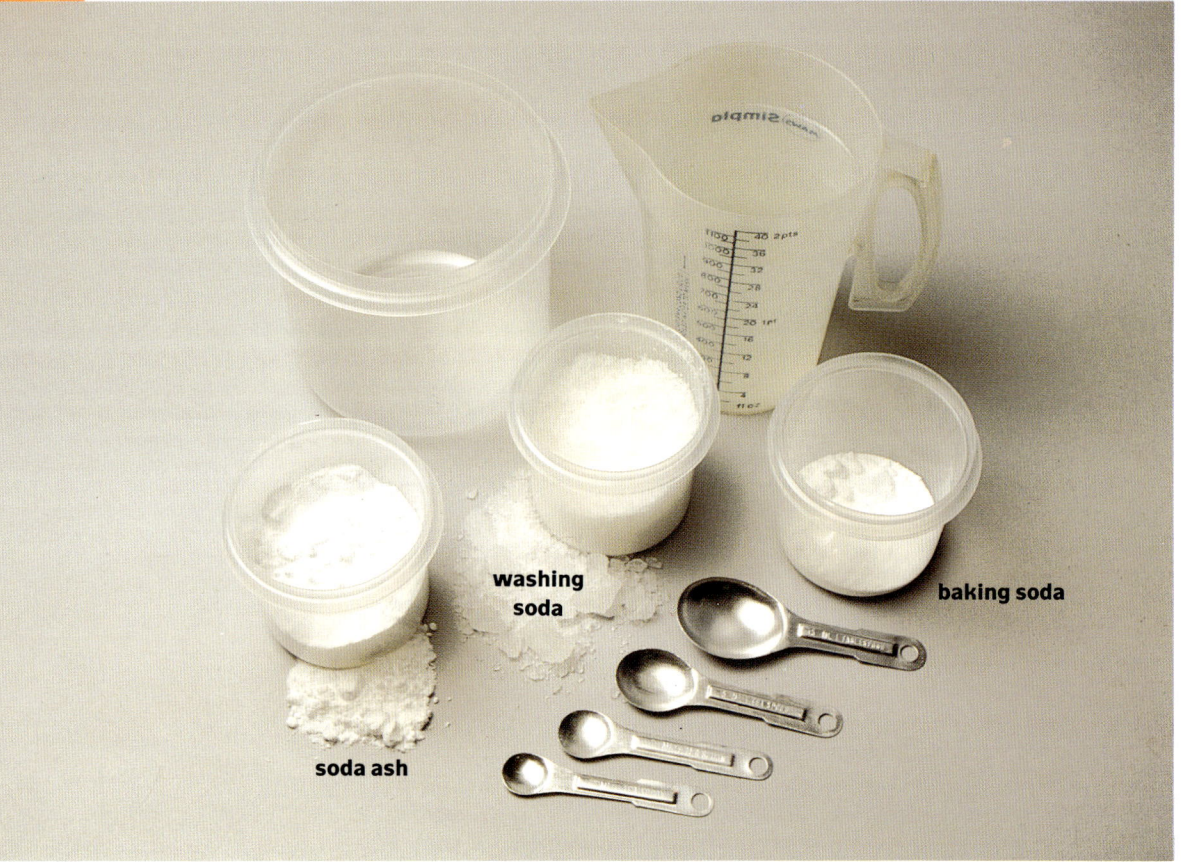

washing soda

baking soda

soda ash

You will need
◊ Basic equipment, first 11 items
◊ Sheets of white paper, 11½ × 8¼in (A4, 297 × 210mm)
◊ Hair dryer (optional)
◊ Two or three white household candles
◊ Card to make a viewing window (use an empty cereal packet)
◊ Ready-made, cut-out window cards to mount your finished work
◊ Stick glue or spray adhesive for fixing

1 So that the dye penetrates the paper properly you should prepare it with a solution of 1 teaspoon baking soda and 1 teaspoon washing soda dissolved in 1½pt (900ml) warm water. You can use soda ash instead of washing soda, but it is twice as strong so you need add only ½ teaspoon to the water. If it is kept in an airtight container this solution remains usable for 10–14 days.

2 Lay a sheet of paper on a flat, non-absorbent surface, such as formica or glass. Use cotton wool to apply the soda solution evenly over the paper. Soak the paper thoroughly but do not rub it so hard that you begin to roughen the surface. Leave the paper to dry completely; wax will not penetrate where there is water. If you want to speed up the drying time use a hair dryer, or iron the paper between sheets of newspaper with the iron set to low. Ironing may cause the paper to crinkle, but this often adds more interesting effects. You could try both ways — smooth and wrinkled.

3
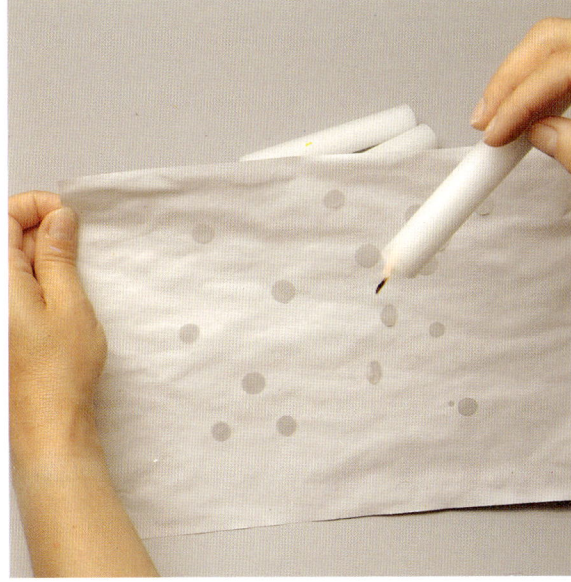

4

5
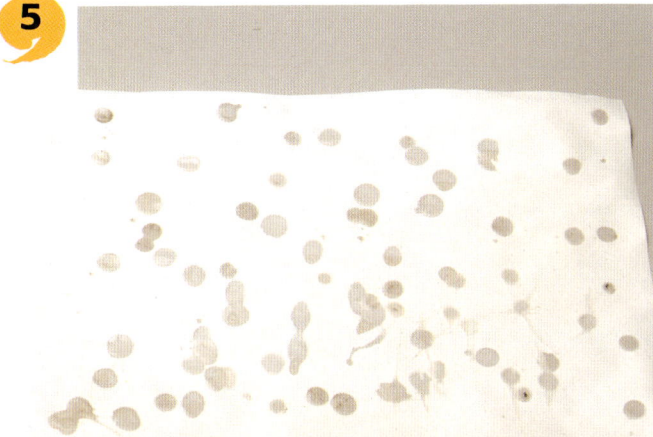

6

7

8
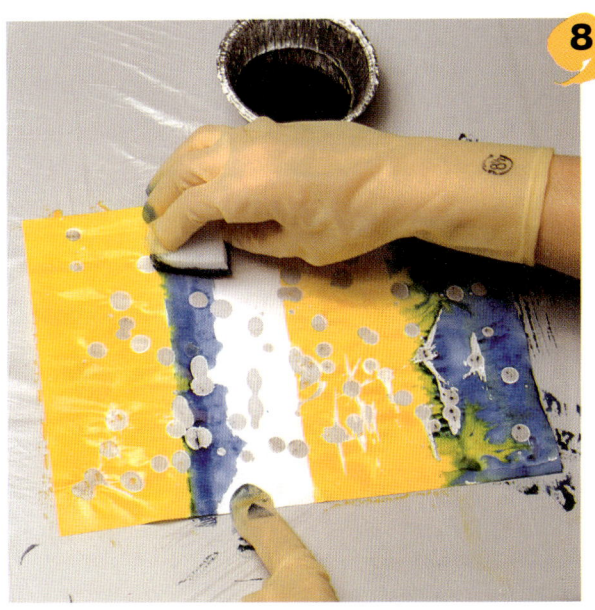

3 Place your prepared sheet of paper on the work surface. Light a candle and, as the wax melts, let it drip onto the paper. Experiment, holding it 3in (7.5cm) above the paper, then 12in (30cm) above the paper. Tip the paper at an angle, and move the candle quickly across the sheet.

4 Use a piece of cardboard to push the molten wax around the paper.

5 Notice the changes in the tone and degree of transparency of the paper as the hot wax cools.

6 Cover your work surface with plastic sheeting to protect it from the dye. Mix ¼ teaspoon yellow dye powder to a paste with a few drops of the soda solution. Add 2 tablespoons (30ml) soda solution to this paste. The dye is ready to use. If you want a paler colour dilute the dye powder still further.

7 Use a large brush or a piece of cut sponge to colour two stripes of yellow on your waxed paper. Wear rubber gloves when you do this or your fingers will go yellow, too.

8 Mix blue or turquoise dye powder in the same way and paint or sponge on two blue stripes. Leave it to dry completely. You can speed this up with a hair-drier, but don't hold it so close that you melt the wax.

SAFETY FIRST

● Good ventilation is important at all times but especially when you are ironing off wax. Work with your iron to one side so that your face is not directly above it. You may even wish to wear a mask as protection against the wax fumes released by the heat of the iron.

9

10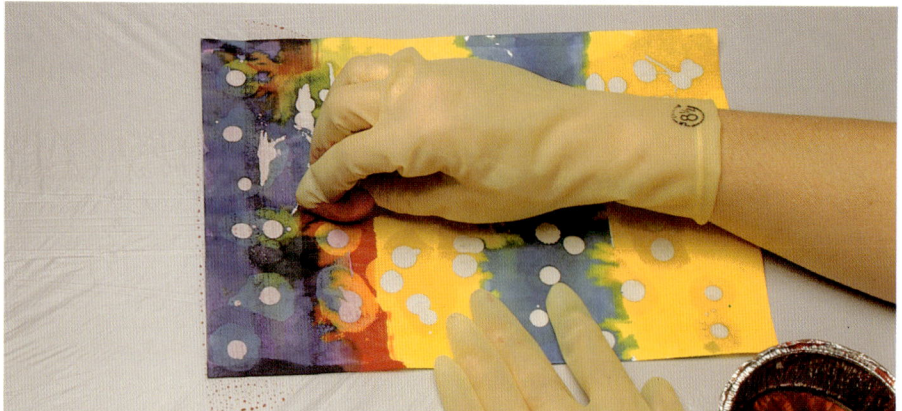

11

9 The wax is removed by ironing out between sheets of newspaper. Always make sure that there is a thick layer of newspaper under your batik to protect the surface below. Place two sheets of newspaper on top and use the iron on cotton heat. You will see the wax melting and being absorbed into the newspaper. Continue to iron, putting fresh sheets of newspaper above and below your work, until no more wax comes out.

10 When the wax is ironed out it also spreads into the paper around the original waxed areas, creating a "halo" effect. These "halo" areas will now also resist the dye, leaving abstract, unwaxed shapes, which can be dyed a third colour if you wish.

11 When the dye has dried completely use a viewing window to select areas, and you will have three or four "alien landscape" cards to send to your friends.

GIFT WRAPPING

◆

How about making some exclusive wrapping paper for a special present or a waterproof jacket for a precious book? You can melt some ordinary candles or use bought batik wax, which comes in the form of granules and which is a mixture of paraffin (candle) wax and beeswax. Paraffin wax is brittle, cracks easily and sometimes flakes off. Beeswax is soft and pliable when it is cool and adheres well to fabrics. The combination of the two balances out their properties so that the wax will crack to give the traditional batik effect when it is folded but not so much that it flakes away. The ratio is about 70 per cent paraffin to 30 per cent beeswax. This project involves using a soft bed, mixing colours and applying extra wax to remove "halos". It also introduces you to using caps.

You will need
◊ Basic equipment, plus
◊ Sheets of soda-treated paper,
   16½in × 11½in (A3, 420 × 297mm)
◊ Small blanket or towel

Cap-making kit
◊ Masking tape
◊ Scissors/craft knife
◊ Empty cereal packets
◊ Boxes
◊ Corrugated card
◊ Kitchen rolls
◊ Corks

1

2

1 Whichever kind of wax you decide to use you will need a way of melting it and keeping it hot. The safest, most reliable equipment is one of the thermostatically controlled, electric wax pots that are available from specialist suppliers. Here, the batik wax granules are beginning to melt.

2 To apply the wax make some home-made versions of Indonesian caps, the copper printing blocks developed by the Javanese to print repeat patterns on lengths of fabric and so speed up the process of batik. Your caps can be made from cardboard rolls or from cut and folded card, held with masking tape if necessary. Cutting with pinking shears gives an interesting tool, and corrugated card is a good material to use because the loops serve as a reservoir for the wax. You could also use corks or wooden cotton reels, but do not use any form of plastic, which will melt in the hot wax.

3

4

5

6

7

8

3 To get the best print from your caps there should be a soft surface under your paper to press into. Lay a folded blanket or towel under the plastic sheeting on your work surface to give a soft bed.

4 Lay a sheet of paper on top of your printing bed. Heat the wax until it has melted, and put your cap into the wax. Cardboard sometimes fizzes the first time you put it in, so don't worry. Count to 10 to allow the wax to penetrate and warm the card.

5 As you lift it from the wax gently shake off the excess wax once or twice. Hold a pad of material underneath it to catch any further drips as you take it to the paper.

6 Print the wax onto the paper by pressing the cap down firmly. If the wax stays white and opaque it is not hot enough. The paper should go darker and become more translucent when it comes into contact with the wax.

7 You can do more than one print before going back to the wax pot, but each successive print will leave a finer deposit as the wax is used up and cools. Three or four impressions are usually the maximum.

8 Combine different cap prints to build up a pattern.

9

10

11

1st colour	resulting colour	2nd colour

SAFETY FIRST

- Whichever way you use to melt the wax do not allow it to smoke – the fumes are unpleasant, unhealthy to breathe in for long periods and unnecessary, for the wax is hot enough before it smokes. A temperature of 270°F (132°C) is an ideal constant temperature, and you can test this with a wax thermometer.
- If the wax becomes overheated and ignites, smother the container with a fireproof lid. **Never** introduce water, which will spit and spread.
- Always work in a well-ventilated area.

The colours and patterns you achieve will be as varied as your imagination.

9 Mix the dye using ¼ teaspoon of dye powder and 2 tablespoons (30ml) soda solution for each colour (see page 92). Red, yellow and blue have been used here. You can apply the dye in stripes or paint different colours inside the various wax-surrounded shapes.

10 When the dye is dry, iron out the wax. If you do not want the "halo" shapes, cover the unwaxed areas with wax while they are still warm from ironing, which makes it quick and economical on wax, and then iron out again. All the "halos" will disappear.

11 Try mixing your dyes to see what other colours you can get.

SUN CALENDAR

Working on fabric is slightly more complicated than producing batik paper, but it is not difficult and the process can still be kept simple while giving effective results. The fabric must be 100 per cent natural fibre — cotton, linen, silk, for example — or viscose rayon. Any man-made fibres in the fabric, as in cotton polyester, may appear to take up the dye only for it to wash out at a later rinse stage, giving disappointing results. When the dyes are mixed with an alkali (the solution of sodas), a chemical reaction takes place that allows a permanent bonding of dye and fibre — hence the name, fibre-reactive dyes. Once the chemical reaction between dye and alkali has begun it continues for 2—4 hours, after which the dyestuff will no longer be fibre-reactive. As with synthetics it may appear to take up, only to wash away later, although it can be used up on paper batiks if you can't bear to throw it away. The dye powder, however, can be stored indefinitely if it is kept in closed containers, in a cool atmosphere and away from the light.

You will need
◊ Basic equipment, plus
◊ 2 squares in prepared fabric, 8 × 8in
  (20 × 20cm) and 3 × 3in (7.5 × 7.5cm)
◊ Small blanket or towel

Cap-making kit
◊ Masking tape
◊ Scissors/craft knife
◊ Empty cereal packets
◊ Boxes
◊ Corrugated card
◊ Kitchen roll

1 Burning a small sample of a fabric is a good way of testing the fibre content, and the kitchen sink is a safe place to do this. Hold a lighted match to a piece of the fabric. Synthetic threads will burn quickly and leave a hard plastic residue; natural fibres burn slowly, leaving a soft ash.

2 You will need a piece of prepared cotton about 8in (20cm) square. Any oils or dressings in the fabric may prevent the dye from penetrating, and they must be removed by scouring. This is achieved by boiling the fabric for 5 minutes in a solution made to the proportions of 2 teaspoons detergent to 2pt (1 litre) water. You can use 2 teaspoons washing soda crystals instead, but this may affect the surface of your boiling saucepan. Rinse the fabric in clear water, allow it to dry and iron to a smooth finish. The fabric is now prepared and is also pre-shrunk.

3

4

6

5

3 Lay the prepared fabric on a soft bed and heat the wax to approximately 270°F (132°C). Have your home-made caps ready, and wax the areas you wish to remain white. If the wax is at the right temperature you will see the change in tone of the fabric just as you did with the paper. If the wax is white and opaque the fibres are not being penetrated by the wax and will not resist the dye.

4 Mix ¼ teaspoon yellow dye with 2 tablespoons (30ml) soda solution (see page 92).

5 Apply the dye with a piece of cut sponge. Remember to wear rubber gloves.

6 Dye the test piece for experimenting with overdyeing later. Leave it to dry naturally; this will depend on the temperature of your room. You can speed up the drying time with some warm air, placing the fabric in an airing cupboard, for example, or hair-drier, but if you use a hair-drier take care not to melt the wax. Apply wax to the dried fabric in the areas you want to keep yellow. The facial detail can be added with a small brush.

7 Mix red dye as yellow above. Try it out on your test piece of fabric. Add more dye powder if the colour is too weak or more soda solution if the colour is too strong. Apply to your square and allow to dry.

8 Use a brush and cap to wax the areas you want to stay orange.

9 Mix blue dye and test it on your sample piece before applying it. When the dye has dried completely remove the fabric from the plastic sheeting and iron out the wax between sheets of newspaper.

You can mount your finished piece and perhaps attach a calendar below it. You can buy ready-made window mounts, or you could get the piece mounted at your local art shop.

CALENDAR

DOLLY BAGS

◆

When you apply the colours all over the fabric each time the range of colours you can achieve is limited to the shades resulting from overdyeing. Painting on the dye in "pools" of fabric surrounded by wax, in the technique known as pool dyeing, gives tremendous possibilities for colour combinations to exist side by side, and the opportunities are limited only by your dye-mixing abilities. Using the dye in this way requires the addition of urea, which is a by-product of natural gas. In this process small amounts of dye are painted onto the fabric, rather than the fabric being immersed completely in a dye bath as in traditional batik, and urea is used to delay the drying process. This is important because fibres and dye react while the fabric is wet, and the longer this process takes the better the fixation of the dye will be — so, no speeding up of the drying from now on. Urea also helps to dissolve the dye more easily and thoroughly, maximizing the colour intensity. This project also involves the use of a sponge "brush", saving colours with wax and boiling out wax.

You will need
◊ Basic equipment, plus
◊ Prepared cotton, 21¾ × 16½in (52 × 39cm); the bag made to imperial measurements will be slightly larger than the metric dimensions in order to keep the figures simple
◊ Lining material, 21¾ × 16½in (52 × 39cm)
◊ Blanket or towel
◊ 2 wooden sticks, 6in (15cm) long — old brush handles, straight twigs, for example
◊ Small paint brush (optional)
◊ Soft pencil, 4B
◊ Ruler

Cap-making kit
◊ Masking tape
◊ Cardboard tubes
◊ Corrugated paper/cereal box card
◊ Scissors/craft knife

Making up the bags
◊ Scissors
◊ Pins
◊ Thread
◊ Sewing machine or needles if you prefer to sew by hand
◊ 1yd (1m) lacing to make the drawstring handles

1 To make up a urea solution dissolve 1 teaspoon of urea with 1pt (600ml) warm water. If you are going to use it straight away do not use water warmer than 122°F (50°C) because fibre-reactives are cold dyes and must not be heated above this temperature. This, like the soda solution, is usable for 10–14 days if it is kept in an airtight container.

2 Using the selective dyeing process you can make three bags with different colour schemes. The bags have a base with a diameter of 5in (12cm) and the sides are 5 × 15¾in (12 × 38cm) (all seams are included in the specifications). Mark the three strips and bases on the prepared cotton with a soft pencil and lay it on a soft bed.

3

4

5

urea solution

soda solution

6

3 Make a sponge "brush". Push one of the wooden sticks into a piece of sponge and strap it firmly in place with masking tape. Trim it to a point, and it is ready for use. The sponge will hold more wax than a normal brush, enabling you to work for longer before having to recharge it with wax. These home-made tools are also excellent for applying dye. Heat the wax and use your sponge "brush" to apply a continuous line of wax, following your pencil lines, to separate the three strips. If you do not do this dye will spread to areas it is not wanted.

4 Make your cap prints in each section, making sure that each shape has a continuous wax boundary. If the wax sticks to the plastic beneath the fabric you know it has penetrated! It will also keep your work in place while you are dyeing, preventing the unwanted transfer of colour.

5 Colour fastness is obtained by combining the urea solution with the soda solution in the ratio of 1 part urea to 2 parts soda. For this project add a few drops of urea solution to $\frac{1}{4}$ teaspoon of dye powder to form a paste, then add 2 teaspoons urea solution and 4 teaspoons soda solution. This will be about full strength; if you want paler colours reduce the dye powder.

6 When all waxing and dyeing is completed and dried remove the fabric from the plastic sheet and iron out the wax. You will probably have noticed that the fabric becomes soft while it is warm from ironing but stiffens again as the residue of wax in the fibres cools. You may wish to retain this quality, because the residue makes the fabric water-repellent. However, if you want the fabric less stiff, more wax can be removed by boiling the fabric in water in an old saucepan for 5 minutes, then plunging it into cold water, using wooden tongs to transfer it from saucepan to bowl. The wax solidifies on the surface of the cloth and can be rubbed or scraped off. This process can be repeated to remove more wax. Finally, boil in soapy water to remove all surplus dye. Allow the dye to set in the fabric for 24 hours before using this method.

Leave the saucepan of water in which you have boiled the fabric to cool, and the wax will form a skin on the surface, which can be removed, dried and used again. You must dry wax thoroughly before reusing it, otherwise it will spit in the wax pot, like hot fat in a frying-pan.

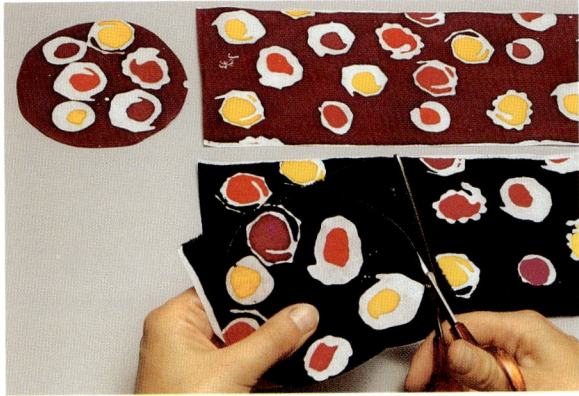

7 Once the wax has been removed to your satisfaction, cut out the fabric ready to make up your bags. Allowing ¼in (5mm) seams, sew the sides together. On each side make a buttonhole ½in (1cm) long and running from ¾in (2cm) to 1¼in (3cm) from the top edge.

8 With right sides together, sew the base to the bottom edge. Turn right side out. Cut and sew the lining material in the same way but omit the buttonholes. Leave unturned.

9 Put the lining inside the bag, turn in ¼in (5mm) seams on both and sew together. Sew two lines of stitching around the top of the bag, one at the top edge of the buttonholes the other at the bottom edge to provide a channel for the drawstring. Thread through

the drawstrings, one entering and one exiting from each buttonhole.

If you want to make a larger bag, multiply the radius of the base, by 6.284 (approx 6¼) to give you the appropriate length side.

HINTS AND TIPS

REMOVING DYE

An easier and more effective way of removing wax is to put your work through a dry-cleaning machine. The chemicals dissolve all the wax but the brightness of the colour is not lost, as does happen to some extent with boiling out. Your waxy batik will have no effect on other items in the dry-cleaning machine, and the dyes will not run.

PILLOWCASE

◆

You can personalize a ready-made garment or article, as long as it is 100 per cent natural fibres, by adding batik decoration of your choice. I have worked on a pillowcase here, but you can work on any article you like. However, as with all the other fabrics, it must be prepared and then laid on a soft bed that is large enough to accommodate the whole of it.

You will need
◊ Basic equipment, plus
◊ Blanket
◊ Dye brushes or sponges
◊ Prepared cotton pillowcase
◊ Caps — two sizes of cardboard tube, flat card to bend into shape and masking tape to hold small shape in position

1 When you use your found or home-made caps to apply the wax you must bear in mind that you have two layers to penetrate. Recharge the cap with wax for each stamp and make sure that it is hot enough by counting to five each time you put the cap into the wax pot.

2 If the wax does not penetrate properly the underside of the completed article may be disappointing. As with the dolly bags, if the wax sticks to the plastic sheeting, leave it to hold your fabric in place while you apply the dye.

3 You will need more dyestuff for this article. Use ½ teaspoon dye powder with 2 tablespoons (30ml) urea solution and 4 tablespoons (60ml) soda solution. If you want paler shades reduce the amount of dye powder or increase the chemical solutions.

4 Remember to wear your gloves. Dye the lightest areas first and allow to dry. If the colour has leaked at all, wax again before adding the dark background, which will cover up any unwanted dye.

5 When the design is completed and dry, remove the pillowcase from the plastic sheeting and iron out the bulk of the wax. Put it in for a dry-cleaning cycle so that the fabric regains its original softness.

There is no need to start with a white background. Immersion dyeing, which is introduced in the next project, will allow you to start with any colour you like, but you must remember that all subsequent colours will be affected by the original shade.

GARMENT FABRIC

◆

Large pieces of fabric can be quite easily batiked. The waxing is done in stages on a soft bed, and the fabric is then immersed in dye to ensure full penetration and evenness of colour.

You will need

◊ Basic equipment, plus
◊ Blanket
◊ Plastic bucket with a minimum capacity of 1 gallon (4.5 litres)
◊ Bowl with a minimum capacity of 1 gallon (4.5 litres)
◊ Paper and fabric for experimenting with caps and dyes
◊ 2yd (2m) prepared fine cotton

Cap-making kit

◊ Masking tape
◊ Scissors/craft knife
◊ Empty cereal packets
◊ Corrugated card
◊ Kitchen roll
◊ Empty card from wide roll of adhesive tape

HINTS AND TIPS

FIXING COLOURS

● Fixing is improved in a humid atmosphere. Short bursts of steam from an electric kettle, introduced intermittently over the 2–3 hour drying period, can provide the necessary humidity.
● The evenness of colour can be enhanced by adding the salt in three stages in the first 15 minutes of the dyeing process. However, the fabric must be removed each time more salt is added, which makes the procedure a bit too complicated for a beginner. For this reason I have suggested that all the salt be added at the same time.

1

2

3

1 Make some cardboard caps and experiment on paper with them until you have a design you are happy with.

2 Try the caps on fabric to see how many prints you can get from each dip in the wax and how they change as the wax cools and runs out.

3 Make as large a soft bed as your blanket and work surface will allow. Lay down the first section of your fabric, and arrange a chair at either side to hold it off the floor while you are waxing. Lift the fabric at intervals as you work to prevent it from being stuck to the plastic when you want to move on to the next section.

4 When the first waxing is complete prepare the dye bath. These ingredients are enough for about 6oz (150gm) dry weight of fabric, which is about what 2yd (2m) cotton should weigh. Dissolve 6 tablespoons (150gm) salt in 3fl oz (100ml) warm water and set aside. Dissolve 6 teaspoons (15gm) soda ash (or 12 teaspoons/ 30gm soda crystals) in 3fl oz (100ml) warm water and set aside.

5 Make a paste of 1½—6 teaspoons yellow dye powder in warm water. Do not use water warmer than 122°F (50°C). Add some more water so that it will pour easily.

6 Add 6pt (3 litres) water to the dye and stir. Add the dissolved salt and stir. Salt is added to this dye recipe to facilitate penetration, to promote an even quality of dyeing and to get the best colour from the dye powder.

7 Immerse the waxed fabric and test piece in clean, cold water and shake off the excess.

8 Transfer the fabric to the dye bath. Immerse it completely, agitating it to ensure good penetration of the dye.

9 Remove it after 15 minutes and put it in a bowl.

10 Add the dissolved soda to the dye bath, then return and immerse the fabric for a further 45 minutes, stirring occasionally. Remove the fabric, rinse in cold water until the water runs clear, then hang to drip dry. This is part of the fixing process.

11 When the fabric is completely dry return it to the soft bed and do the second waxing. This time wax everything you want to stay yellow.

12 Follow the same recipe and procedure as before, but using blue dye powder instead of yellow. Test the colour on your sample piece first.

13 As the fabric moves around in the dye bath some of the wax will be bent and crack, and dye will be able to penetrate the fibres. This is what gives batik its traditional crackle effect. Wax cracks more readily and cleanly when it is cold, and this is why the fabric is soaked in cold water before it is immersed in the dye bath. The cracking is further controlled by crushing the fabric to a greater or lesser extent before and while it is being dyed.

It is easier to boil out the bulk of the wax from a large piece of fabric rather than ironing it. Dry clean it to restore the original softness, and then it will be ready to make up into the article of your choice. If you machine-wash the article at home afterwards do so on a cool wash — 104°F (40°C) — and wash separately for the first few washes, especially if you have used intense colours.

CUSHION COVER

◆

As we have seen, it was the Javanese who invented the canting. Although it is not easy to use, once you have mastered the techniques you will find that the canting will provide a continuous flow of hot wax that will enable you to fine line or dot work that would not otherwise be possible. There are many different shapes of these metal wax reservoirs available, but they all have one or more spouts through which the wax flows. The diameter of the spouts is one of the factors dictating the width of a line or the size of a dot of the wax applied to the fabric; speed, heat and angle of use are others.

Wax can be most easily applied to fine cottons and silks because the wax can penetrate more quickly than on thicker or more coarsely woven fabrics like linen. You will draw a more confident, freer and finer line if the tool can move smoothly and easily across the surface. If you go more slowly to allow wax to penetrate a thicker fabric you will be more likely to produce wobbly, more uneven and thicker lines. The heat of the wax also affects the speed with which it flows through the spout and how much it spreads in the fabric, and this is particularly evident when you are working on fine fabrics, such as silk. Remember that the same spout will produce lines of different widths on different fabrics and with the wax at different temperatures.

You will need
◊ Basic equipment, plus
◊ Soft pencil, 4B
◊ Wooden frame
◊ Drawing pins
◊ Prepared cotton, 17 × 17in
   (43 × 43cm)

1 An abstract design, which will give you maximum freedom to experiment with the cantings, is suggested for a cushion cover. Lay the prepared piece of cotton on your work surface and use a soft pencil to mark the diagonal and horizontal crosses lightly as a guide to keep the design symmetrical.

2 At first you will find that canting work is easiest on stretched fabric. You can use an old picture frame, if it is firmly jointed and not warped. Pin the centre of each side and then the corners. The fabric needs to be taut, but take care that you do not pull the weave out of alignment, or the image will be distorted when you take the fabric from the frame.

3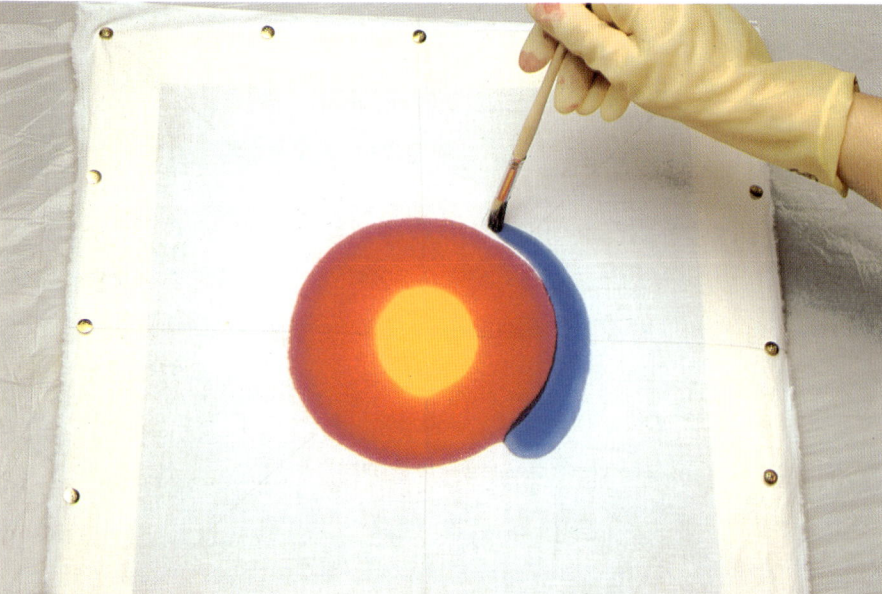

4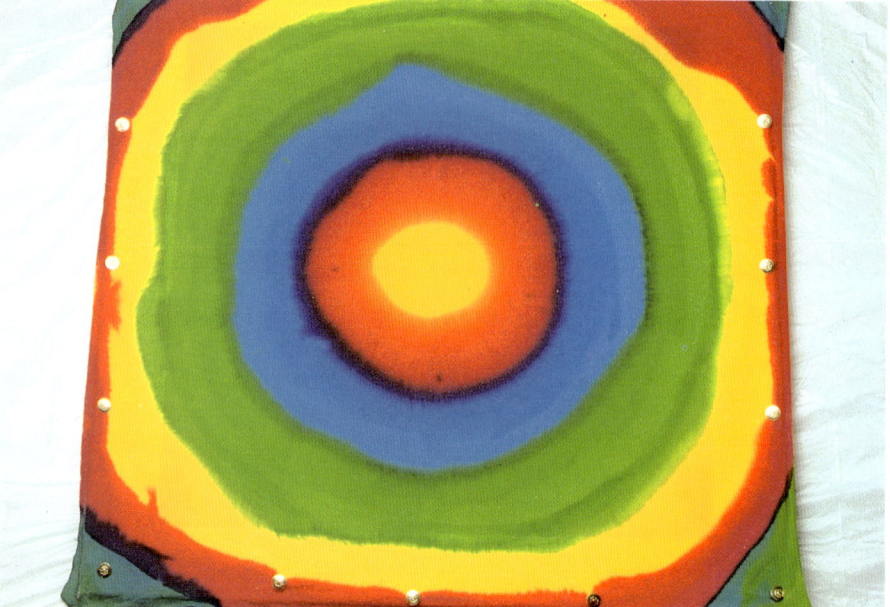

5

HINTS AND TIPS

USING A CANTING

- If you get some unwanted drips, do some on purpose to match on the other side so that the "mistakes" are incorporated into your design or used to accentuate a motif.
- Do not travel so fast that the wax does not have time to soak in at all. Experiment with the lines and marks that the different cantings can make.

3 Before you begin waxing, mix the dyes – 6 tablespoons (90ml) of each should be plenty. I have used red, yellow and turquoise (see page 104). Apply the dyes to the fabric, allowing them to mingle with each other at the edges to create a colourful, softly diffused effect.

4 Keep the colours light and bright. Allow the fabric to dry completely.

5 Heat the wax and put the canting in it for at least 30 seconds so that the metal bowl can warm up and help to keep the wax hot. Fill the reservoir about half full so that wax does not flow over the top while you are working. Use a piece of soft, absorbent cloth to remove excess wax and to catch any drips as you carry the canting from the wax pot to the fabric.

6

7

6 Rest your frame at an angle and also hold the canting at an angle as you work. The angle affects the flow of wax from the spout, and you will have to experiment to get the flow you want, but do not hold it at such a sharp angle that wax flows out of the back onto your fingers!

7 When waxing is complete, mix up 3fl oz (90ml) of black dyestuff using ½ teaspoon dye powder and apply it over the fabric with a sponge. Remember to have the sheet of plastic underneath to catch any drips and to wear rubber gloves to protect your fingers. Fibre-reactive dyes increase in intensity when they are overdyed, and this is particularly true with black, which looks darker and richer when it is applied twice, as was done here to cover the underlying bright dyes. When the fabric is completely dry, iron out and dry clean before making up into a cushion cover.

FISH ON SILK

◇

Silk is a much more delicate fabric than cotton, and it requires a different treatment and a different technique. It has to be prepared for the same reasons as cotton, but it should never be boiled. A rinse in warm water containing detergent is sufficient. The wax can be cooler because the weave is so fine, and you can use a canting with a smaller spout because the wax will penetrate the fabric easily. The dyes will look less intense than on cotton and linen, and they will also react differently.

You will need
◊ Basic equipment, plus
◊ Prepared silk, 6 × 6in (15 × 15cm)
◊ Sheet of acetate, 11½ × 8¼in (A4, 297 × 210mm)
◊ Cardboard frame with an image area 5¼ × 5¼in (13.5 × 13.5cm)
◊ Masking tape
◊ Mixing palette
◊ Small, soft dyebrush – watercolour brush size no. 4

1

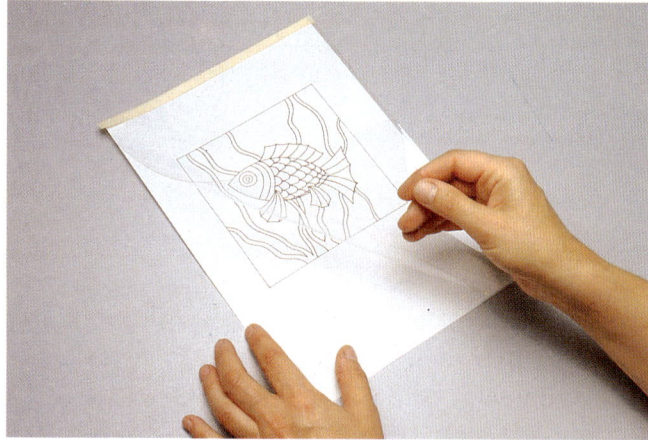

1 Keep to quite a simple image to begin with. You can use the fish shown here or draw an image of your own. Because silk is so fine you will be able to see through it and use it as you do tracing paper to do your waxing. Put a layer of acetate between the image and your silk to prevent the wax picking up any ink, which might transfer to the silk when you are ironing out the wax.

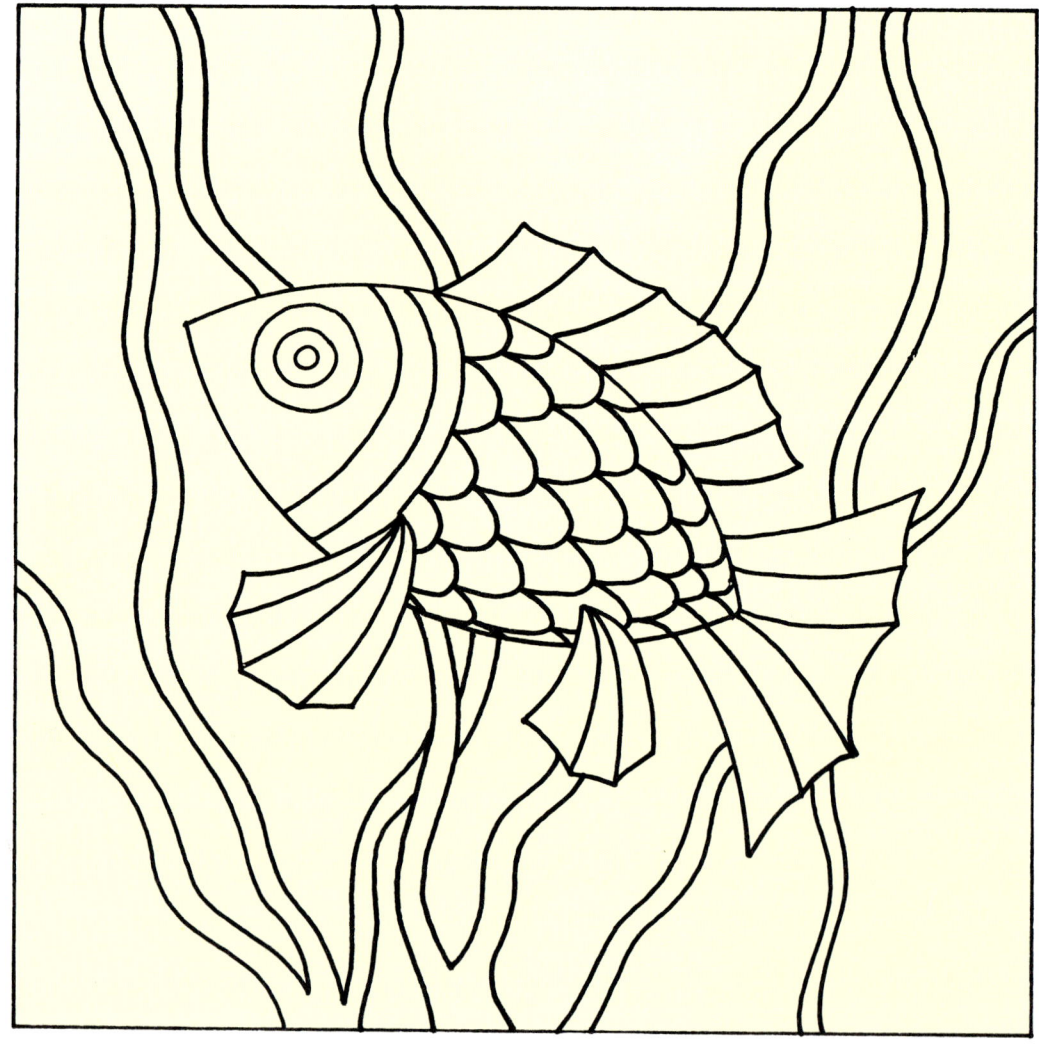

2 You can use a cardboard frame on which to stretch the silk. Although you can use corrugated box card, the best kind is heavy mounting board or the card used for shop displays. If you use the fish the cut-out window needs to be 5¼ × 5¼in (13.5 × 13.5cm). Tape the prepared fabric to the frame so that it is taut but not distorted. Position the stretched fabric over the image.

3 Tape it securely at the top, but just catch the sides and bottom with small pieces of tape so that you can separate the layers to check your progress.

4 Working with the fabric and canting at an angle, draw a line of wax around the perimeter of the image area, using the edge of the frame to guide the canting. This line will prevent the dye from spreading into your cardboard frame.

5 Following the lines of the image underneath, wax around the different "pools" of colour that you want. Make sure there are no gaps in the lines themselves or at the points they join to prevent dye from spreading to unwanted areas.

6 You will need very small amounts of dye for the fish. Mix a solution of 1 teaspoon urea solution and 2 teaspoons of soda solution and use them to mix the colours you want. Use a palette and treat the dye powder as if it were powder paint, mixing it with the chemical solutions as if they were water.

7 Test the colours on a sample.

8 Remove your stretched fabric from the acetate-covered image and paint on the dyes.

9 When the dye is completely dry, which happens much more quickly on silk than on cotton, wax the whole area before ironing out to prevent "halos" from forming.

10 Be very careful when you iron out silk. Creases that form at this stage are very difficult to remove. It is better to use unused newsprint, and do not pick up your ironed piece until it has cooled completely, otherwise it will be distorted when the wax cools. Ironing flat again can sometimes be difficult.

You could sandwich your finished batik between two layers of perspex and hang it against a window or mount it on a white backing sheet and frame it. Spray adhesive is an efficient and easy way of mounting silk on paper.

WINDOW BLIND

◆

When cotton batik is held against the light the effect is similar to that of stained glass windows. The dyes are seen at their very best, the light giving extra vibrancy to all the colours. A window blind is, therefore, a good way of displaying your batik expertise. Choose a small window for your first attempt. This project will cover an area 26in (66cm) wide and 44in (112cm) long.

The materials allow ½in (12mm) at the side edges for turning and 4in (10cm) at the top and bottom for fixing to the blind kit. The fabric may shrink when it is boiled, so cut the material at least 1in (2.5cm) larger all round than the measurements given for the prepared fabric.

You will need
◊ Basic equipment, plus
◊ Prepared fabric, 27 × 52in (69 × 132cm)
◊ Wooden frame, 27 × 27in (69 × 69cm)
◊ Drawing pins
◊ Tape measure
◊ Long ruler or straight edge
◊ Masking tape
◊ Soft pencil, 4B

Plan of window blind

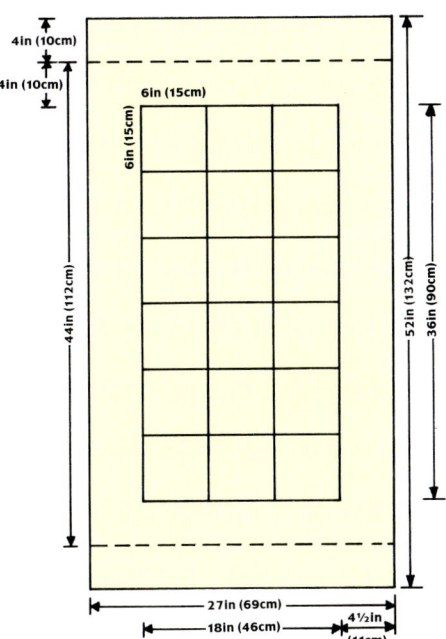

1

2

3

4

5

1 Lay the fabric on a firm surface and use a soft pencil to mark off 4in (10cm) at top and bottom. Draw a margin inside these lines of a further 4in (10cm) and on each side a margin of 4½in (11cm). The inside area is 18in (46cm) by 36in (90cm), so the repeat motif has been made 6in (15cm) square to fit three times across and six times down. Mark these squares. The border pattern needs only a ruler's width line marked in to keep the width of the snake line constant, with the points 1in (2.5cm) along the edges.

2 A frame about 27in (68cm) square would be ideal for stretching your fabric so that it can be worked in two manageable sections. These adjustable frames, which slot together, are available from most craft shops in a range of sizes; although you could use an old picture frame.

3 Wax in the border pattern. When the first section is complete move the fabric up the frame and position the second half. Move it carefully so that you do not crack the wax lines; otherwise the colours will seep where you do not intend them to.

4 The only extra guides you might need are the vertical and horizontal crosses so that you can place the points of the diamond shapes in each square. Let your canting run freely and enjoy applying the undulating lines. They will all look sufficiently similar to work well visually but different enough to add interest.

5 It is easier to apply dye if the fabric is in a complete length. If it is laid on a plastic sheet the dye may collect and cross over the wax lines. Laying it on an absorbent surface, such as newspaper, can make this less likely, but tends to suck the dye away from the fabric. If

6

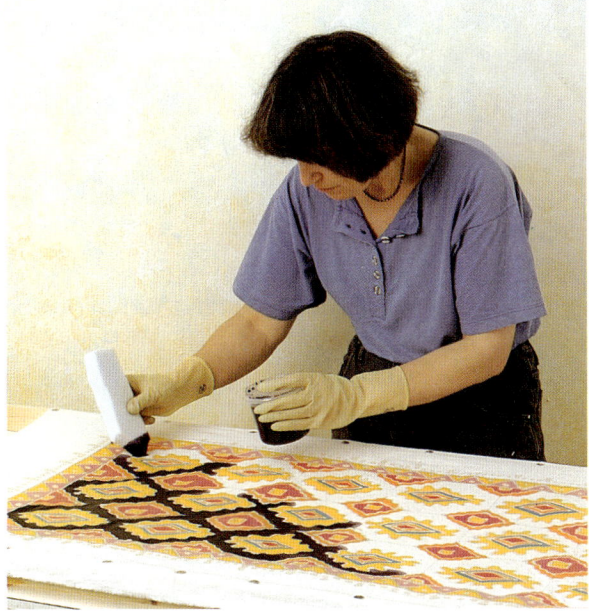

7

8

you can suspend the material in some way there will be fewer colour accidents and the finished design will look more the way you intended. You can suspend the fabric from a shelf or door lintel, which is how I applied the smaller areas of colour here. Remember to work from light to dark with your dyes and wax them as they dry to prevent any accidents with darker colours later.

6 The final background was applied with a sponge while the fabric was suspended between two lengths of 2in (5cm) square wood resting on the work surface.

7 It is better to work horizontally when larger areas are being dyed because the fabric will hold the dye, which will not drain away to the base, as happens when hanging vertically, resulting in some colour loss at the top.

8 When all the dye is completely dried, wax all over to avoid "halos", remembering to lift the fabric between applications of wax. Iron out and either leave the fabric stiff and waterproof, or get it dry cleaned after ironing and spray it with fabric protector and water repellant so that the blind can be wiped down. Your batik fabric is ready to turn into a roller blind and bring the beauty of stained glass to your window.

PORTRAITS

◆

The techniques you used to make the Sun Calendar — successive waxing and dyeing to build up the image — can be used to reproduce photographs. This time, instead of using caps on cotton, you will wax with a canting onto silk. Silk is used because of its transparency, which allows you to see the image easily through the fabric. Choose an image with quite a lot of contrast — it could be your partner, child, pet or even the car! It doesn't matter if it is in black and white or colour.

You will need
◊ Basic equipment, plus
◊ Image — photograph or picture from a magazine, for example
◊ Enlarged photostat of the chosen image
◊ Acetate
◊ Prepared silk, 11in (2.5cm) wider all around than projected finished image
◊ Cardboard frame with inside dimensions of projected finished image
◊ Unprinted newsprint

increasing strength of dyestuff ➞

1 Enlarge the image on a photostat machine. As a guide, increase the face to measure at least 6in (15cm) from crown to chin. Cover the image with acetate.

2 Plan to have three tones in addition to white. These do not have to be greys — you might like to work in tones of one colour by mixing different strengths of dyestuff.

3 Prepare and attach your silk to the cardboard frame (see page 113). Tape the image in position behind the stretched silk and draw the line of wax around the image area (see page 113). Wax in the areas to be kept white using a brush or sponge for large areas and soften the edges by applying the wax as dots with the canting.

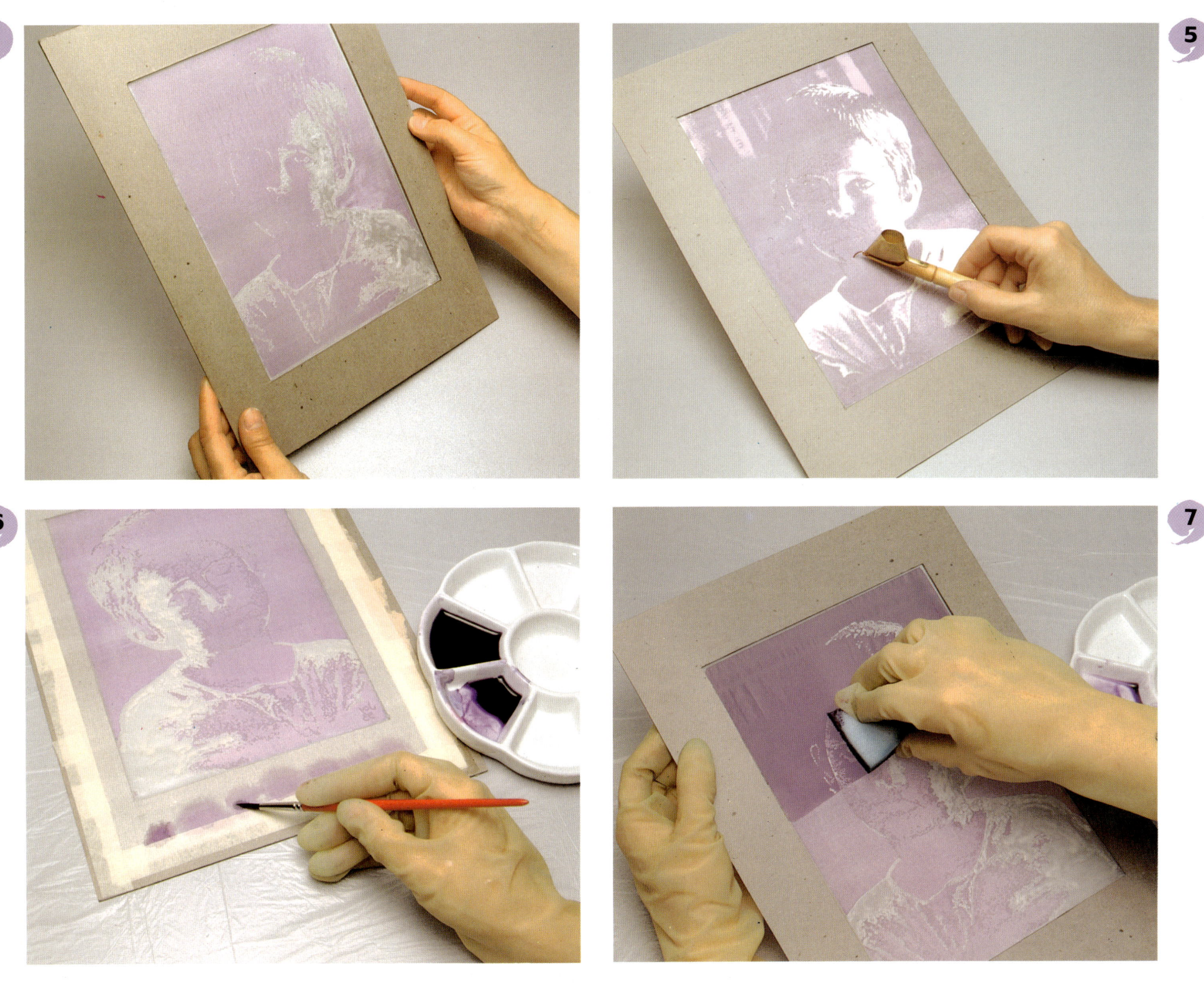

4 Remove the silk from the image ready to dye the first tone. Mix the lightest dye (tone 1) and apply it with a piece of sponge. Do not overload the sponge with liquid or the wax outline to your image will be unable to contain the dye. Remember to wear rubber gloves.

5 Use the dotting technique to wax the areas to be saved as tone 1.

6 Mix the next dye, tone 2 and test on the reverse side of the picture.

7 Apply the tone with a soft sponge.

8 Apply wax to save the areas of tone 2.

9 Mix the last and darkest dye, tone 3, and apply as before. When it is completely dry, wax the remaining areas to avoid "halos" forming after ironing out.

Iron out the wax, leaving the silk to lie flat until it is cool. Mount for display.

OWL PICTURE

◆

In all the other projects in this book you have used wax as a resist so that you could selectively dye areas of paper or fabric. Another use for this resist is to "undye" areas of an image. By using ordinary household bleach on fabric that is already dyed a strong colour, you can "discharge" the dye — that is, remove the dye already in the fabric.

Varying the dilution strength of the bleach and/or the length of time it is in contact with the fabric allows you to create an image in varying tones of the original colour. The strength of the bleach solutions and contact times given here are only approximate, and you will have to experiment on the particular fabric you are using because dyes react in different ways.

You will need
◊ Basic equipment, plus
◊ Prepared, pre-dyed cotton 11 × 11in (28 × 28cm)
◊ Household bleach
◊ Wooden frame
◊ Drawing pins
◊ Plastic tray larger than the fabric
◊ Sodium metabisulphite
◊ Masking tape
◊ Soft pencil, 4B

SAFETY FIRST

● **If any bleach gets onto your skin or into your eyes, rinse immediately in lots of cold, clean water.**

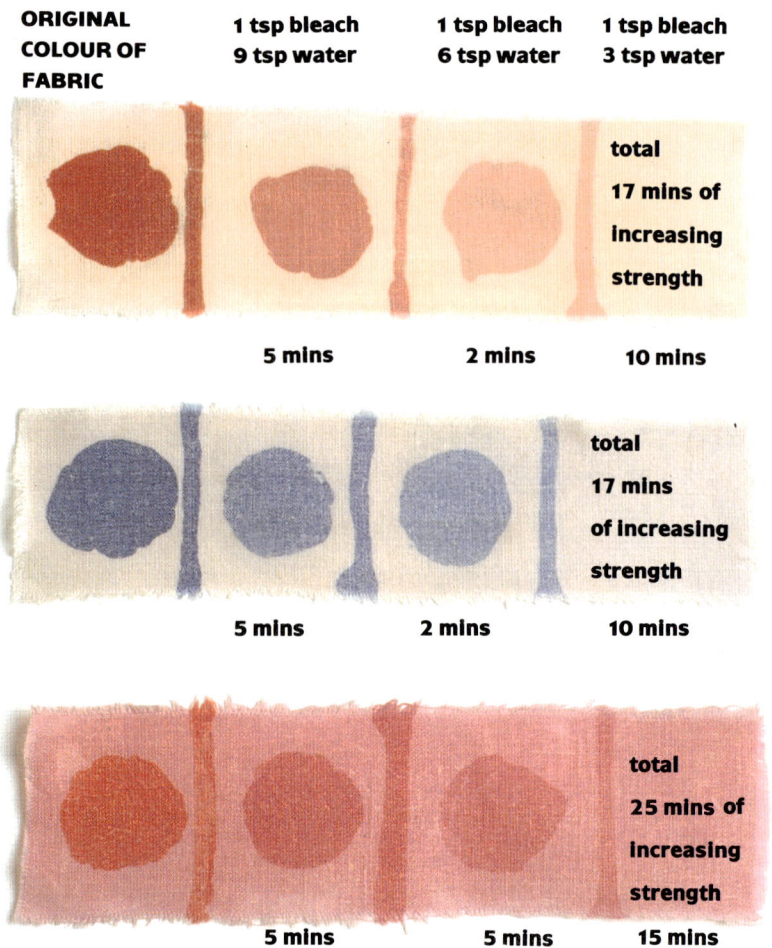

ORIGINAL COLOUR OF FABRIC	1 tsp bleach 9 tsp water	1 tsp bleach 6 tsp water	1 tsp bleach 3 tsp water
	5 mins	2 mins	10 mins	total 17 mins of increasing strength
	5 mins	2 mins	10 mins	total 17 mins of increasing strength
	5 mins	5 mins	15 mins	total 25 mins of increasing strength

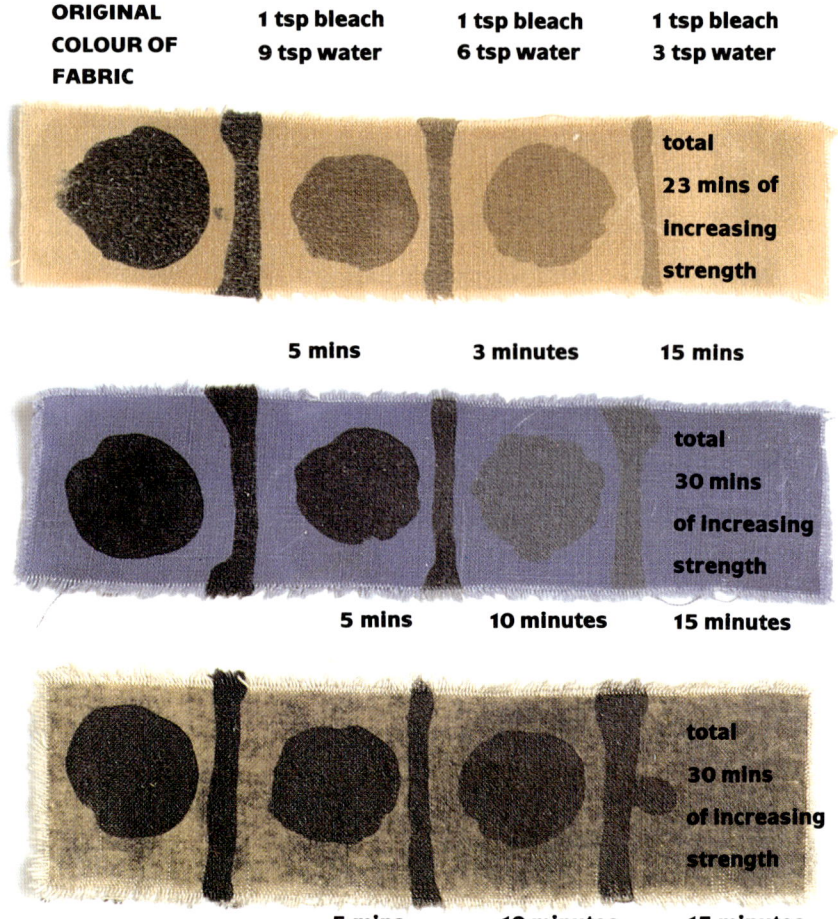

ORIGINAL COLOUR OF FABRIC	1 tsp bleach 9 tsp water	1 tsp bleach 6 tsp water	1 tsp bleach 3 tsp water
	5 mins	3 minutes	15 mins	total 23 mins of increasing strength
	5 mins	10 minutes	15 minutes	total 30 mins of increasing strength
	5 mins	10 minutes	15 minutes	total 30 mins of increasing strength

1 Some dyes discharge more readily than others, so always do a test on a small piece of your fabric before you start your main work. Never use neat bleach — it will rot the fibres — and never use bleach on silk — it will rot the fabric completely. The strongest solution you should use is 1 part bleach to 3 parts water. It is better to extend the time than to increase the strength of the bleach.

2 Black dyes discharge to very different colours according to the bias of colour in the make-up of the dye.

3 Transfer your image to the fabric using a light box or using masking tape to keep everything in place against a window. Until you are confident enough to draw freehand, it might be sensible to avoid black fabric, because it is harder to see through. If pencil does not show up on your fabric use white chalk or pastel.

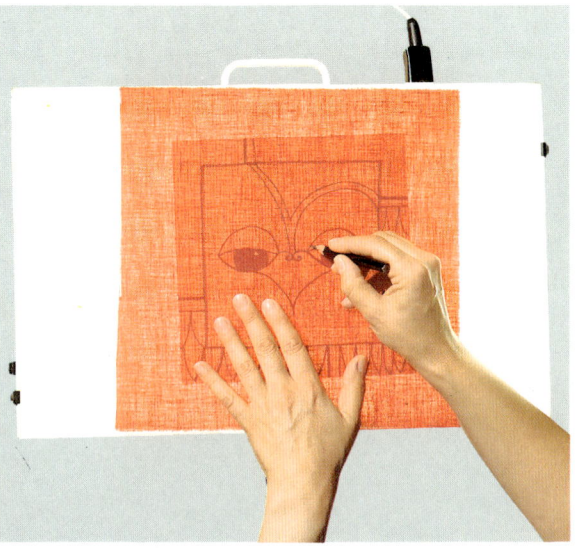

4 Pin your prepared fabric to the frame and use cantings or brushes to wax the areas or lines that are to be the darkest tone.

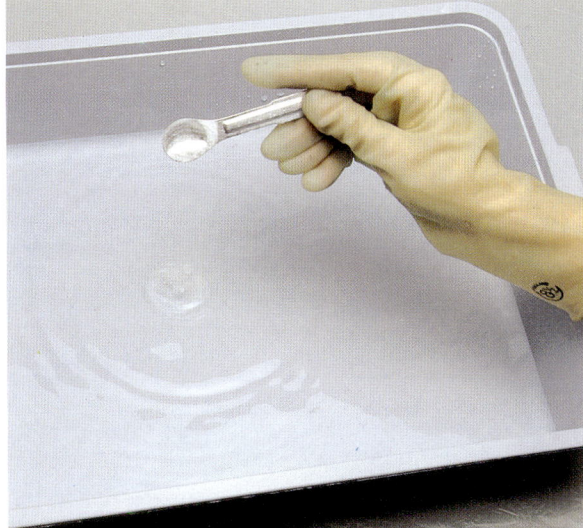
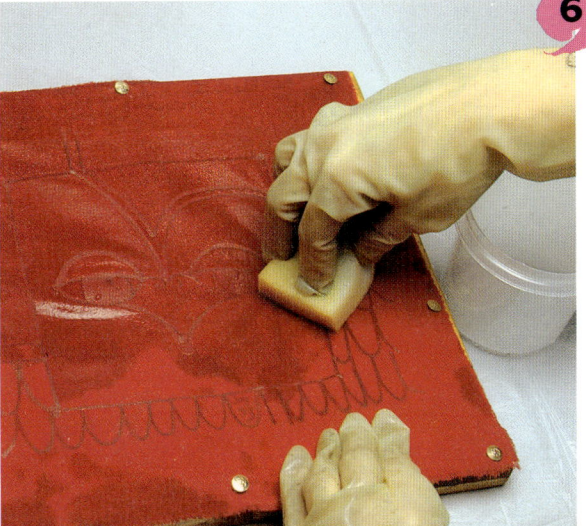
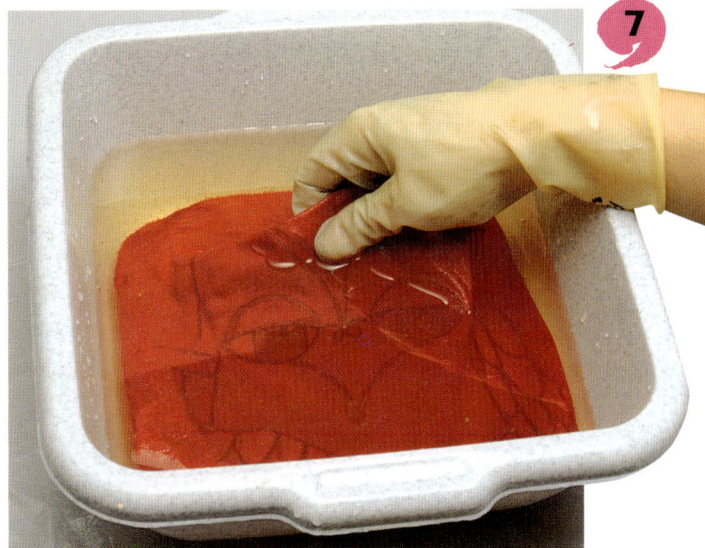

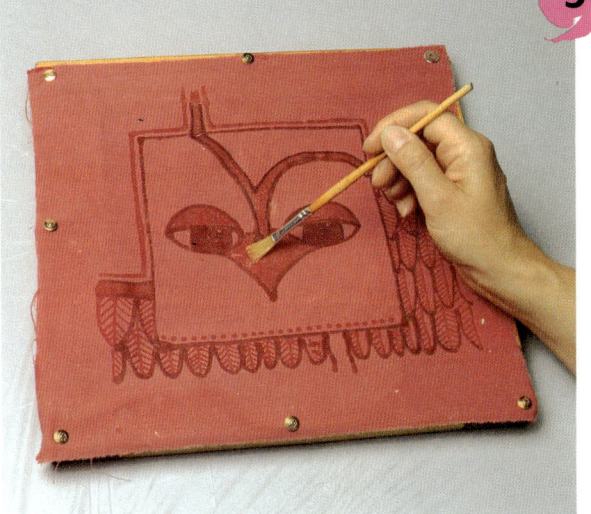

5 Prepare the neutralizing solution in readiness for step 8 later. Dissolve ½ teaspoon of sodium metabisulphite to 2pt (1 litre) water, which should be at a temperature of 105°F (40°C). You will find sodium metabisulphite on the home-brew counter, where it is sold for sterilizing equipment.

6 Mix a weak bleach solution of 1 teaspoon bleach to 3 tablespoons (45ml) water and apply it with a sponge or cotton wool. Protect your hands with rubber gloves.

7 When enough dye has discharged, which should take 5–10 minutes, rinse the fabric in cold water.

8 Transfer the fabric to the sodium metabisulphite solution and leave for 15 minutes. This will neutralize the bleach and prevent it from damaging the fibres. Rinse again in cold water.

9 Remount the fabric on the frame and when it is completely dry, wax the areas you want to stay the tone achieved by the first bleaching/discharging.

10 Mix a stronger bleach solution of 1 teaspoon bleach to 2 tablespoons (30ml) water, and apply as before. After 5–10 minutes rinse in cold water, then transfer to a fresh solution of sodium metabisulphite, which must be renewed each time it is used. Wax to save the last tone before the final bleaching.

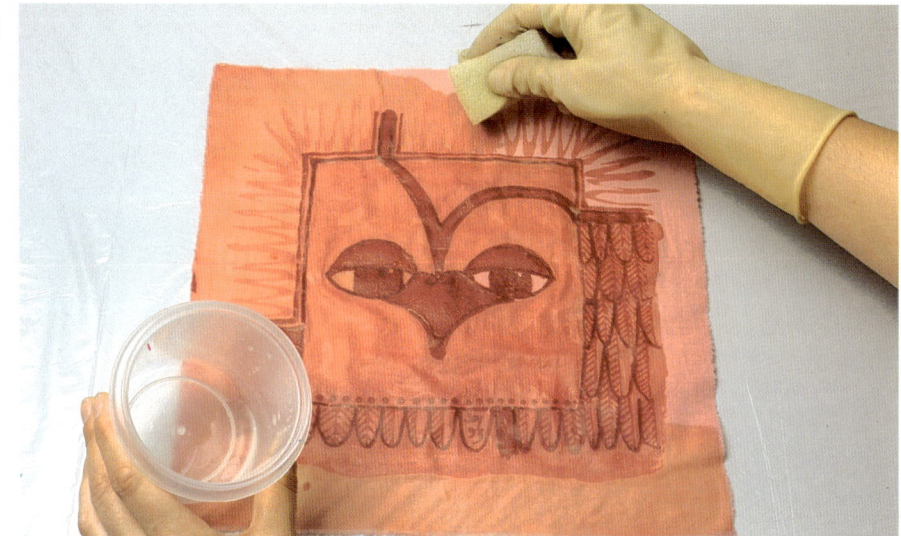

11 This time mix a strong bleach solution of 1 teaspoon bleach to 1 tablespoon (15ml) water.

12 When all the dye has been removed, rinse and neutralize as before.

13 When it is completely dry, iron out the wax.

Mount and frame.

WALL HANGING

◆ ———

Bleach can also be used to increase the possible range of colours when you are working on images that you do not want to be outlined by a white wax line. When you do successive immersions in dye some colours are lost — for example, if the first colour is yellow, subsequent dyeing with blue will create green; if the first colour is red, subsequent dyeing with blue will create purple, and in neither case will any of the fabric be blue. In this project, which uses red and blue dye, the discharge process is used to regain the blue.

You will need
◊ Basic equipment, plus
◊ Prepared cotton, 24 × 36in (60 × 90cm)
◊ Soft pencil, 4B
◊ Blanket
◊ Plastic bucket with a minimum capacity of 1 gallon (4.5 litres)
◊ Bowl with a minimum capacity of 1 gallon (4.5 litres)
◊ Cork
◊ Kitchen roll (cardboard)
◊ Plastic tray
◊ Bleach
◊ Sodium metabisulphite
◊ 2 pieces of ½in (14mm) dowel, each 2ft (60cm) long

To make up
◊ Scissors
◊ Pins
◊ Thread
◊ Sewing machine or needles

1 On the prepared fabric use a soft pencil to mark margins of 2½in (6.5cm) at the top and bottom to form the channels for the rods to fit in, and a 1in (2.5cm) margin on either side for a hem. These lines will act as guidelines for waxing. Lay the fabric on a soft bed and wax the white border pattern with cork and kitchen roll caps.

2 Draw an oval in the centre. It does not have to be perfect, and an uneven shape will be more interesting.

3 Position the eyes about halfway up the "face". Support this area over a frame so that you can hold the fabric at an angle to wax in the white part of the eyes.

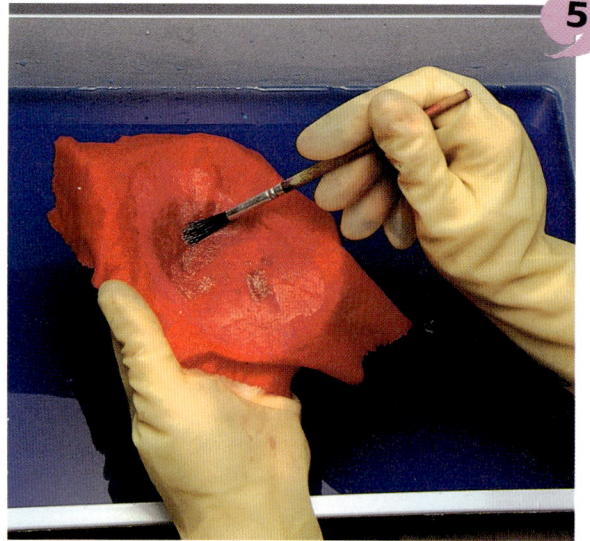

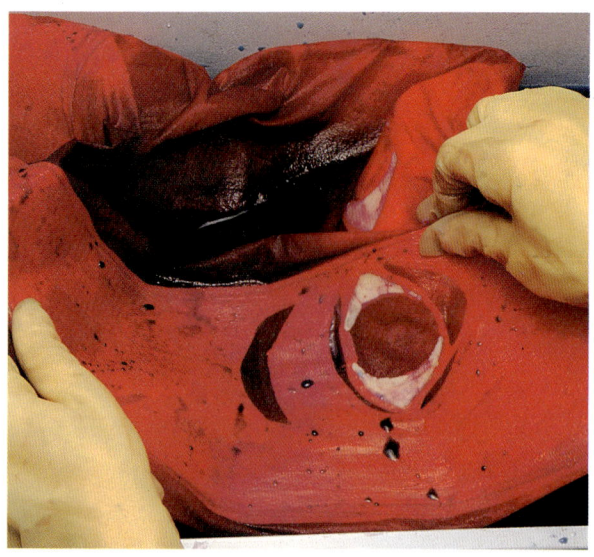

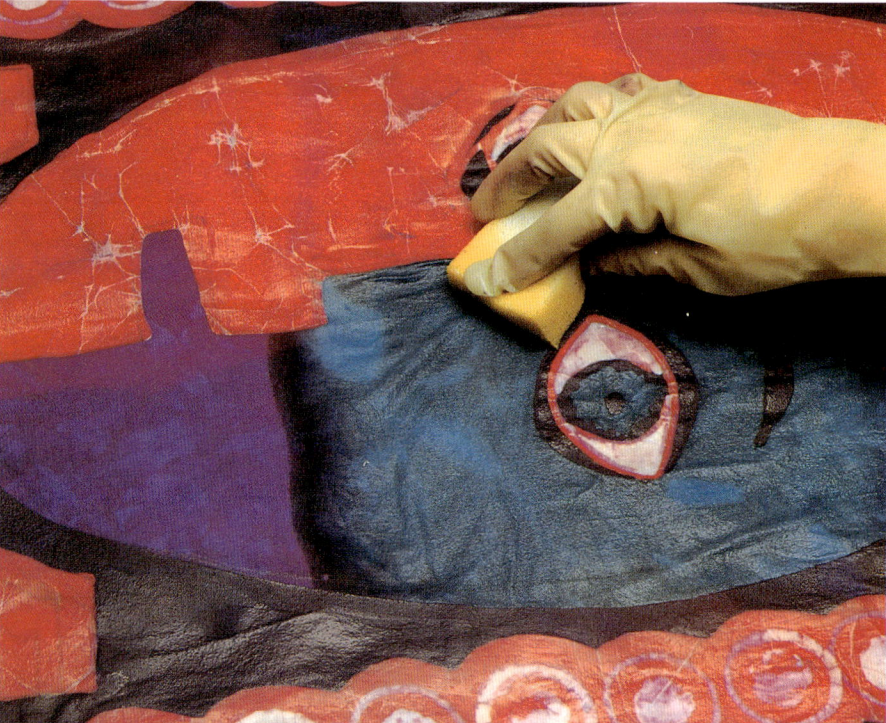

4 Prepare a red dye bath (see page 25). Remember to dye a test piece to try out overdyeing colours and discharge strengths and times. Complete the border, using a brush to wax areas to stay red. Use a sponge "brush" to wax in the side of the mask face that is to stay red. This will allow you to apply the wax quickly, making it easier to draw the lines.

5 Prepare a blue dye bath and test the colour on your sample. Adjust as necessary.

6 If you want to avoid too much crackle on the face, use a tray to hold the dye because it will be easier to keep the fabric flat.

7 When the fabric is rinsed and completely dry, return it to the work top and wax the areas that are going to stay purple. To avoid wax sticking to the plastic sheeting, lift the material as you wax. You may find it easier to mount the fabric on a frame.

8 Mix a medium strength solution of bleach, preparing enough to cover the unwaxed areas and using proportions of 1 tablespoon bleach to 6 tablespoons water. Test on your sample piece to check the timing. You will find that the red dye discharges completely before the blue, so as soon as all the red is gone you can rinse out the bleach solution. Neutralize and rinse (see page 43).

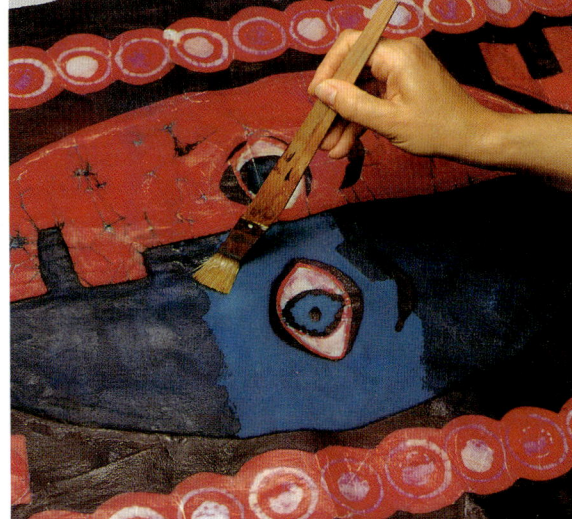

9 If you want to intensify the blue dye, apply it as in pool batik. When it is completely dry, wax over to avoid "halos" forming after ironing out.

10 If you want to iron out so that the fabric retains a residue of wax for waterproofing do so on a surface that is large enough to accommodate the whole piece so that it will cool flat. Otherwise, such a large piece may distort like silk.

Turn in and sew the sides. Turn over wide hems at the top and bottom to take the wooden dowel by which the finished piece will hang. The bottom rod will weight the work, making it hang better. If you prefer a softer finish have the work dry cleaned then spray it with a fabric protector.

GALLERY

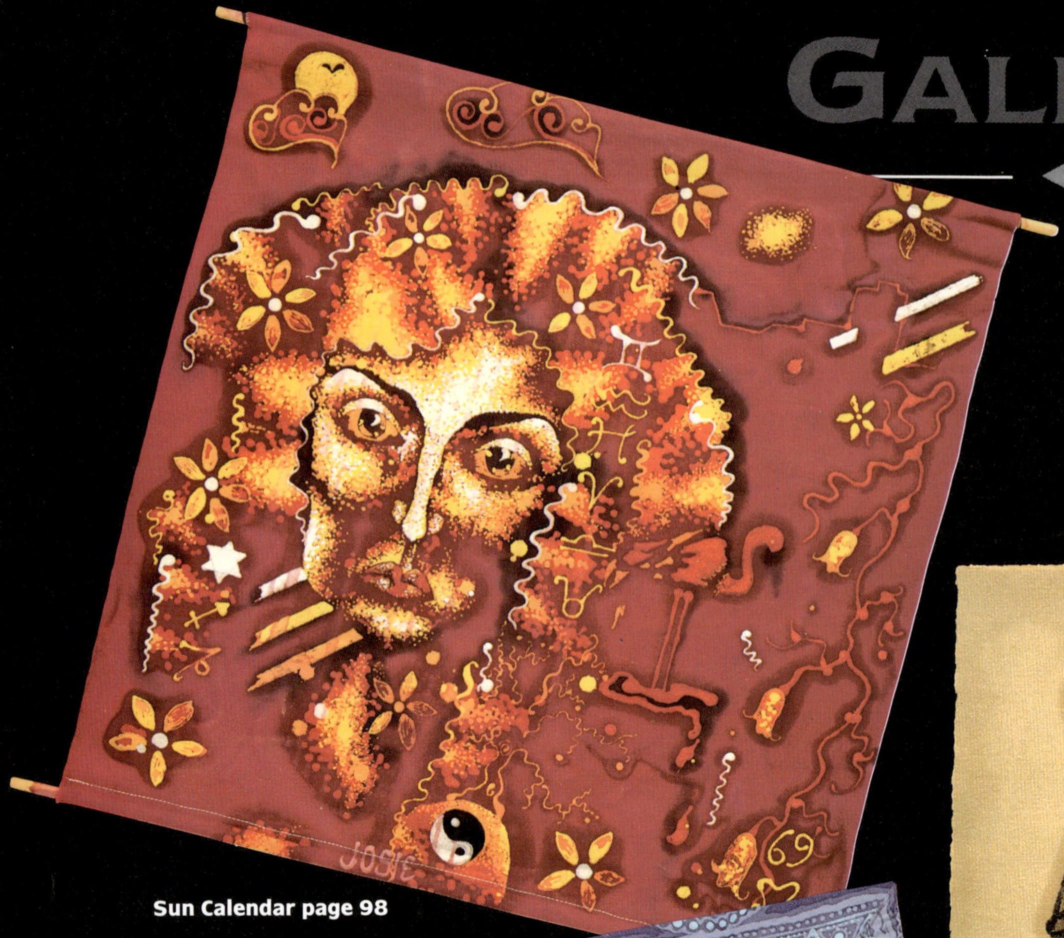

Sun Calendar page 98

Owl Picture page 121

Cushion Cover page 109

Portraits page 118

Here are some inspirational ideas to take you
further with your newly acquired skills. Each piece refers
you back to the project that uses similar techniques.

Wall Hanging page 125

Fabric Painting

Master a whole range of techniques such as sponging, stencilling and printing to create sensational effects

Introduction

Painting on fabric offers you the opportunity to create sensational effects on ordinary household items. Liven up a dull T-shirt or an old pair of jeans; design table linen to match your china, cushions to match your wallpaper and loads of other exciting things.

You don't have to be a great artist to master the art of fabric painting as many simple and effective designs can be done freehand. As your skills develop you can attempt more ambitious designs which require a steady hand, such as copying a motif from a book or magazine, or even making up your own design and transferring it onto fabric.

There are numerous ways of applying the paint to the fabric. Stencilling is an excellent way of covering a large area or creating a repeat pattern, for example on a tablecloth. Printing with sliced vegetables, fruit and flowers is a novel way of creating abstract patterns onto fabric – and it's dead easy: simply apply paint to the surface or edge of the object with which you are painting and print it directly onto the fabric. Throughout the book there are projects that incorporate masking, sponging, printing and painting on dark fabric so you become familiar with a whole range of fabric painting techniques.

Fabric paints come in many forms so you can create many different effects with puff, glitter and pearly paint. Colours can be easily mixed and applied to both natural and synthetic material. Furthermore, by ironing the newly-painted fabric on the wrong side, the article becomes colour-fast which means that it can be machine-washed time and time again. For best results new fabrics should be washed and ironed before paint is applied so that any dressing is removed which would prevent the paint from being absorbed. Remember to always place a piece of paper underneath the fabric onto which you are painting.

This book is specially designed for beginners: no expensive equipment is needed nor any special skills. Although suggestions have been given for colours and designs in all the projects there is no reason why you shouldn't try different combinations of colours and patterns. In many of the projects there are illustrations of alternative ways of painting the items to encourage you to use your imagination and, more importantly, to have fun with the paints.

Basic equipment you will need for painting on fabric.

Painted Espadrilles

Plain espadrilles come in a variety of bright colours, and they are inexpensive to buy. Decorating lighter colours – pale blue, green, pink and white – tends to be more successful than applying paint to darker shades. I have suggested using masking tape as a guide, but you may feel confident enough to apply the paint freehand.

You will need
◊ 1 pair of plain espadrilles
◊ Newspaper
◊ Masking tape
◊ Scissors
◊ Fabric paints (I used red, yellow and blue)
◊ Mixing palette
◊ Brushes (small and medium sizes)
◊ Tailor's chalk or coloured pencil
◊ Iron
◊ Cloth

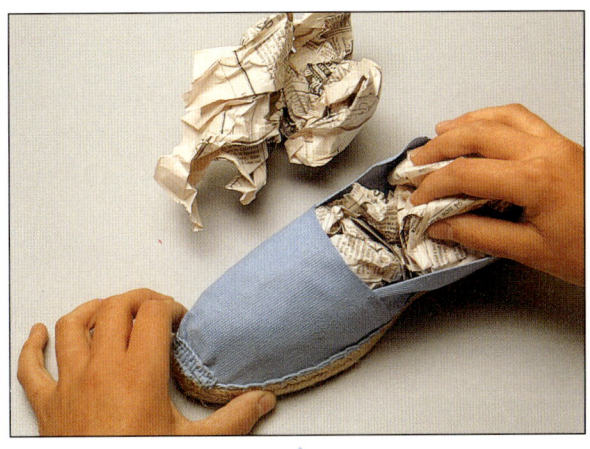

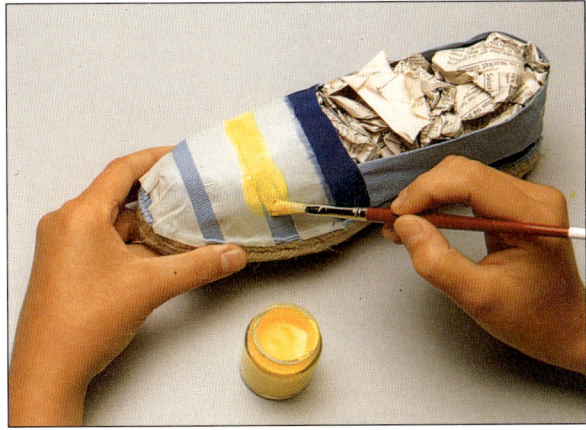

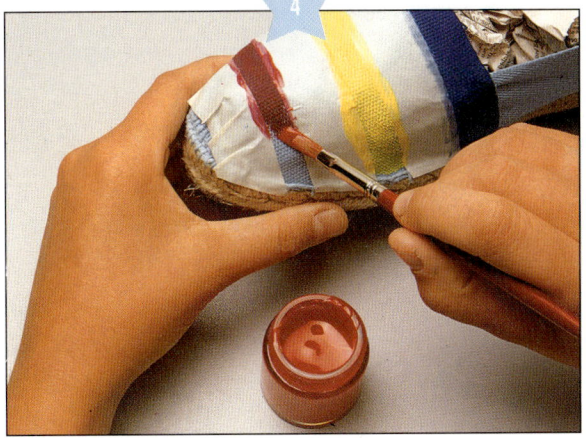

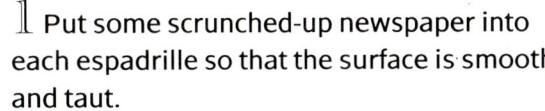

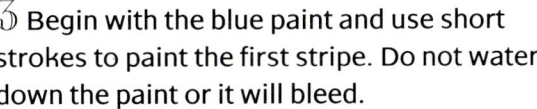

1 Put some scrunched-up newspaper into each espadrille so that the surface is smooth and taut.

2 Place three strips of masking tape across the front of the shoe, varying the distance between the pieces or using narrower tape if you want narrower or wider lines.

3 Begin with the blue paint and use short strokes to paint the first stripe. Do not water down the paint or it will bleed.

4 When you have painted the red and yellow stripes, leave the paint to dry before removing the masking tape.

5 Add the details to the stripes.

6 I added bumps to give a wavy effect; this can be done freehand.

7 Use tailor's chalk or a coloured pencil to draw a pattern of random circles on the sides of each espadrille.

8 Paint in the circles using a small brush to give a neat outline.

9 Place a piece of cloth over the espadrille and iron to seal the paint.

Customized Jeans

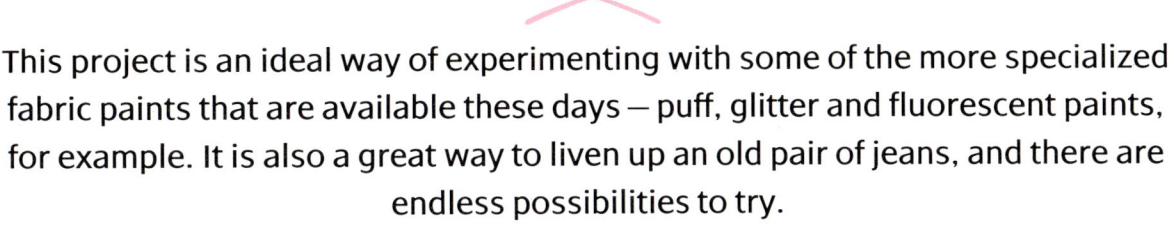

This project is an ideal way of experimenting with some of the more specialized fabric paints that are available these days — puff, glitter and fluorescent paints, for example. It is also a great way to liven up an old pair of jeans, and there are endless possibilities to try.

You will need
◊ Pair of jeans
◊ Newspaper
◊ Fabric paints (including puff, glitter and fluorescent)
◊ Mixing palette
◊ Paint brushes (various sizes)
◊ Hair-drier

1 Place a few sheets of newspaper inside the jeans to protect them from paint seeping through.

2 Use puff paint to draw zigzag lines around the pockets.

3 Add green dots to the inside of the zigzags.

4 Paint on a patch using a mixture of yellow and white. Draw on some cross-hatched squares using a mixture of blue and purple paint.

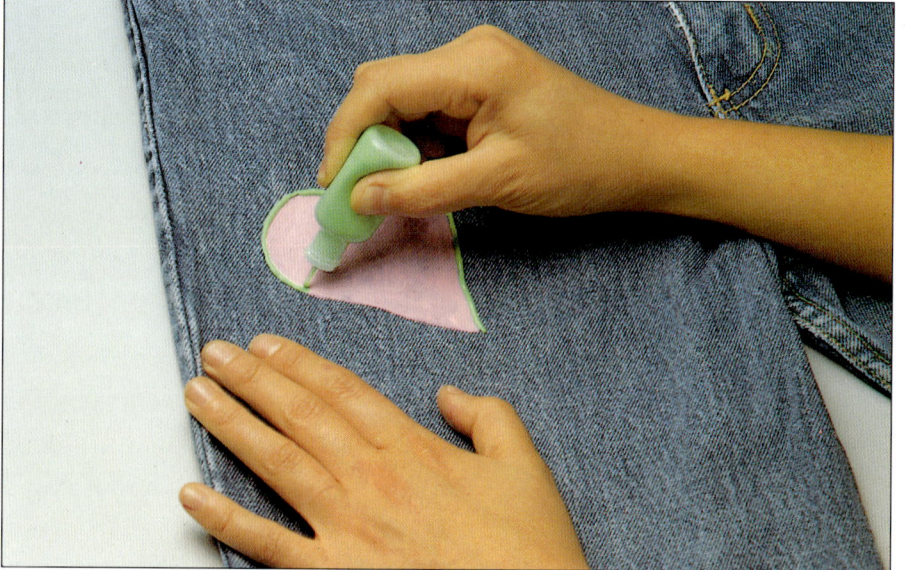

7 Add green puff paint crosses inside the heart and white dots around the edge. Add more patches down the legs of the jeans if you wish. When the paint is completely dry puff up the paint using a hair-drier.

5 Paint on "stitches" around the patch using pink puff paint.

6 Draw another motif on the other leg of the jeans — a pink heart, for example. Use green puff paint to draw a border around the heart.

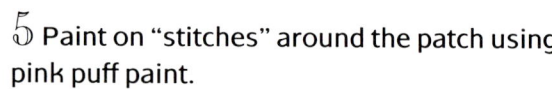

Butterfly T-Shirt

Plain T-shirts in a wide range of colours and sizes are available all over the place, and if you buy them from a market they cost very little. Alternatively, you could give a new lease of life to an old T-shirt. I have drawn a butterfly design, but there is no limit to the patterns and motifs that you can try. This is an ideal project for experimenting with some of the specialized fabric paints, such as glitter paints, and puff paints, which change when they are exposed to the warmth of a hair-drier.

You will need
◊ Tracing paper
◊ Pencil
◊ Scissors
◊ Plain T-shirt
◊ Newspaper
◊ Pins
◊ Tailor's chalk or coloured pencil
◊ Fabric paints (including puff and glitter paints)
◊ Mixing palette
◊ Paintbrushes (various sizes)
◊ Hair-drier

1 Trace the butterfly template from the outline on page 165 and cut it out. Cut out the holes in the wings.

2 Put newspaper inside the T-shirt to stop paint seeping through to the back. Pin the template to the front of the T-shirt and draw around the shape with a coloured pencil or tailor's chalk. Use a coloured pencil to add other details — the antennae, for example — freehand.

3 Paint in the wings using whatever colours you wish. Use a no. 6 paintbrush for the small dots and a ¼in/5mm brush for the larger ones.

4 Add other colours. Allow the paint to dry for about 20 minutes before painting another colour next to it.

5 Add lines of puff paint around the patterns on the wings.

6 Add some spots of glitter paint around the neckline.

7 Outline the wing shapes in a different colour puff paint. Puff up the paint using a hair-drier.

Abstract Patterns

This is an ideal way of decorating lengths of plain fabric so that you can make them up into curtains, table linen, cushion covers or even clothes. Look around your home and you are sure to find countless bits and pieces – sponges, combs, jar lids, pen tops, pegs – that can be used to make interesting patterns. You could also experiment with food – pasta or potatoes, for example – to create some unusual designs.

You will need
◊ Items for printing – combs, cotton reels, pen tops, etc.
◊ Newspaper
◊ Fabric
◊ Masking tape
◊ Fabric paint
◊ Mixing palette
◊ Paintbrush (medium size)
◊ Iron
◊ Cloth

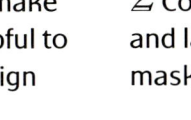

1 Assemble the items you think would make interesting shapes. You might find it helpful to make a rough sketch of your overall design before you begin.

2 Cover your work surface with newspaper and lay out the fabric, if necessary, using masking tape to keep it in position.

3 Mix the colours you want to use in a palette.

4 Apply paint to the object – I used a comb – taking care not to use too much paint or the outline will not look crisp and neat.

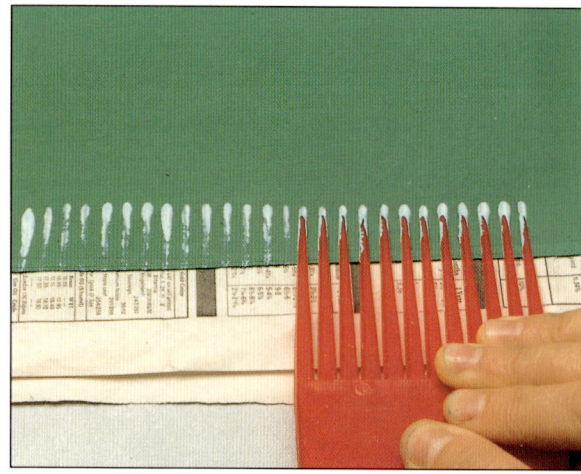

7 Incorporate the shape into your design. Leave to dry.

8 Use a different colour with your next object. I used a small piece of sponge, which gives an interesting and uneven texture.

9 Leave the third colour to dry before you apply the next series of coloured shapes. When you are satisfied with the pattern, iron under a cloth to fix the paints.

5 Use the comb to transfer the paint to the fabric. Continue all around the edge of the fabric, then leave to dry for about 20 minutes.

6 Take your next object – I used a wooden cotton reel – and paint the surface with a different colour.

Vegetable-printed Apron

Vegetables that have a distinctive shape, such as cabbage, mushrooms, chilies and broccoli, are ideal for fabric printing. Cut them in half and use them to decorate a plain calico apron of the kind you can buy in catering or do-it-yourself shops. Try experimenting with halved fruit.

You will need

◊ Selection of vegetables (broccoli, mushrooms, cabbage, okra, chili, etc.)
◊ Kitchen knife
◊ Pencil
◊ Plain paper
◊ Plain calico apron
◊ Newspaper
◊ Fabric paints
◊ Mixing palette
◊ Paintbrush (medium size)
◊ Fabric paint pens
◊ Iron
◊ Cloth

4 Test the cabbage on a piece of rough paper to check that the surface is smooth and gives an even impression. You will need to press fairly hard to get a good print, but do not put too much paint on the vegetable or the pattern will smudge.

1 Cut the vegetables you want to include in your design in half with a sharp knife. Include the stalks and cut more than one of each so that you can use several colours.

2 Draw a rough sketch on plain paper of how you want the apron to look.

3 Lay the apron on sheets of newspaper and prepare the paints. Use a paintbrush to paint the surface of, say, the cabbage.

5 Print the cabbage on the apron.

6 Add more vegetable prints to build up your design, taking care not to move the vegetable as you apply pressure. Add fresh paint for every print.

7 Use a fabric marker pen to draw a line around the edge of the apron and to highlight the pocket edge. Iron under a cloth to fix the paints.

Printing with Flowers

This simple project uses flowers and leaves to decorate fabric, which could be used for cushion covers, table or bed linen or even curtains. Some kinds of plant material work better than others – flowers and leaves with sturdy, unfussy outlines give more successful prints than more delicate shapes. Try buddleia, ivy and conifer leaves and flowers such as daisies. The backs of leaves with prominent veins work especially well.

You will need
◊ Rough paper
◊ Coloured pencils
◊ Newspaper
◊ Fabric of your choice
◊ Masking tape
◊ A selection of flowers and leaves
◊ Fabric paints
◊ Mixing palette
◊ Paintbrush (medium size)
◊ Iron
◊ Cloth

1 Position the flowers and leaves in a pleasing design. Make a rough sketch of the design and colour in the shapes so that you have a reference when you start to print.

2 Cover your work surface with newspaper and spread out your fabric, taping it in position if necessary. Mix your paints and paint some of the leaves.

3 Using your sketch as reference, place a leaf on the fabric, pressing it firmly but gently. Hold it down for 10 seconds, then raise an edge to see if the impression has printed. If you are happy with the result, carefully lift the leaf to avoid smudging the paint. Continue building up the design with other leaves.

4 Now paint a flower, placing it as indicated on your rough sketch. Fill in any gaps in the design and don't worry if some of the flowers look rather abstract. Leave to dry before ironing under a cloth to fix the paints.

Folk Art Picture

This charming image is achieved by applying a series of stencils, one after the other, and painting each in a different colour. You could frame the completed image, as I have done, or you could paint two and make up a pair of cushion covers.

You will need
◊ Tracing paper
◊ Pencil
◊ Stencil card
◊ Masking tape
◊ Craft knife or scalpel
◊ Piece of canvas or calico, approximately 13 × 11in/33 × 28cm
◊ Scissors
◊ Newspaper
◊ Stencil brush (¼in/5mm or ½in/12mm)
◊ Fabric paint
◊ Mixing palette
◊ Iron
◊ Cloth
◊ 4 buttons

3 Cut out a piece of canvas or calico and place it on some sheets of newspaper. Tape the first stencil – the background to the picture – securely in position over the canvas and paint it – I used blue. Carefully remove the stencil so that you do not smudge the edges. Leave to dry for a few minutes.

4 Tape the second stencil – the house front and chimney piece – accurately in position and apply dark blue paint. Use a paintbrush to paint around the window areas.

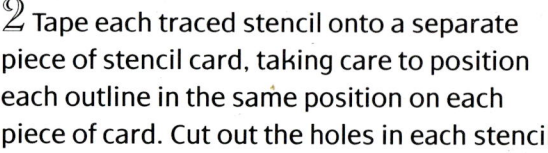

1 Trace the stencil designs on pages 166 to 168, drawing each of the outlines onto equal-sized sheets of paper so that they will all fit together accurately.

2 Tape each traced stencil onto a separate piece of stencil card, taking care to position each outline in the same position on each piece of card. Cut out the holes in each stencil.

5 Leave the paint to dry before you use the next stencil.

6 Tape the next stencil – the front door and roof – in place. This time use brown paint. Again, leave to dry.

7 Tape the next stencil in place and then paint the side of the house purple. Leave to dry before using the last stencil, the foreground and trees, which are painted green.

8 Iron under a cloth to fix the paint and sew a button in each corner.

Child's Wall-hanging

This charming parade of stencilled animals would look great on a child's bedroom wall. The project uses simple, colourful hand-stitching and stencilling, which combine to give an old-fashioned, slightly folksy effect. You could make a similar piece using numbers or letters instead of animals.

You will need

◊ Tracing paper
◊ Pencils
◊ Stencil card
◊ Masking tape
◊ Craft knife or scalpel
◊ 8 pieces of cream-coloured fabric, each measuring approximately 5 × 5 in/12.5 × 12.5 cm
◊ Fabric paints
◊ Mixing palette
◊ Stencil brushes ¼ in/5mm and ½ in/12 mm
◊ Sponge (natural sponge is best)
◊ Iron
◊ Cloth
◊ 2 pieces of coloured fabric, each measuring approximately 50 × 8 in/128 × 20 cm (I used blue)
◊ Pins
◊ Scissors
◊ Needle
◊ Coloured embroidery silks
◊ 2 buttons
◊ Bias binding, tape or ribbon, approximately 4 in/10 cm

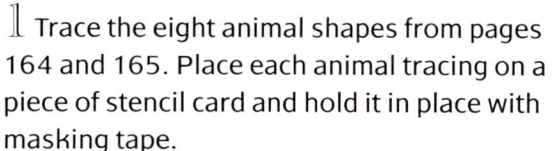

1 Trace the eight animal shapes from pages 164 and 165. Place each animal tracing on a piece of stencil card and hold it in place with masking tape.

2 Use a craft knife or scalpel to cut out each shape. Discard the tracing paper.

3 Cut out eight squares of cream-coloured fabric.

4 Use masking tape to hold each cut-out animal in position on a square of fabric.

5 Prepare your paints, then colour the pig's body using a stencil brush.

6 Colour the pig's feet brown and add a band of brown across its body.

7 The cockerel has a blue-green body and a bright red comb.

8 Add some yellow and orange to the feathers in the cockerel's tail.

9 Colour the cow's body black and its hooves and udder pink. Make some spots by sponging on some white paint.

10 Paint the rest of the animals, using the photograph of the finished wall hanging as a guide. Turn under the edges of each square and iron under a cloth to fix the colours and press down the turned-back edges.

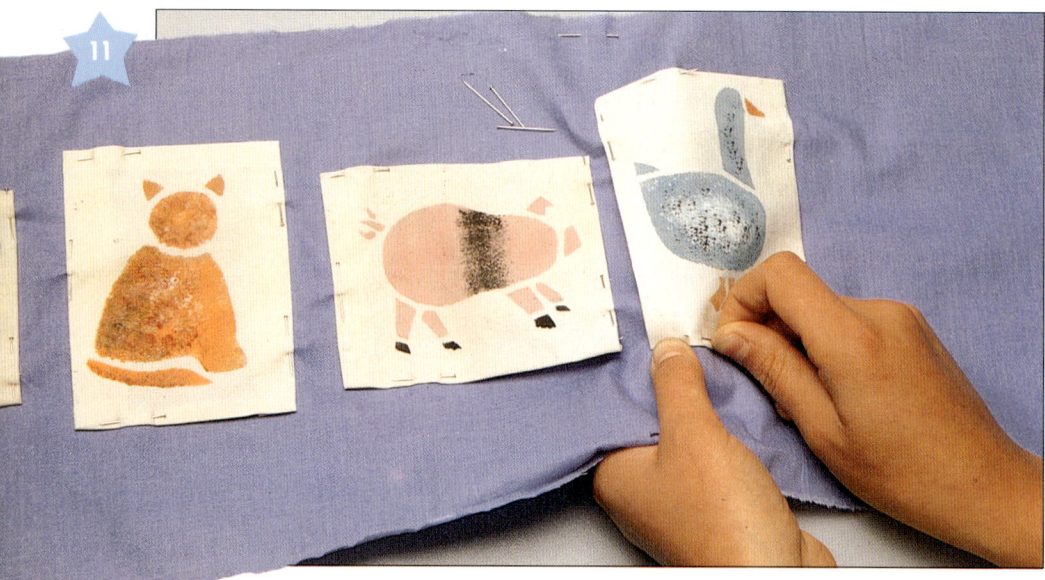

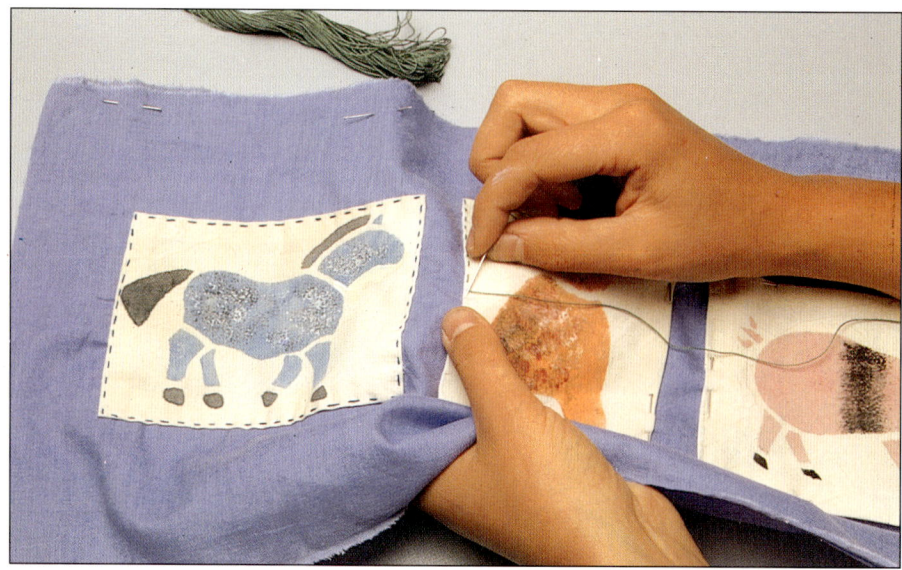

11 Place the two rectangles of fabric together and pin. Space the eight animal pictures evenly along one of the long rectangles of fabric, pinning them in position.

12 Use coloured embroidery silk and straight stitch to sew each square in place.

13 Turn the edge of the large rectangle into a neat hem on the front and hand sew with yellow embroidery silk.

14 Sew a button in each of the top corners and add loops of tape, bias binding or ribbon from which to hang it.

Shopping Bag

The combination of the attractive fruit design and the durable nature of this simple canvas drawstring bag makes it the perfect way to carry heavy fruit and vegetables home from the market. Although I have supplied simple templates for the motifs, you could decorate it with an alternative pattern so that the bag could be used to carry school things or your sports kit.

1 Trace the fruit motifs from the templates on page 163 and cut out.

2 Cut two pieces of canvas. Place the templates on the canvas, pin them in position and use a pencil to draw around the outlines.

3 Use your traced outlines as a guide to fill in the details of the fruit.

4 Use a ruler to add the check tablecloth pattern.

5 Mix your paints. You will need yellow for the bananas, purple for the grapes (you can add some white, yellow and orange for a lighter shade of purple) and green for the apples.

You will need
◊ Tracing paper
◊ Pencil
◊ Scissors
◊ 2 pieces of canvas, each
   18 × 16in/45.5 × 40.5cm
◊ Pins
◊ Ruler
◊ Fabric paint
◊ Mixing palette
◊ Paintbrushes (3 sizes)
◊ Fabric paint pen (blue)
◊ Iron
◊ Cloth
◊ Sewing machine
◊ Sewing thread
◊ ¼in/5mm cord,
   30in/76.5cm long
◊ Safety pin

6 Use short strokes to apply the first colour. Aim to create a three-dimensional effect.

7 Paint the apples and bananas.

8 Colour the stalks and leaves of the apples.

9 Add the detail to the grapes, using dark green for the tendrils and brown for the stalks.

10 Add detail in brown to the bananas to make them look as natural as possible. Leave

the paint to dry for about 20 minutes, then iron under a cloth.

11 Paint in the white squares of the tablecloth border pattern and outline the squares with a blue fabric painting pen.

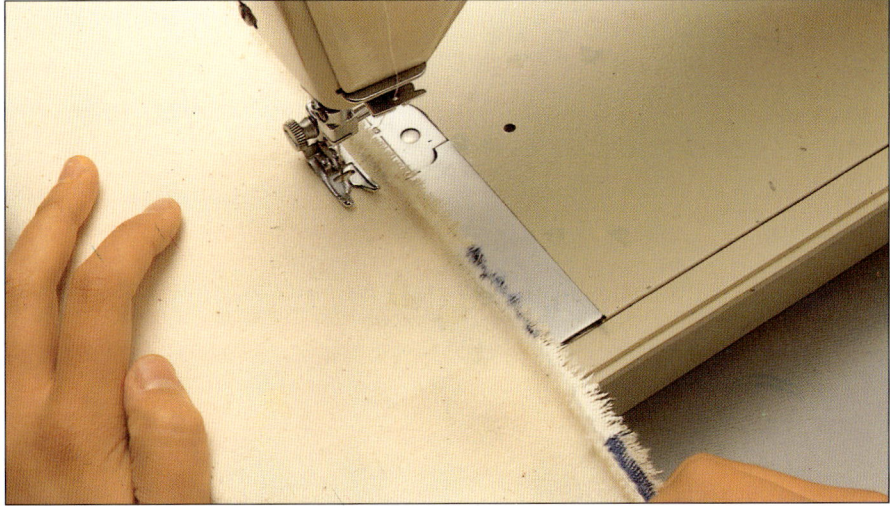

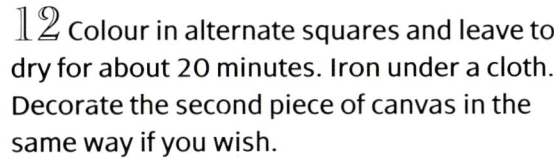

12 Colour in alternate squares and leave to dry for about 20 minutes. Iron under a cloth. Decorate the second piece of canvas in the same way if you wish.

13 With right sides together, sew one side of the bag with a sewing machine.

14 Open the bag so that the middle, inside seam faces you. On each side at the top, turn 2in/5cm of the raw edge inwards at an angle. Machine stitch into place. Fold back the bag with right sides together and machine stitch along the bottom and side. Turn right side out.

15 Use a safety pin to thread through the cord as a drawstring. Bind the ends of the cord to stop it from unravelling.

Animal Cushions

Scatter these lively animal cushions on a child's bed or arrange them in a group on a chair. Watered-down fabric paints have been used to achieve the background colours, while thicker paints are used for the detailed markings. Simple embroidery stitches in brightly coloured threads have been added to enhance the details of feathers, whiskers and so on.

You will need

◊ Tracing paper
◊ Pencil
◊ Scissors
◊ Pins
◊ White cotton fabric, approximately
  20 × 10in/51 × 25cm for each cushion
◊ Newspaper
◊ Fabric paints
◊ Mixing palette
◊ Paintbrushes (small and medium)
◊ Coloured embroidery silks
◊ Needle
◊ Sewing thread
◊ Sewing machine
◊ Kapok or other toy stuffing
◊ Buttons for eyes
◊ String for pig's tail

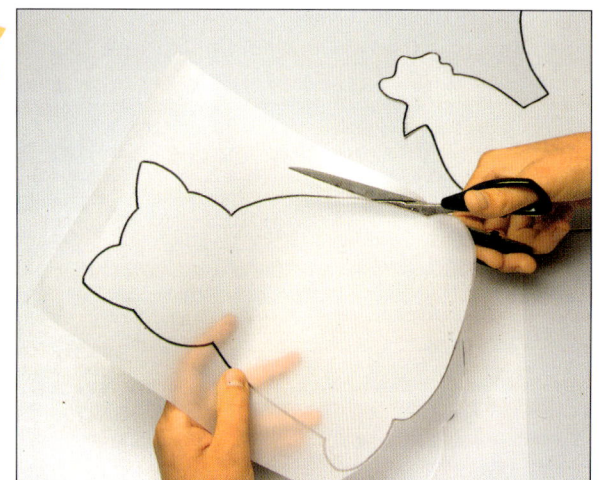

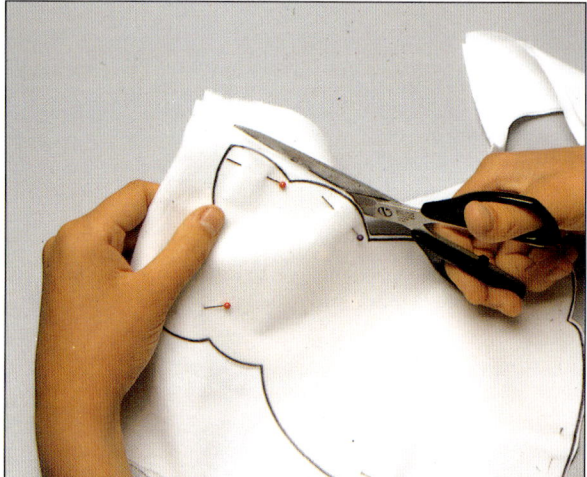

1 Trace the animal templates on pages 160 to 162 and cut out.

2 Pin each template to a double layer of fabric and cut around it.

3 Place each animal shape on some newspaper and prepare your paints.

4 Water down the paints that you are going to use for the background — for example, use orange for the cat — but do not make the colour flat; it will look more natural if it is quite streaky.

5 Add spots on the back and head and a nose and tail, using the photograph on page 53 as a guide.

6 Make the pig in the same way and remember to include two ears.

7 Use brown paint for the pig's feet and the spots on its flanks.

8 The cockerel is more difficult. The background is a combination of green, purple, pink and yellow. Apply each colour separately but try to achieve a soft, feathery effect with no harsh edges to the colours.

9 Add a yellow beak and bright red comb.

10 Iron both sides of each of the animals under a cloth when you have finished them to seal the paints.

11 Use embroidery silks to stitch details on the cockerel's neck feathers.

12 Stitch some additional feather detailing to the cockerel's back.

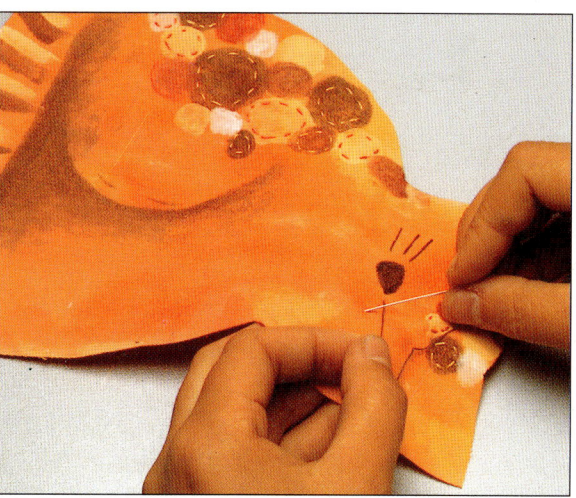

13 Stitch around the spots on the cat and embroider the whiskers. Remember to stitch the cat's paws.

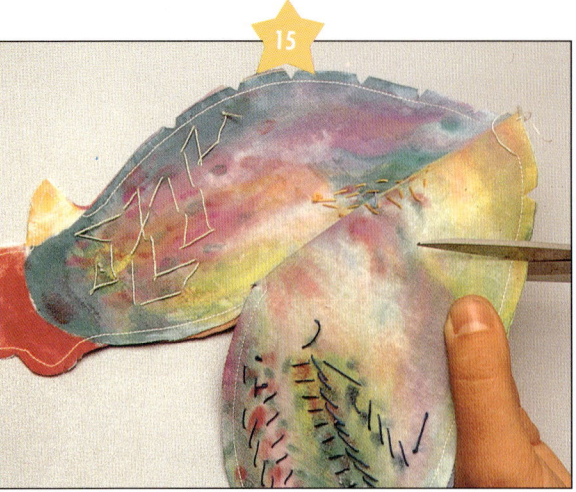

14 Pin the two pieces of the cushion together and use a sewing machine to stitch around the edge, leaving about 2in/5cm open along the bottom edge.

15 Carefully snip the curved edges up the stitching line so that the seams lie flat.

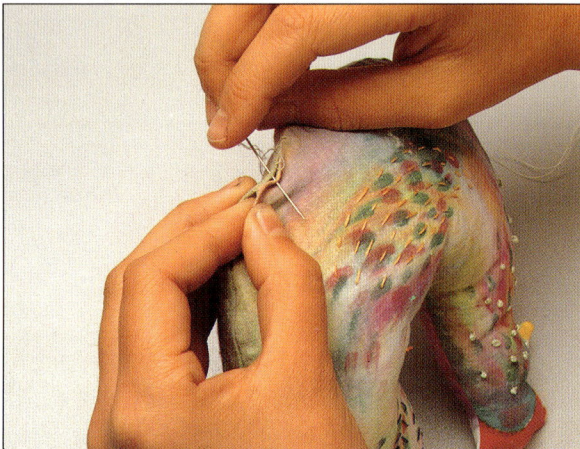

16 Turn the cushion to the right side, using the wrong end of a paintbrush to push out the seams, especially around the cockerel's beak and comb. Fill the cushion with Kapok or any soft toy stuffing material, pushing it into the head and tail with a piece of wooden dowel or the wrong end of a knitting needle.

17 Sew up the open seam. Repeat steps 14–17 for the pig and cat.

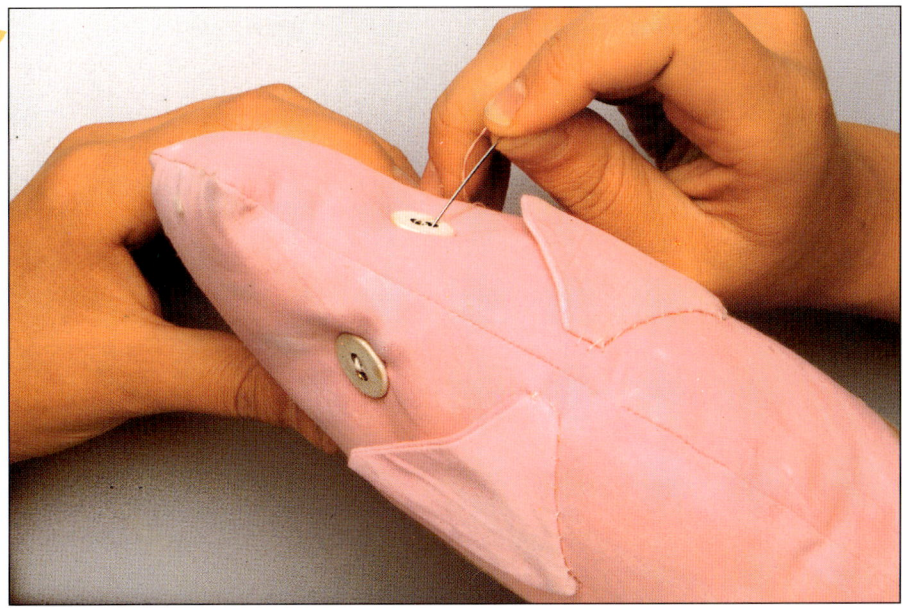

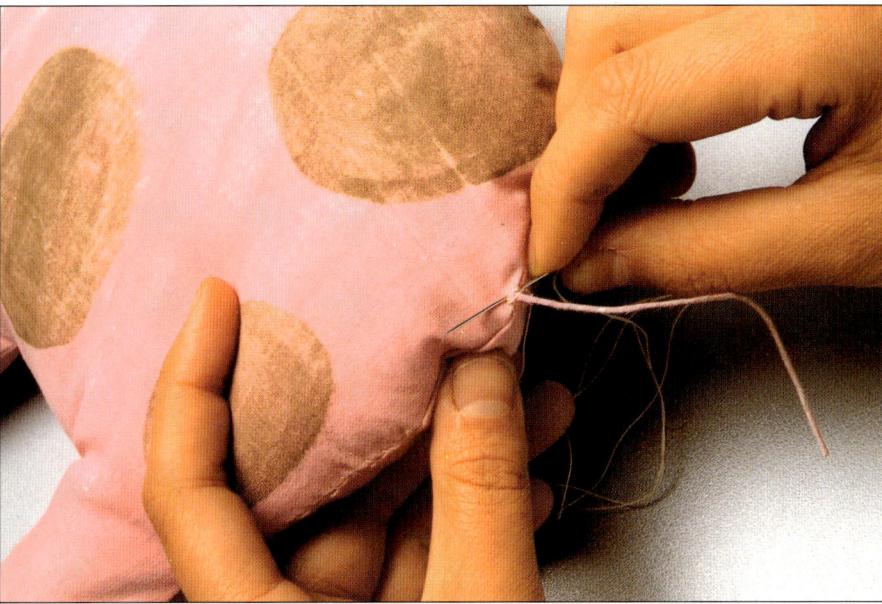

18 Stitch on buttons for eyes and remember to add the pig's ears.

19 Make a tail for the pig by painting some string pink and sewing it onto the pig's back.

Pillowcases

Simple stencilling techniques allow you to decorate plain cotton pillowcases with a fresh floral design, and once you have mastered the techniques there is no need to stop at pillowcases: you can decorate a duvet cover and sheet to match. I have supplied templates for the flowers, but you may prefer to design your own motifs.

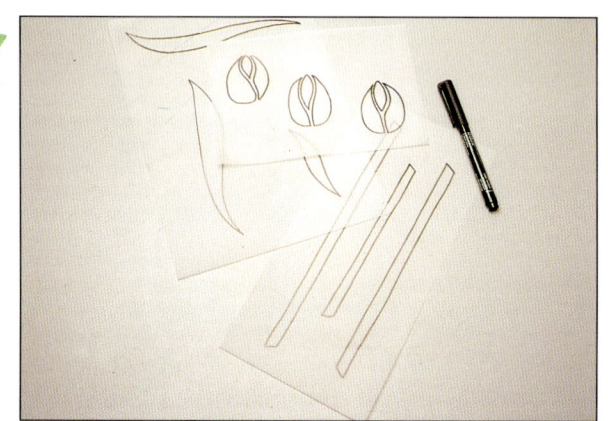

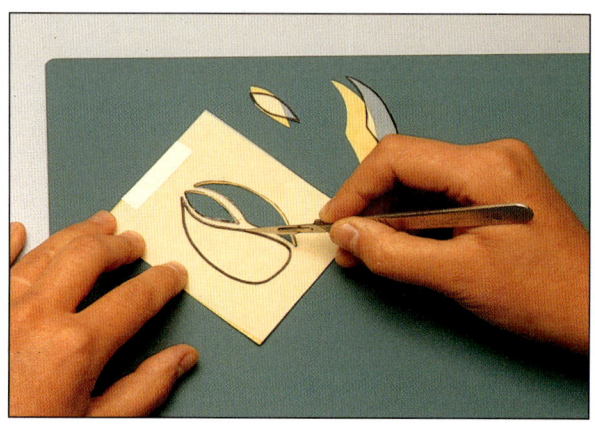

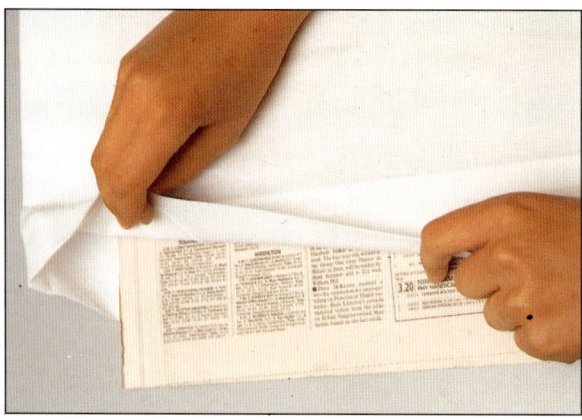

You will need
◇ Marker pen
◇ Tracing paper
◇ Masking tape
◇ Stencil card
◇ Craft knife or scalpel
◇ 2 plain cotton pillowcases
◇ Newspaper
◇ Fabric paint
◇ Mixing palette
◇ Stencil brush
◇ Iron
◇ Cloth

1 Use a marker pen to trace the stencil patterns from the outlines on page 158.

2 Use masking tape to hold the traced shapes securely in position on the stencil card.

3 Cut around the shapes with a craft knife or scalpel, working on a cutting mat or a piece of thick cardboard. Discard the tracing paper.

4 Put some pieces of newspaper inside the pillowcase to protect the other side from any paint that seeps through.

5 Position the stem templates on the pillowcase, securing them with masking tape.

6 Mix the paint colours. Paint in the stems with a small (¼in/5mm) stencil brush and use different shades of green.

7 Dab rather than use brush strokes for a "sponging" effect and take care not to splash the paint onto the rest of the pillowcase.

8 Repeat until there are stems across the pillowcase — about eight in all. Remove the stencils.

9 Position the leaf stencils and secure them with masking tape. Colour the leaves as you did the stems, holding the stencil firmly down with your fingers so that paint does not bleed under the cut edge.

10 Position the flower stencils and hold them in place with masking tape. You could paint them all the same colour or in various shades of red — add orange, yellow or purple, for example.

11 Allow the paint to dry, then iron with a piece of cloth over the paint to fix the colours.

Doll

This simple doll makes a delightful gift for a child older than five or six years of age. You could design a different outfit if you preferred, or you could base the doll's appearance on someone you know. If you wish you could add extra details such as a hair ribbon, a hat or a piece of jewellery.

You will need
◊ Sketch pad
◊ Coloured pencils
◊ Tracing paper
◊ Pencil
◊ Piece of white fabric, 13 × 10in/33 × 25cm
◊ Pins
◊ Scissors
◊ Newspapers
◊ Kapok or other toy stuffing
◊ Sewing machine
◊ Sewing thread
◊ Fabric paints
◊ Mixing palette
◊ Paintbrushes (various sizes)
◊ Iron
◊ Cloth
◊ Needle
◊ Buttons

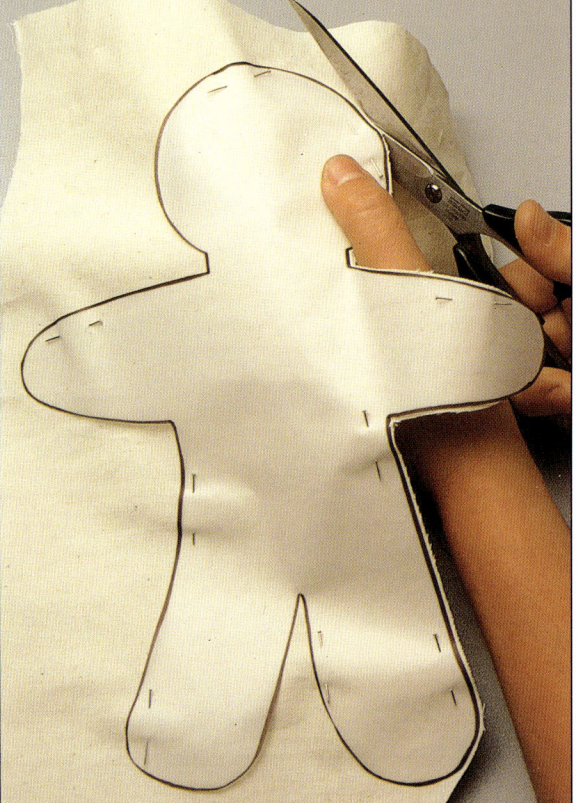

1 Sketch a design for your doll's clothes, keeping to the shape of the doll.

2 Trace the doll's template from page 159 and cut out. Fold the white fabric in half (so that it measures 13 × 5in/33 × 12.5cm) and pin the template to it, making sure that the pins go through both layers. Cut out the outline, adding a seam allowance of 1/8in/3mm all round.

3 Using your sketch as a reference, pencil guidelines on the cut-out doll — hairline, top, trousers, shoes and so on. Add the details to front and back.

4 Cover your work surface with newspaper and paint the front of the doll. Begin with the background colour of the blouse — I used blue.

5 Next paint in the shoes and trousers and then the mouth, cheeks and hair.

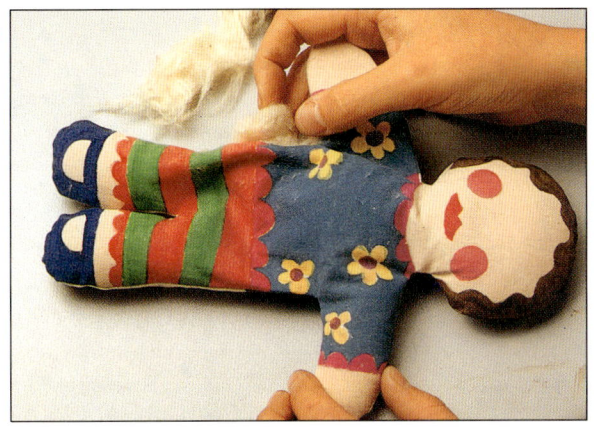

6 Allow the paint to dry, then add details such as the flower pattern to the top and the frills around the neck and trousers.

7 Paint the face pale pink and leave to dry. Paint the back of the doll to match. Iron.

8 Place the two pieces, right sides together, and machine stitch all the way around the doll, leaving a gap of about 2in/5cm under one arm. Carefully snip into the curves, up to the sewing line, at the neck, between the legs and at the ends of the arms and legs so that the seams lie smoothly.

9 Turn the doll the right way out. You may find it helpful to use the wrong end of a paintbrush to push the arms and legs through. Fill the doll with Kapok or any other soft toy stuffing, adding little pinches at a time and using a piece of wooden dowel or the wrong end of a knitting needle to push the filler down into the arms and legs. Stitch up the underarm seam opening.

10 Sew on buttons for the eyes.

11 Paint on the eyebrows.

Templates

PILLOWCASES

DOLL

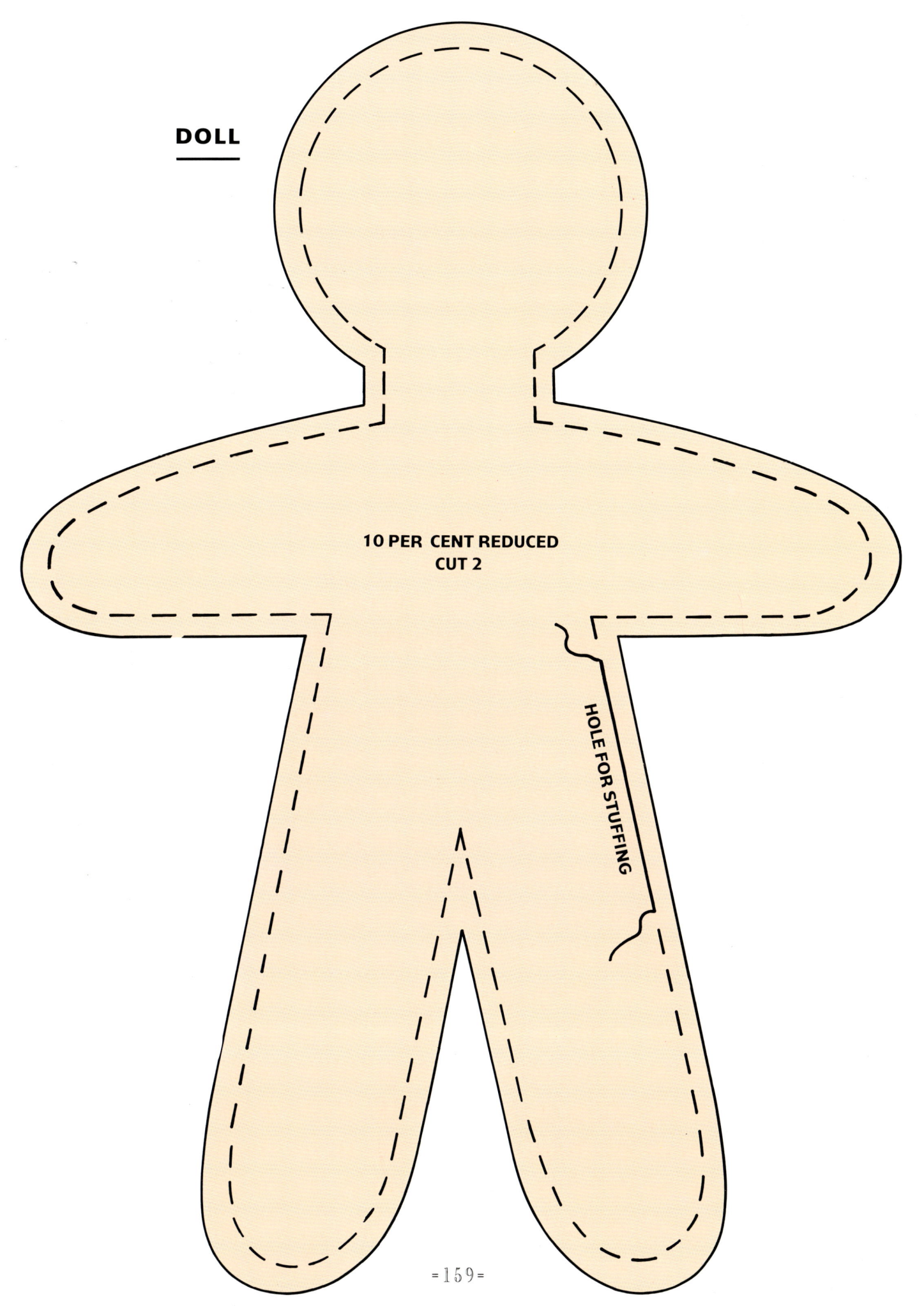

10 PER CENT REDUCED
CUT 2

HOLE FOR STUFFING

ANIMAL CUSHIONS

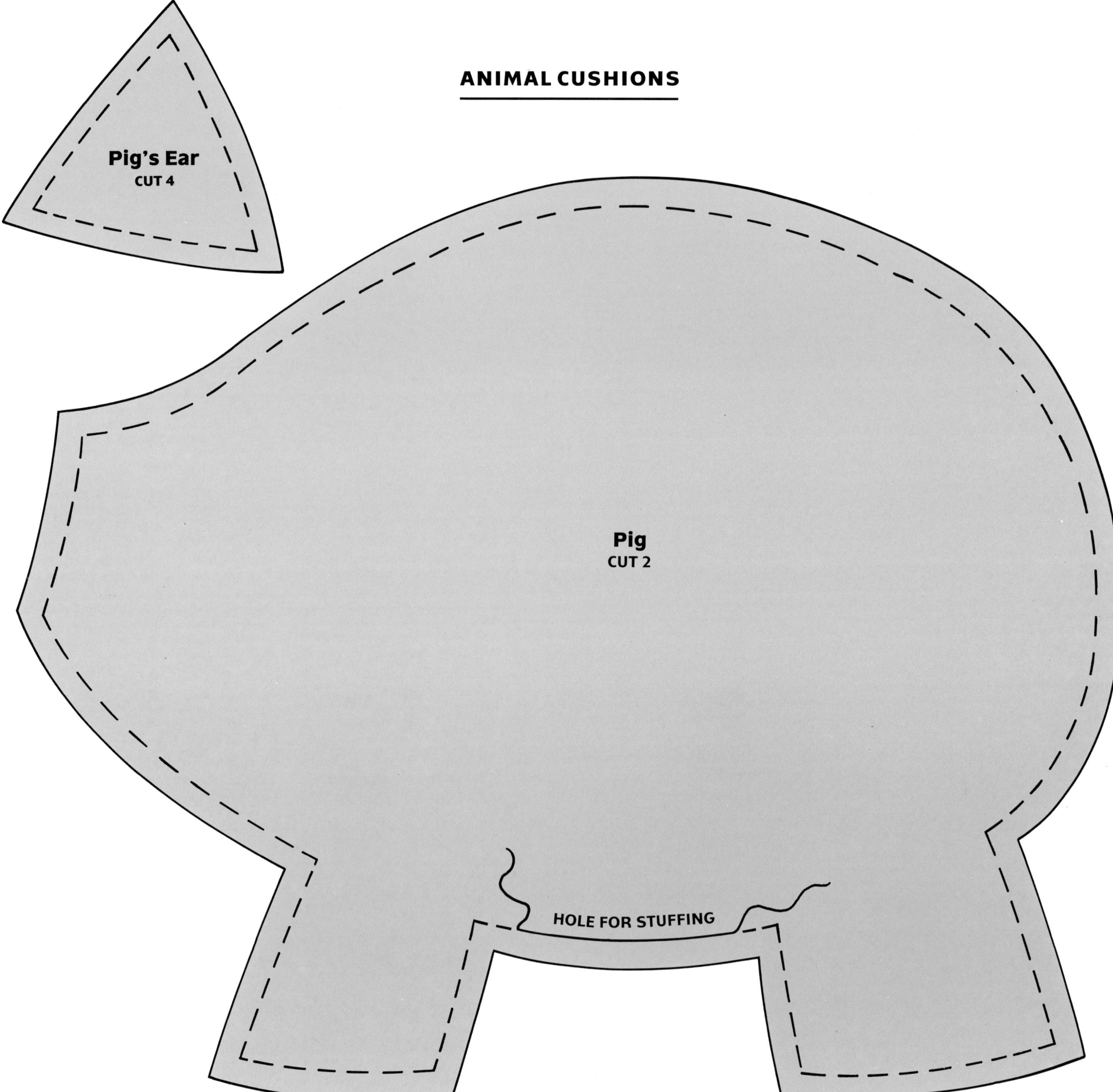

Pig's Ear
CUT 4

Pig
CUT 2

HOLE FOR STUFFING

ANIMAL CUSHIONS

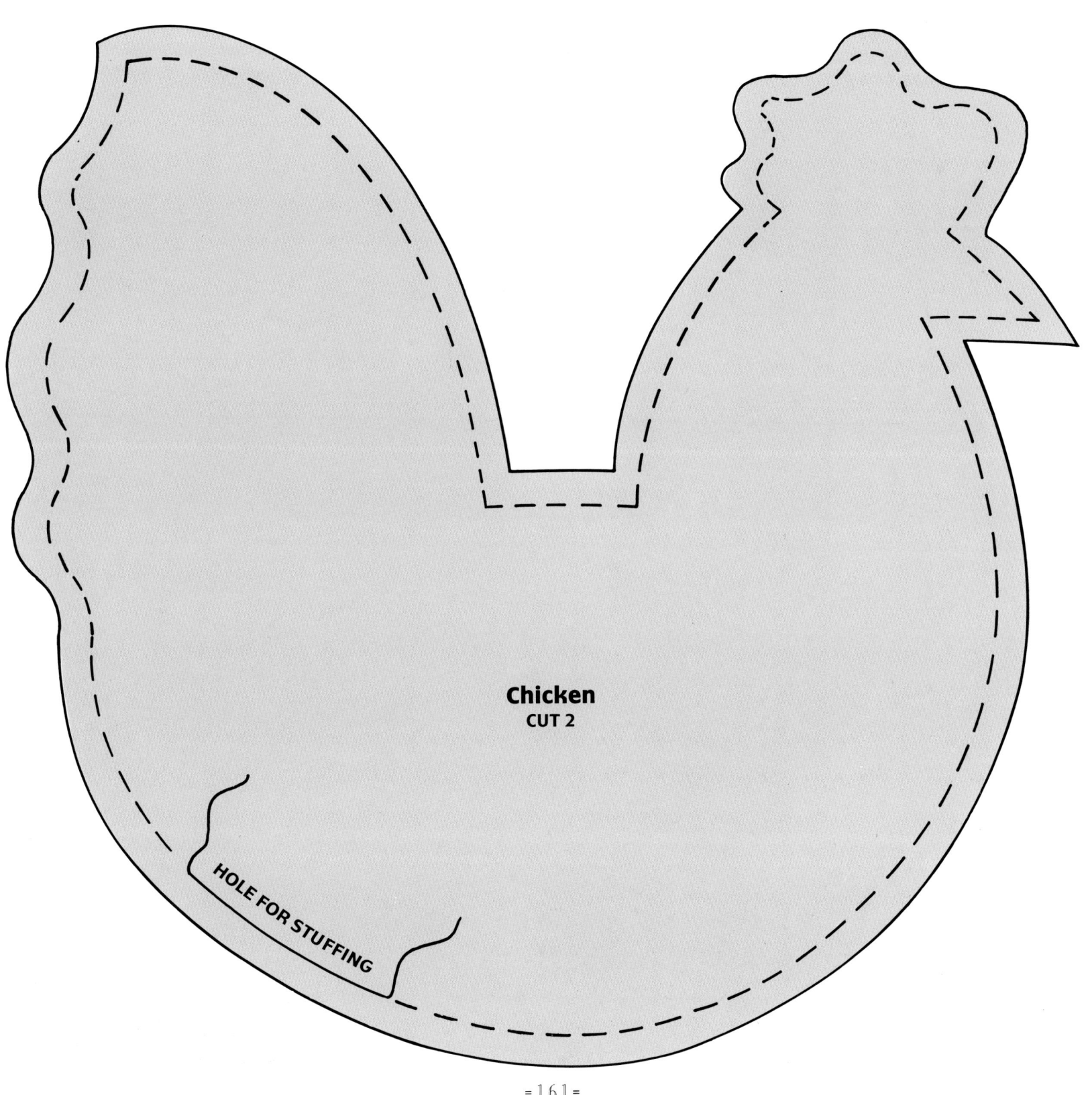

Chicken
CUT 2

HOLE FOR STUFFING

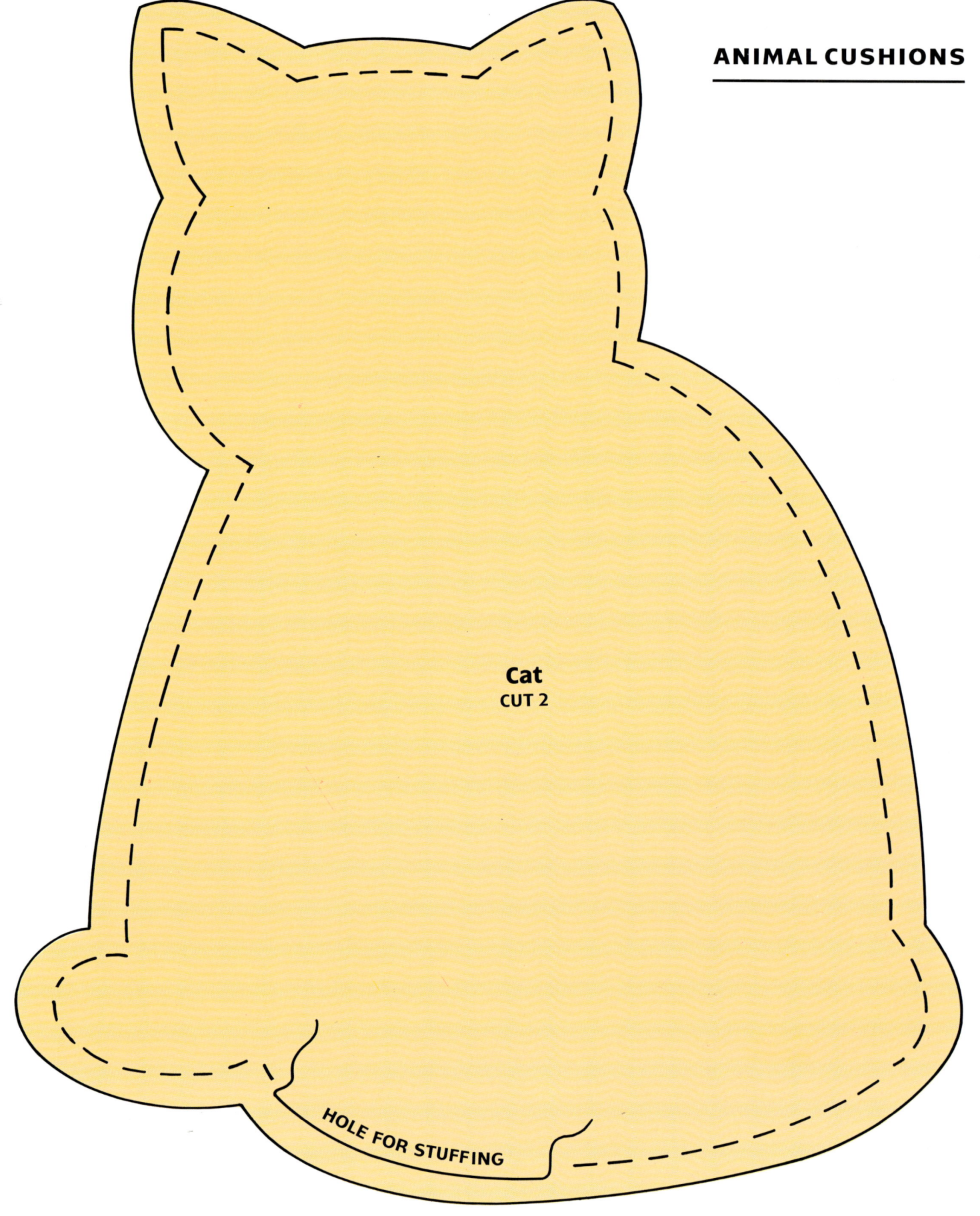

ANIMAL CUSHIONS

Cat
CUT 2

HOLE FOR STUFFING

SHOPPING BAG

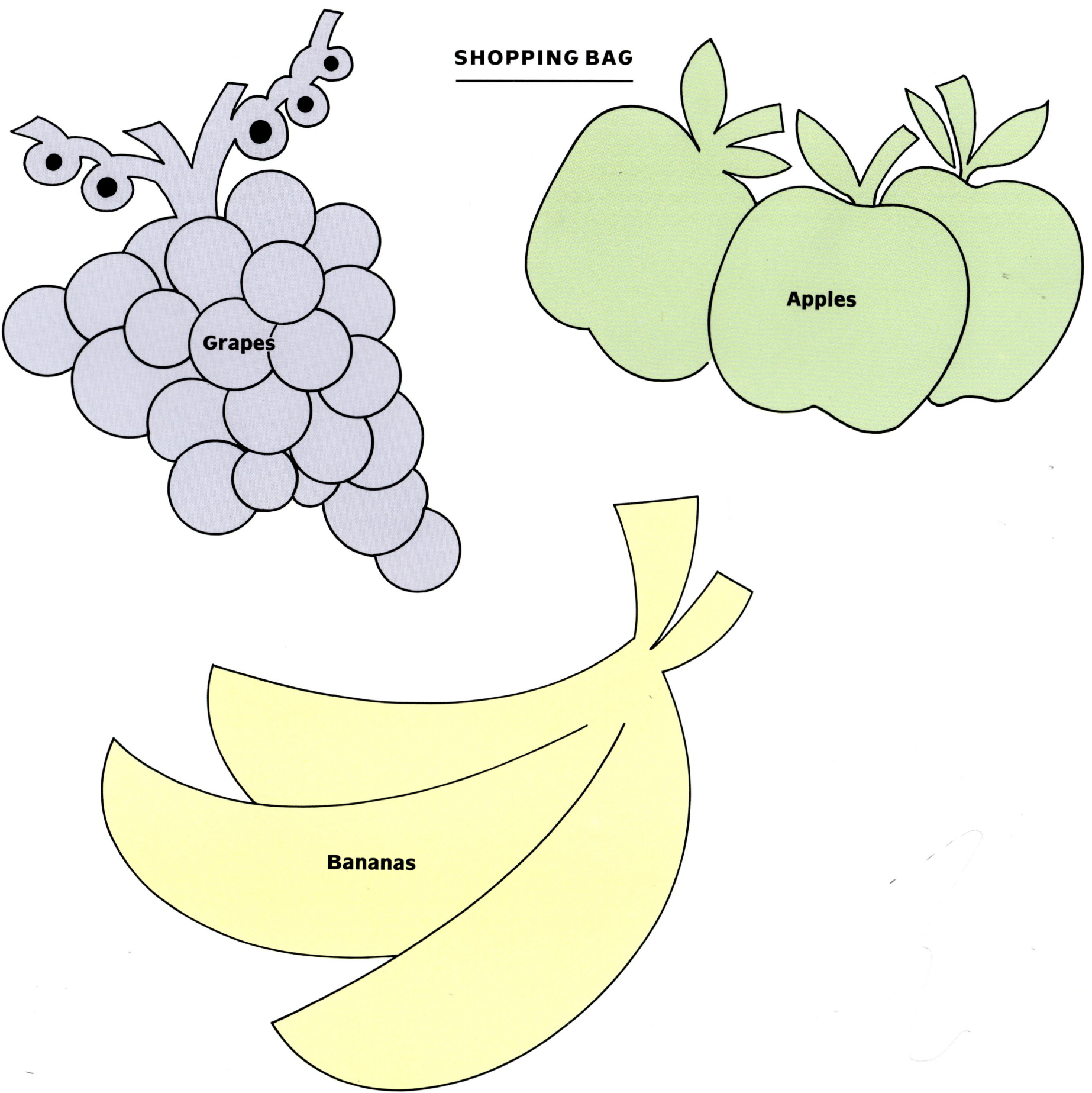

Grapes

Apples

Bananas

ANIMAL WALL HANGING

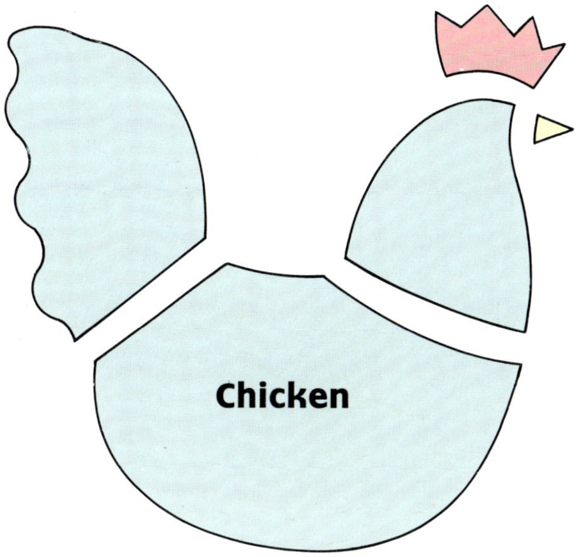

**BUTTERFLY
T-SHIRT**

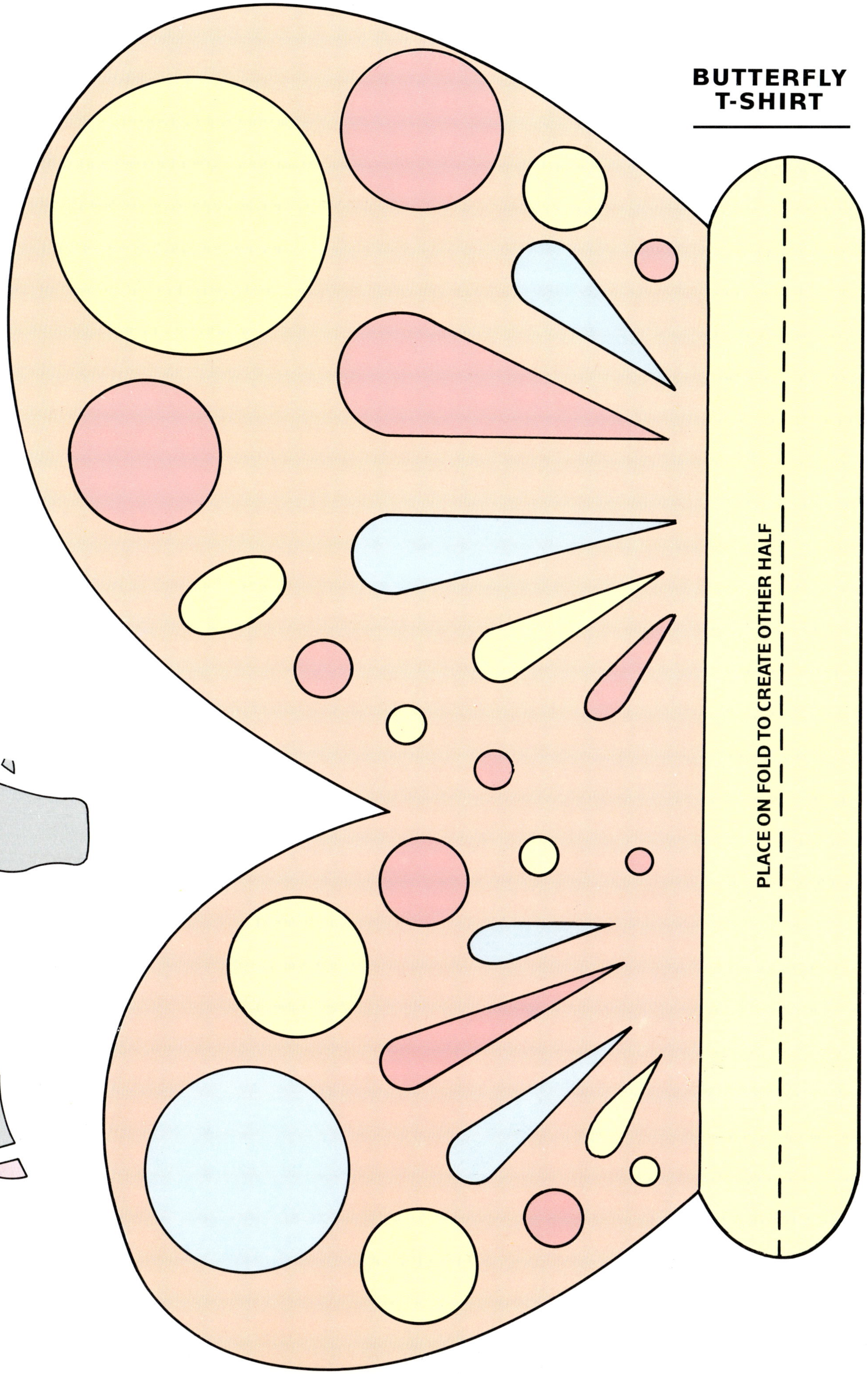

Chicken

Cow

PLACE ON FOLD TO CREATE OTHER HALF

FOLK ART PICTURE

FOLK ART PICTURE

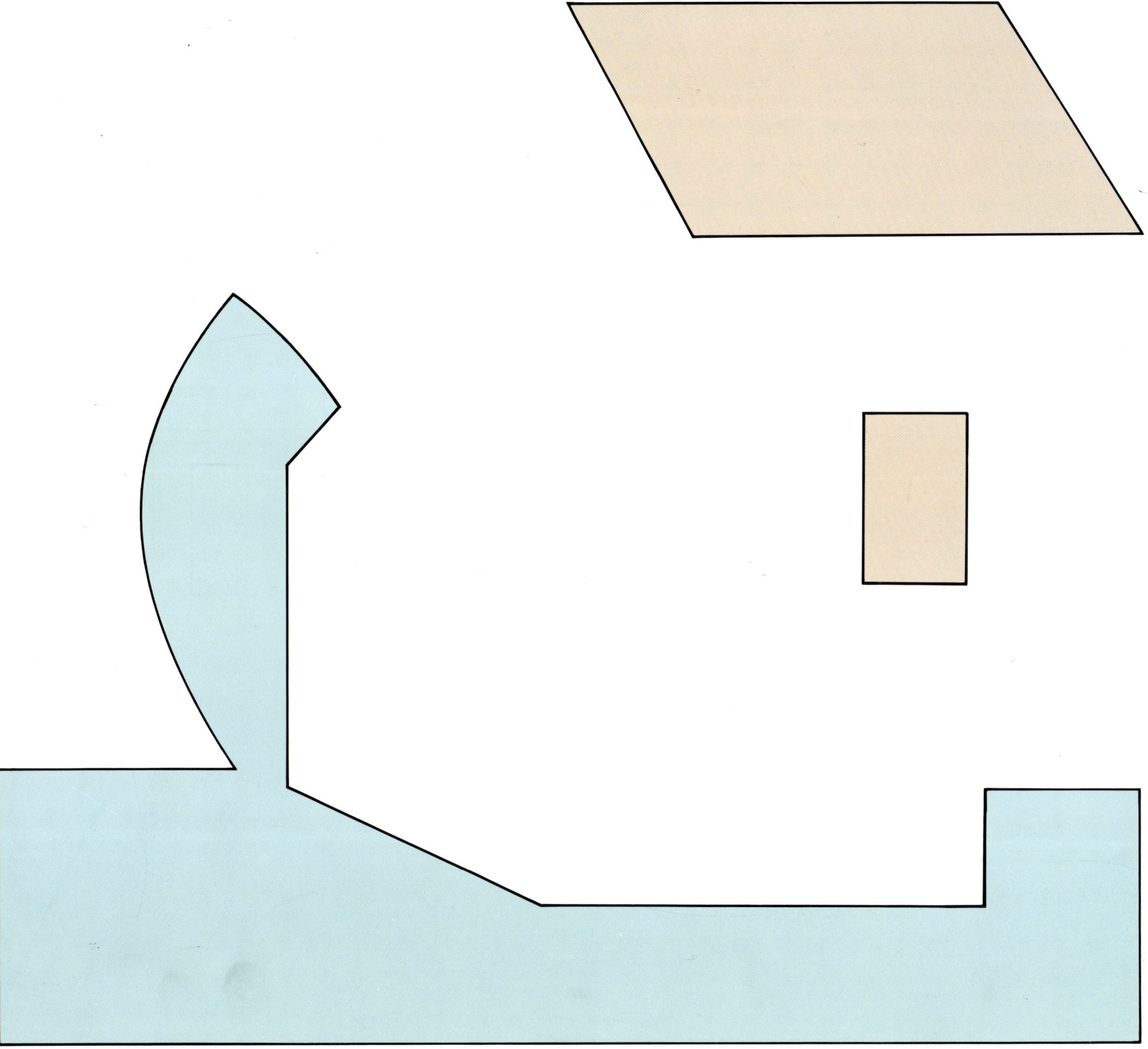

FOLK ART PICTURE

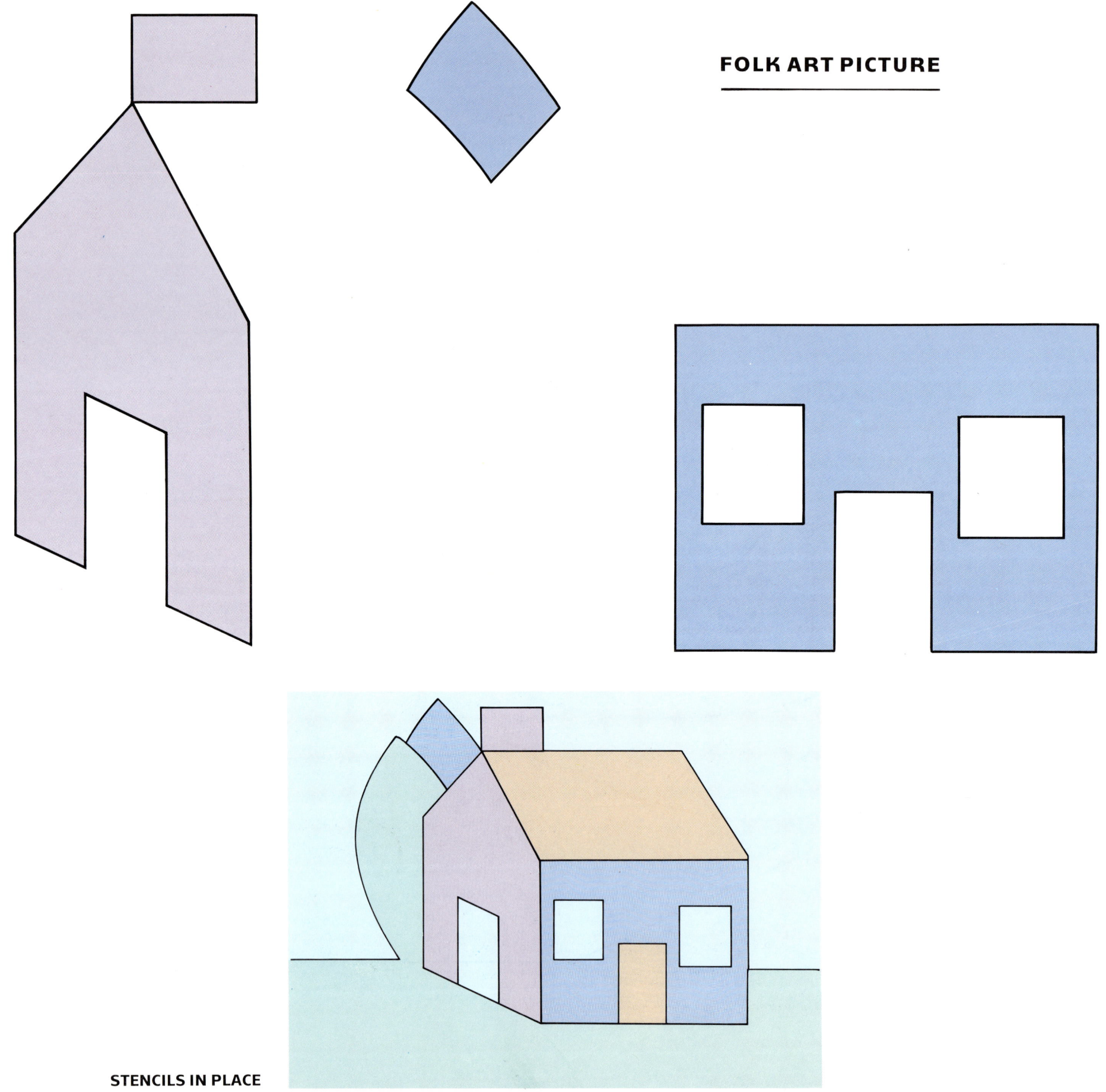

STENCILS IN PLACE

Tie-Dyeing

Give your wardrobe and surroundings a new lease of life with this inspiring and creative craft

INTRODUCTION

◆

Tie-dyeing, one of the oldest and one of the simplest methods of producing patterned fabric, is considered to be a "resist" method of dyeing, similar to batik. Many types of pattern can be achieved by binding or folding the fabric, then immersing it in a dye bath. Complex-looking, multicoloured patterns can be made by refolding and rebinding the fabric each time a new colour is added, and modern cold water dyes allow spectacular effects to be obtained easily and safely. You will find most of the materials you need in your home, so you will not need to buy expensive equipment before you can get started.

Early evidence that tie-dyeing was widely used to produce patterned fabrics can be found in the *sima* charters from Indonesia, which mention tie-dyers as one of the five different kinds of textile worker producing fabric in the early 10th century. It is likely, however, that tie-dyeing was used as a method of patterning fabric in that region even before that date. One of the earliest techniques of tie-dyeing to be used was *ikat* – a method of tying resist material around yarn and dyeing before weaving – which added subtle variations of colour to simple geometric designs. *Ikat* was also extensively used in Africa, and some of the most elaborate uses of the technique can be found among the people of western Madagascar.

Pelangi, the technique most often associated with tie-dyeing, produces the familiar circular and striped patterns that can be found on many modern tie-dyed fabrics. Traditionally, fabric decorated with circular patterns was hung on poles outside the houses of dead people, and these sacred textiles, known as *poritutu coto*, were produced by the people of the Rongkong region of the island of Sulawesi in eastern Indonesia. Similarly, in Morocco Berber women made head scarves with rectangular or mirror patterns, which were used to ward off the evil eye.

One of the more complicated methods of tie-dyeing is *teritik,* which involves stitching areas of the fabric to resist the dye. Some of the earliest evidence of the trade in this type of tie-dyed fabric was found in a list of fabrics exported from Indonesia in 1580. The Indonesian word *teritik* means "to drip consecutively in little drops", and this phrase accurately describes the effect that can be achieved by the technique. The use of stitching in *teritik* means that, unlike in *pelangi*, a more controlled, sometimes even pictorial pattern can be achieved.

In the West the technique became fashionable in the 1960s and 1970s, often resulting in some rather garish designs. More recently, however, western designers have been adapting the traditional methods of *pelangi* and *teritik* to produce elaborate and subtly coloured patterns. Spectacular results can be produced by over-dyeing, and rainbow-coloured designs are easily achievable.

Pinching, folding and binding or sewing the fabrics prevents the dye from reaching those areas of the material that are covered by the resist material, and those parts that are not exposed to the dye remain uncoloured. The end result is determined by the way in which the fabric is folded, bound and stitched before dyeing, and subsequent re-folding and dyeing enables a variety of patterns and colours to be built up.

As with other forms of surface patterning or dyeing, the best results are usually obtained when the fabric is decorated before it is made up into the garment. However, if simple garments are selected, it is possible to overcome the problems that are caused by seams so that even those with only limited sewing abilities can produce some really eye-catching patterns.

Even in its simplest forms tie-dyeing offers a way of achieving a wide variety of patterns, and vibrant or subtle colours can be used to give different effects. Combining these simple, ancient processes with modern materials allows an enormous range of personal and individual patterns to be produced by this versatile craft.

EQUIPMENT AND MATERIALS

The projects in this book have been designed to demonstrate a variety of tie-dyeing techniques, and each project takes you through the steps involved in creating the finished items. The materials and techniques required for each project are described in detail, and as you work through the projects you will build up your own "library" of dyeing techniques. Slightly more complex methods and articles are introduced in the later projects, and newcomers to the craft can work through the early pieces to develop their confidence and expertise so that they will be able to design and create their own items, and experimenting with different materials and techniques will show just what a versatile and enjoyable craft this is.

You will find most of the equipment you will need in your home. Several different kinds of fabric dye are available, although those most suitable for tie-dyeing are the cold water dyes. (Before you begin make sure that the dye you intend to use is suitable for the fabric with which you will be working.) In general, it is easier to dye 100 per cent natural fibres – silk, cotton, wool and linen, for example, or a combination of these. Synthetic fabrics or mixes of natural and synthetic fibres do not dye evenly, and you will have to use special dyes for these fabrics.

You will need

◇ Old newspaper or a plastic sheet to protect your work surface
◇ Scissors and a craft knife
◇ As wide a variety of winding materials as possible – string, thread, wool, twine, strips of fabric (from old sheets etc) and elastic bands
◇ 30 wooden or plastic clothes pegs (those with metal springs are best)
◇ 50 paper clips in various sizes
◇ Glass marbles or balls or stones (about 30 small, 10 medium sized and 4 large)

◇ 5 corks in various sizes
◇ Old buttons in various sizes
◇ Rubber gloves (the thin, surgical ones are best)
◇ Plastic bucket or large plastic bowl
◇ Electric kettle or saucepan and hot plate
◇ 5ml measure (1 teaspoon) and a 15ml measure (1 tablespoon)
◇ Large, heat-proof measuring jug that holds 1 litre (2 pints)
◇ 500g (1lb) table salt
◇ 0.5 litre (1 pint) vinegar

You will also need some cold water dyes. When you select your dyes weigh the fabric and check the quantity of dye you need for each item or items. Each manufacturer gives specific recipes and instructions for its own products, so although general instructions of mixing cold water dyes are given in the instructions for each project, you must always check the manufacturer's instructions for the dye you are using. The quantities given in these mixing instructions will dye approximately 270 x 270 cm (64 x 64 in) of fabric.

You will also, of course, need materials and garments, as well as a few accessories, and these are listed for each product.

MIXING DYES FOR COTTON

1 Mix each dye, remembering to check the manufacturer's instructions for the dye that you are using. Approximately you will need to add 5g (1 tsp) of dye to each 0.5 litre (1 pint) of boiling water in a heat-proof jug.

2 Add 30g (2 tbsp) of salt and mix thoroughly.

3 Add this solution to a bowl containing 2 litres (4 pints) of hot water and stir.

4 You can check the strength of the dye by placing a strip of the fabric you are using in the dye bath for 10–15 minutes. If the colour is too strong, add more boiling water; if it is too weak, add more dye.

MIXING DYES FOR SILK AND WOOL

1 Add 5g (1 tsp) of dye to each 0.5 litre (1 pint) of boiling water in a heat-proof jug.

2 Add 30 ml (2 tbsp) vinegar and mix thoroughly. Add this to a further 1 litre (2 pints) of hot water and stir.

TYING METHODS AND EXAMPLES

There are numerous ways of tying fabric to achieve patterns, and each one will produce a different end result. Even if you tie several pieces of material in the same way, you will not be able to produce exactly the same pattern each time, and this is one of the exciting things about tie-dyeing – you never know exactly how a piece will turn out, and every one is individual and personal.

MARBLED PATTERN

Crumple the fabric into a hard ball and bind it with twine or string. For each different colour, re-crumple the fabric in a different way. When you are dyeing larger pieces of material, bunch the fabric along its length and bind it into a sausage-like shape. You can add greater definition to the pattern by brushing fabric paint onto the fabric after it is dry but before untying it.

CHECK PATTERN

Evenly pleat the fabric and iron it, then secure the pleats with clothes pegs.

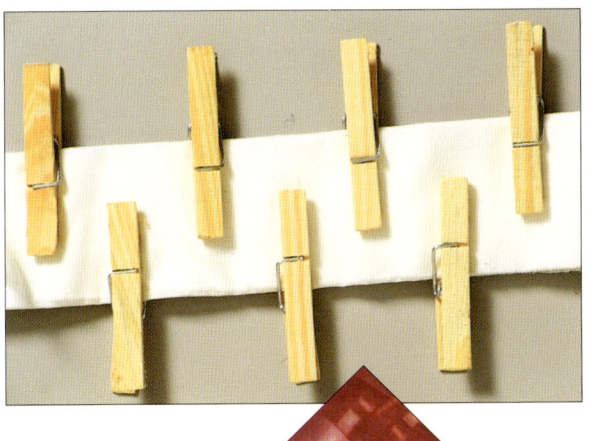

STRIPES

Fold the fabric in half, pleat it and bind it in the centre with string.

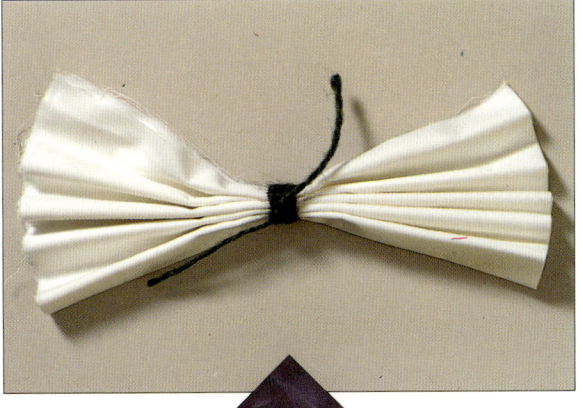

SMALL CIRCLES

Tie small round objects – marbles or stones – into the fabric.

VIGNETTE EFFECTS

Roll the fabric tightly around a cord then ruche it. Repeat the process by wrapping the fabric in opposite directions and re-dyeing it with a different colour.

FRAGMENTED PATTERN

Pinch the centre of the fabric and allow it to fall into drapes like a closed umbrella. Cross-bind it with thread or twine.

RIBS

Make neat folds and secure the pleats at regular intervals with paper clips.

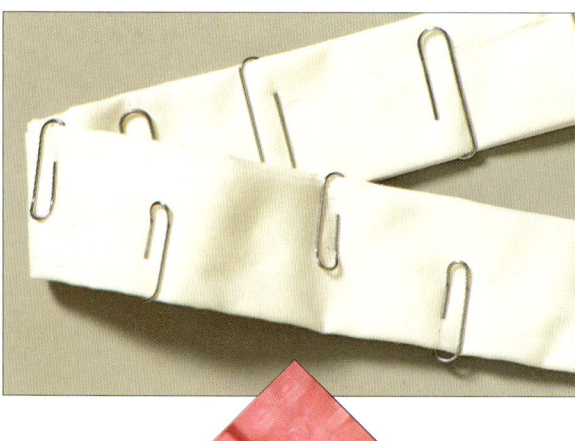

VARIABLE STRIPES

Fold the fabric in half, pleat it and bind it at intervals with twine or thread.

ELABORATE CIRCLES

Wrap a champagne cork into the fabric and tie it with thin twine or thread.

ASYMMETRIC PATTERN

Knot each corner with a piece of fabric from the centre of a square of material. This technique is best done with lightweight fabrics.

BOLD STRIPES

Simply knot the fabric at intervals.

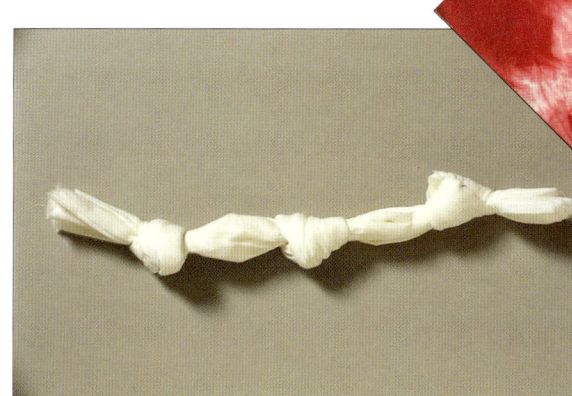

CONCENTRIC PATTERN

Pinch the centre of the fabric and allow it to fall into drapes like a closed umbrella. Bind it at intervals lengthways.

SQUARES

Take a square of fabric and fold it diagonally twice so that it makes a triangle. Pleat the fabric length-ways and bind it with thread.

FRACTURED GLASS PATTERN

Fold the fabric once or twice, then twist and allow it to twist back on itself before binding it with twine.

TABLE NAPKINS

This first project uses a square patterning method and a single colour to make some table napkins. The materials listed below – except the dye itself – are sufficient for one napkin, so if you want to make more, you will need to multiply the quantities accordingly. You can, if you prefer, use ready-made napkins. Remember to use pure natural fibres.

You will need
- ◇ 1 square of cotton, 45 x 45cm (8 x 8in)
- ◇ Electric iron
- ◇ Clothes pegs (optional)
- ◇ 90cm (36in) string
- ◇ 2.5g (½ tsp) cornflower blue cold water dye (sufficient for 6 napkins)
- ◇ 30g (2 tbsp) salt
- ◇ Heat-proof jug large enough to hold 1 litre (2 pints)
- ◇ 1 bowl, large enough to hold 3 litres (6 pints)
- ◇ Rubber gloves

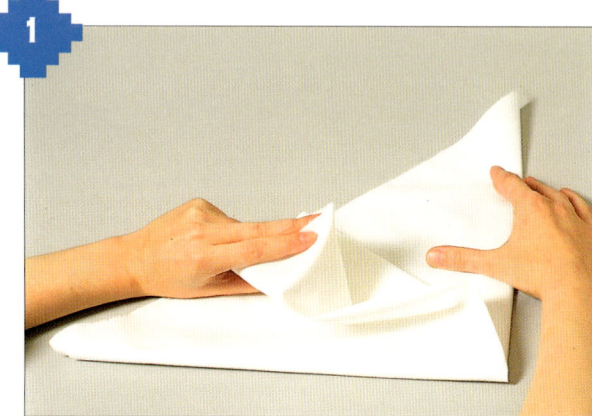

1 Iron the fabric to remove unwanted creases and folds. This will both make it easier to fold the cloth as you want and help to prevent the dye from adhering to areas of the cloth you do not want to be coloured. Fold the square over on itself diagonally to form a triangle then fold it again to make a smaller triangle. To ensure that the pattern was soft, we did not iron these folds in.

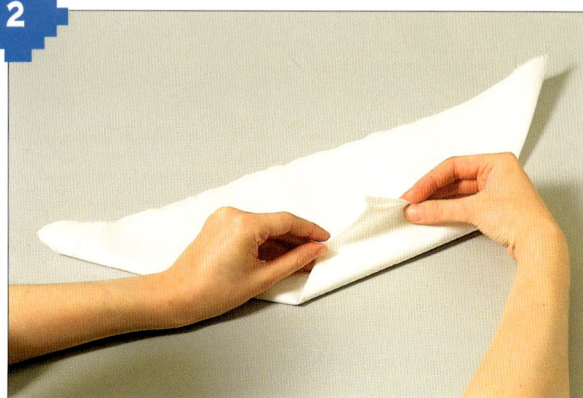

2 Place the folded square in front of you with the apex of the triangle towards you and fold the top over by 2.5cm (1in). Using that as a guide, continue to fold down the material to form a long strip.

3 You may want to hold the pleats with clothes pegs to stop them from unfolding while you work.

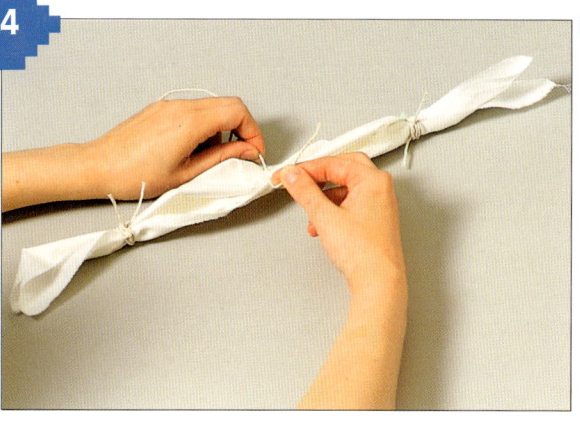

4 Each napkin will require five pieces of string, each about 18cm (7in) long. Bind the first piece of string several times around the centre of the strip and tie it tightly.

5 Repeat this at the ends, then tie pieces about half-way along each end or where the folds are beginning to open.

6 Mix 2.5g (½ tsp) of blue dye to 0.5 litre (1 pint) of boiling water in a heat-proof jug. Add 30g (2 tbsp) of salt and mix thoroughly. Place the bound square in the dye bath for 10–15 minutes – but check the manufacturer's instructions – and stir occasionally to make sure that the dye is even.

7 Once the fabric is the colour you want, remove the bundle or bundles from the bowl and rinse thoroughly under cold running water. When the water runs clear, most of the excess dye will have washed out. Untie the string.

8 When the fabric is completely dry, iron it and hem or overstitch the edges.

TIP

• Some dye manufacturers produce an after-treatment for their products, which prevents too much colour washing out, and you may want to consider using one of these if the items you make are likely to require frequent washing.

CARDS AND JEWELLERY

◆

Now that you have tried one of the basic methods, you can combine several techniques, including over-dyeing, to produce more intricate, multicoloured patterns. Mastering the basic binding and dyeing techniques will make it easier for you to visualize the likely end results, and making personalized gift tags, greetings cards and jewellery from these samples is an ideal way of using your early experimental pieces.

You will need
◇ 2 pieces of habutai silk, finely woven, each 30 x 30cm (12 x 12in)
◇ 5m (15ft) heavy thread or embroidery thread
◇ 2.5g (⅛ tsp) each of red, yellow and blue dye
◇ 45ml (3 tbsp) vinegar (but check manufacturer's instructions)
◇ 2m (6ft) twine
◇ 5 small marbles or glass balls
◇ 2–3 bowls, each large enough to hold 0.5 litre (1 pint)
◇ Electric iron
◇ 1 sheet of A1 (33⅛ x 23⅜in) card or ready-made greetings card and gift card blanks
◇ 1 pair of earring findings or blanks of your choice
◇ 2 brooch findings
◇ 4 blank button covers, 22mm (¾in) across
◇ Scissors and a craft knife
◇ Clear, all-purpose adhesive

1 Take one piece of silk, scrunch it into a tight ball and bind it with embroidery thread. Randomly tie marbles into the second piece with embroidery thread. Mix the blue dye in 0.5 litre (1 pint) of boiling water in a heat-proof jug and add 15ml (1 tbsp) vinegar to the solution (but check the manufacturer's instructions). Because silk does not react well to boiling water, allow it to cool to 50°C (about 120°F) before pouring the dye into the bowl. Place the tightly bound bundle of silk in the blue dye.

2 Mix the yellow dye in the same way and place it in the fabric with the marbles tied into it. Leave both pieces for about 20 minutes. Do not throw away the blue dye because you will need it again. Remove each bundle and rinse thoroughly under the cold tap until the water runs clear. Untie each bundle and allow the silk to dry flat. You can iron damp silk with a medium hot iron, and you may wish to speed up the drying process in this way.

3 When the blue square is dry, find the centre and pinch it so that the fabric falls into folds like a closed umbrella. Cross-bind it down three-quarters of its length, starting at the pinched centre.

4 Fold the yellow square diagonally twice so that it forms a triangle and pleat it along its length, ironing the folds at each turn. Bind it with five pieces of twine along its length.

5

5 Mix the red dye, allow it to cool and place the blue square in the red dye. Place the yellow square in the blue dye. Leave both pieces for at least 20 minutes. Rinse each piece thoroughly in cold running water. Untie, allow to dry completely and iron.

6

6 Use a viewing window or two L-shaped pieces of card to select areas to cut and mount for your cards and gift tags.

7

7 We used a round wooden brooch blank and a semicircular metal blank and oval earring drops, which you can obtain from most good craft shops and some department stores. If you use adhesive to hold the fabric in place, take care not to get it on the front of the silk, which will be spoiled.

8

8 Button blanks usually have removable backs. Make sure that you keep the fabric taut and even over the front while you clip in the back sections.

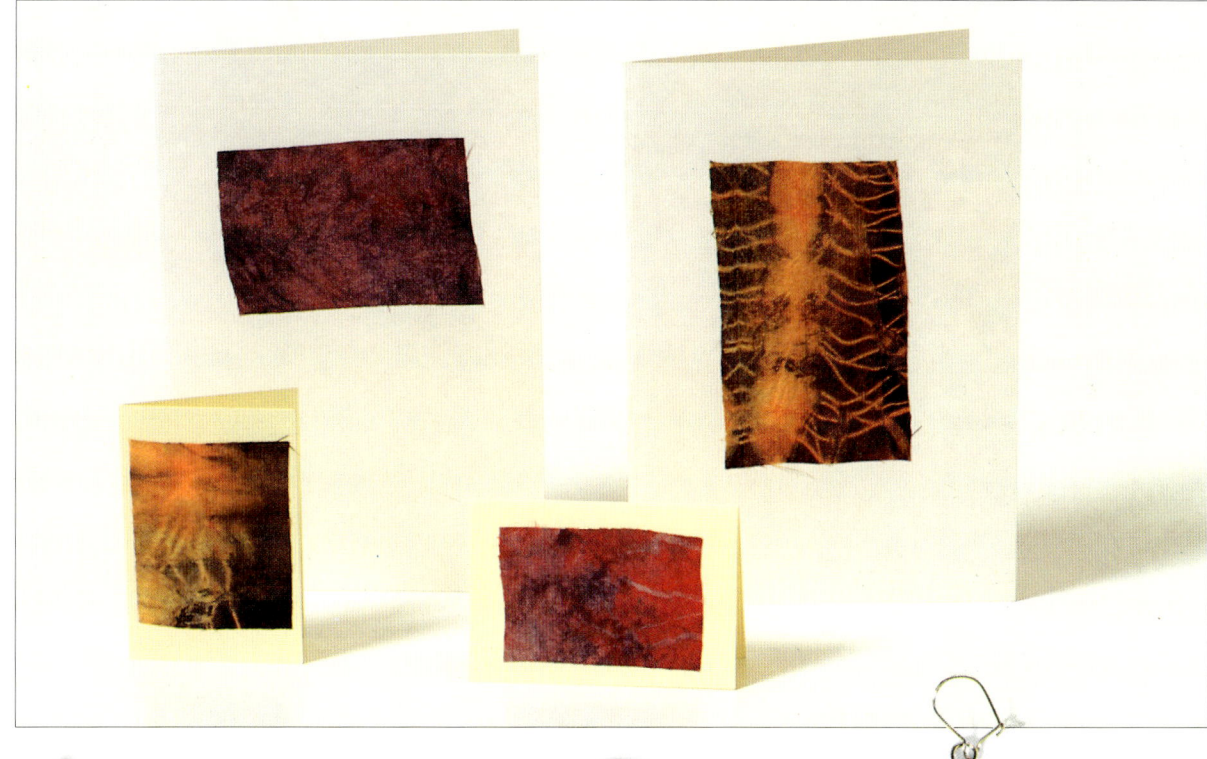

Socks and Hair Scrunchies

The basic principles of tie-dyeing apply no matter what object you choose to decorate, whether it is plain fabric or a ready-made item. When you are selecting a method, however, you should consider the construction of the piece you are planning to make, because some patterns are more effective on a larger scale. In addition, some fabrics, such as cotton jersey and non-woven materials, stretch when they are wet, so you may want to bear this in mind when you plan your design.

You will need
◇ 1 pair of white, plain flat-weave, cotton socks
◇ 3 pieces of fabric, each 1m x 2.5cm (39 x 1in)
◇ 2 hair scrunchies (see opposite)
◇ 1m (39in) string
◇ 1.25g (¼ tsp) each of orange, light green and violet dye
◇ 5g (1 tsp) salt
◇ 10ml (2 tsp) vinegar (but check manufacturer's instructions)

> **TIP**
>
> • When you buy articles such as socks to tie-dye, avoid those made of ribbed cotton jersey, which tends to stretch out of shape when it is immersed in water. A small amount of nylon – not more than 10 per cent – will help to prevent the socks from twisting and bagging.

1 Cut one of the strips of fabric into eight pieces and tie four pieces at intervals around each sock.

2 Use the remaining two strips to cross-bind each sock tightly along its length.

3 Tie three knots along the length of the first hair scrunchy.

4 Cross-bind the second scrunchy with string along its length.

5

6

5 Mix the dyes, adding 5g (1 tsp) salt to the orange dye and 5ml (1 tsp) of vinegar to the others. You will need about 0.5 litre (1 pint) of each colour. Place the socks in one colour and a scrunchy in each of the other colours. Leave them for about 20 minutes.

6 Remove the items from the dyes, rinse thoroughly and allow to dry. If the socks have stretched slightly, try drying them in a tumble dryer to shrink them back into shape.

MAKING 2 HAIR SCRUNCHIES

You will need

◊ 2 pieces medium weight habutai silk,
   each 70 x 10cm (28 x 4in)
◊ Needle and sewing cotton
◊ 10cm (4in) fine string
◊ 35cm (14in) fine elastic
◊ Bodkin or safety pin

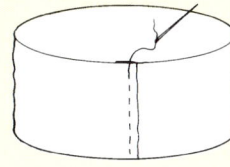
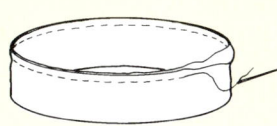

• With right sides together, stitch the two short ends of one piece of silk together to form a circle, then fold the fabric in half lengthways.
• Still with right sides together, stitch along the long edge to form a tube, leaving a small opening. Turn the silk back to the right side and repeat the process with the second piece of silk. Dye the scrunchies as described above.

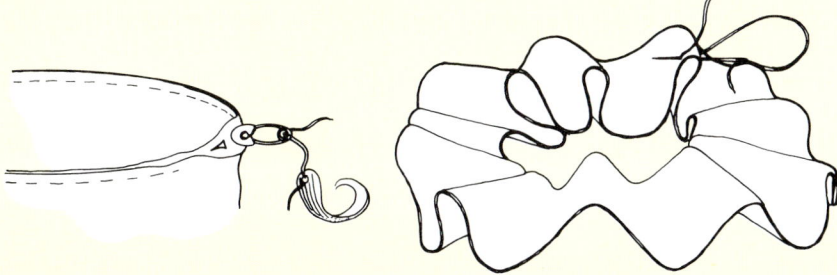

• When they are dry, tie a piece of fine string to the elastic and use a bodkin or safety pin to thread it through the opening in the tube.
• Untie the string, pull up the elastic and tie the ends together, over-sewing them for extra security if you wish. Neatly oversew the opening. Alternatively, use two ready-made, plain scrunchies.

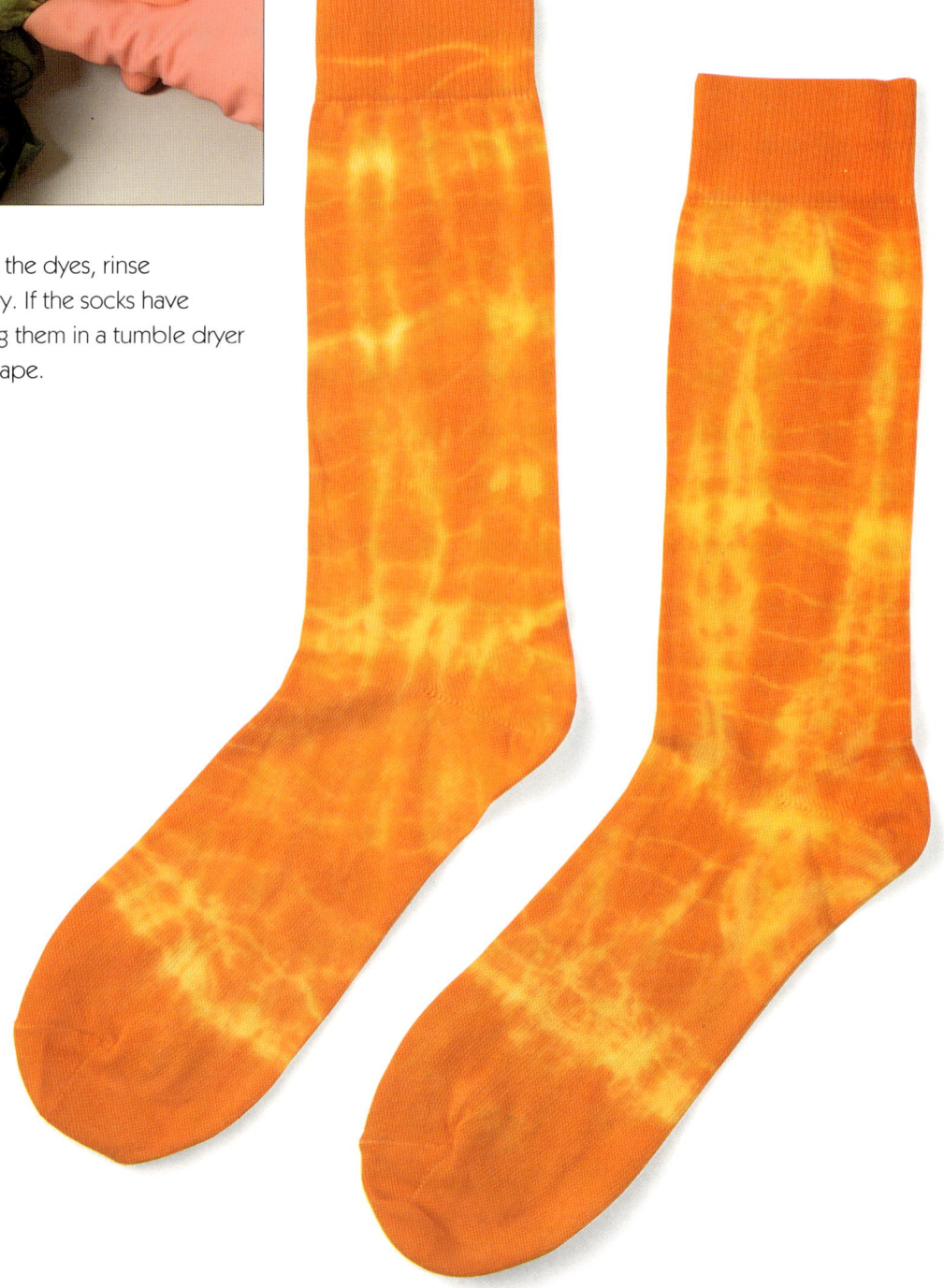

COLOURED T-SHIRT

We have chosen to dye a plain coloured T-shirt a deeper shade of its original colour, and this allows us to develop a range of hues of one main colour. You might prefer to experiment with the other primary colours – red and yellow – but unless you are especially fond of earthy colours, it would be as well to avoid over-dyeing material that is already dyed in a secondary colour – orange, green or purple – with its opposite in the colour spectrum (see the colour wheel on page 187).

You will need
◇ 1 bright blue cotton T-shirt
◇ 1 large and 2 small marbles
◇ 2m (6ft) string
◇ 1 bowl, large enough to hold 1.5 litres (3 pints)
◇ 7.5g (1½ tsp) navy blue dye
◇ 5g (1 tsp) salt

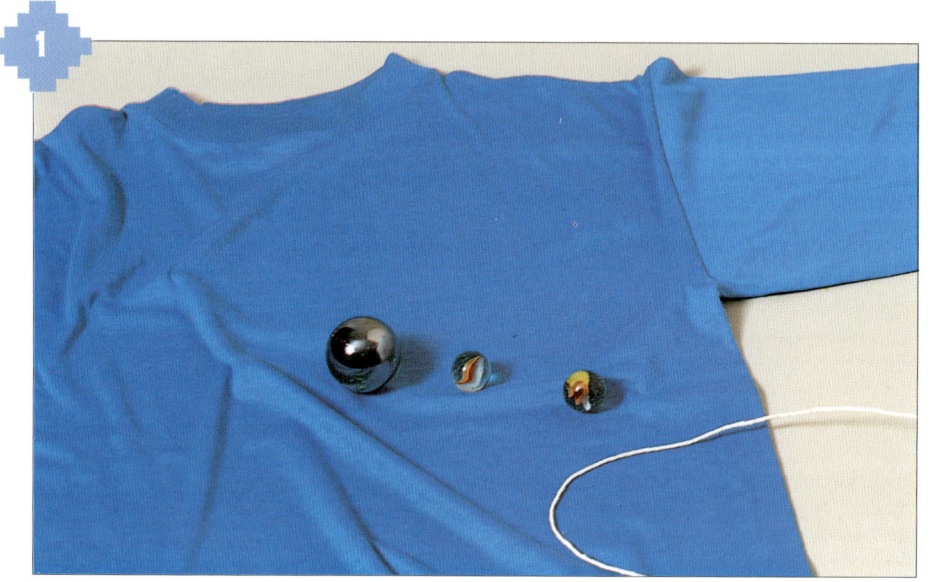

1 If you are using a new T-shirt, wash it in cool water and leave it to dry. This will remove any dressing on the fabric that might resist the dye.

2 So that the pattern appears on the front only, separate the front from the back and use string to bind the large marble into the centre of the front.

3 Wind the string around several times, leave a gap and then bind the fabric twice more to make a concentric pattern.

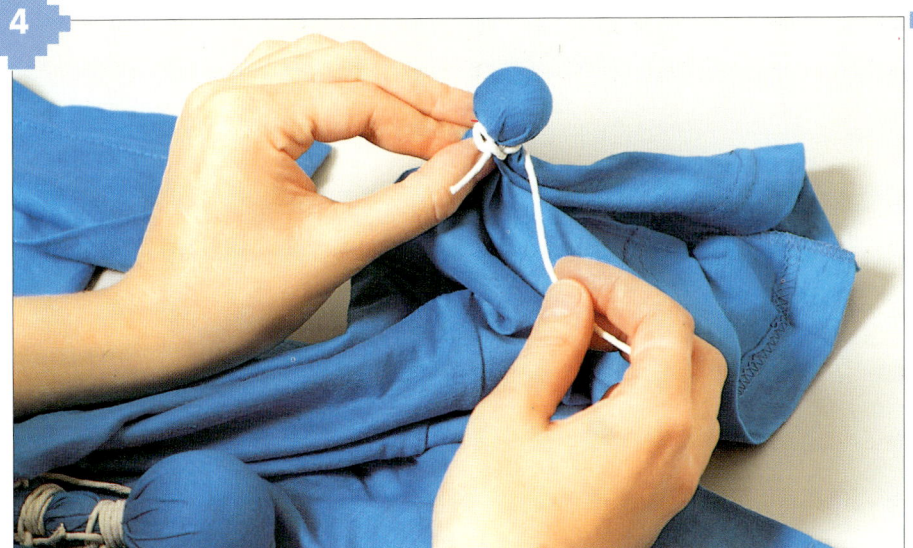

4 Bind a small marble into the shoulder fold of a sleeve, leave a gap and bind again.

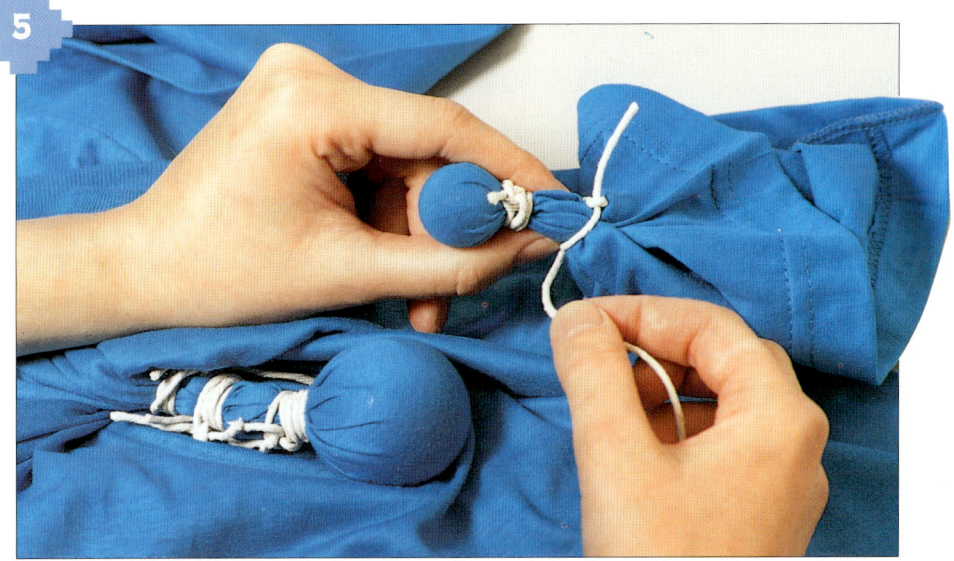

5 Repeat on the other shoulder.

6 Mix the dye according to the manufacturer's instructions and add the salt. Allow the dye to cool. If the T-shirt is not made from good quality jersey, you may prefer to leave the dye until it is cold, which will help to overcome the problem of stretching. Place the T-shirt in the bowl.

7 Leave the T-shirt in the dye for about 20 minutes, stirring it frequently to prevent streaks being created and then rinse the T-shirt until the water runs clear.

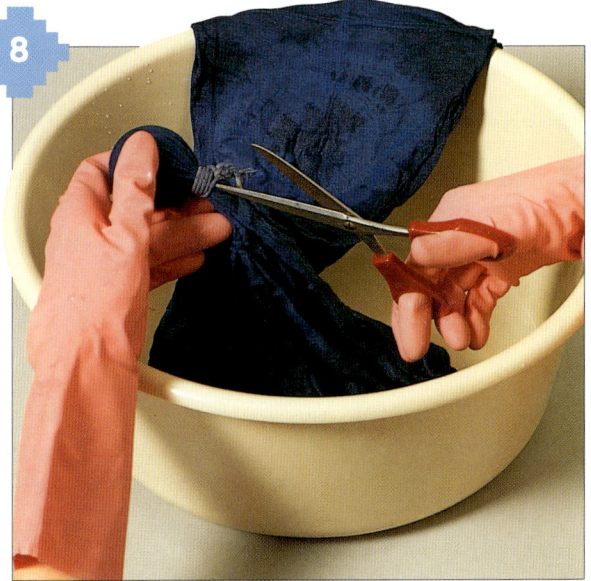

8 Untie the string keeping the T-shirt over the bowl to prevent dripping. If it has stretched slightly, you may want to dry the T-shirt in a tumble-dryer to shrink it a little, and ironing will also help get it back into shape if necessary.

SILK SCARF

There are many different kinds of silk, and these vary greatly in price. You should, however, be able to buy a suitable length of lightweight habutai or pongee silk relatively inexpensively. Alternatively, you may prefer to personalize a scarf that you already own. We have used three different colours and two tying methods to produce a subtle, delicately shaded pattern.

You will need

◇ 90 x 90cm (36 x 36in) undyed, lightweight habutai silk
◇ Electric iron
◇ 4m (13ft) twine
◇ 2m (6ft 6in) heavy thread or 2-ply wool
◇ 5g (1 tsp) each of deep rose, golden yellow and marine blue dye
◇ 90ml (6 tbsp) vinegar (but check manufacturer's instructions)
◇ 1 bowl, large enough to hold at least 1 litre (2 pints)

TIP

• If you choose to dye a scarf that is already coloured, remember that the original colour of the fabric will affect the result. A blue scarf dyed with yellow will, for example, become green (see the colour wheel on page 187)

1 Before binding your scarf, iron it to remove any creases; you may find it easier to iron silk that is slightly damp. Fold the silk square diagonally to form a triangle, then fold it in half again to make a smaller triangle.

2 Pleat the silk lengthways and bind the folded strip with pieces of twine, placed at intervals of about 6cm (2½in), and fasten securely. Mid-way between each piece of twine, tie lengths of heavy thread tightly around the silk.

3 Mix 5g (1 tsp) deep rose dye in 1 litre (2 pints) of hot water and allow it to cool to 50°C (about 120°F). If the kind of dye you are using requires the addition of vinegar when silk is dyed, add 30ml (2 tbsp) to the solution. Place the pleated and bound silk scarf into the dye bath, making sure that the bowl is large enough to allow the material to move freely and that the dye solution is sufficiently deep to cover the material completely to ensure that it is evenly coloured.

TIP

• If you are using dye colours that are either very strong or very dilute, you may wish to alter the dye to water ratios. In general, the final colour is determined both by the concentration of the dye and by the length of time that the object is immersed in the dye.

4 Leave the scarf in the bowl for at least 15 minutes, stirring it occasionally. When you have achieved the shade you want, remove the dye from the bowl and rinse the scarf under cold running water until the water runs clear. Then untie the twine and thread.

5 Allow the silk to dry flat. You may iron it when it is still slightly damp to remove all creases. Find the center of the square, pinch it and allow the silk to fall into drapes as if it were a closed umbrella.

6 Cross-bind the silk tightly with twine from top to bottom, mix the yellow dye and proceed as before.

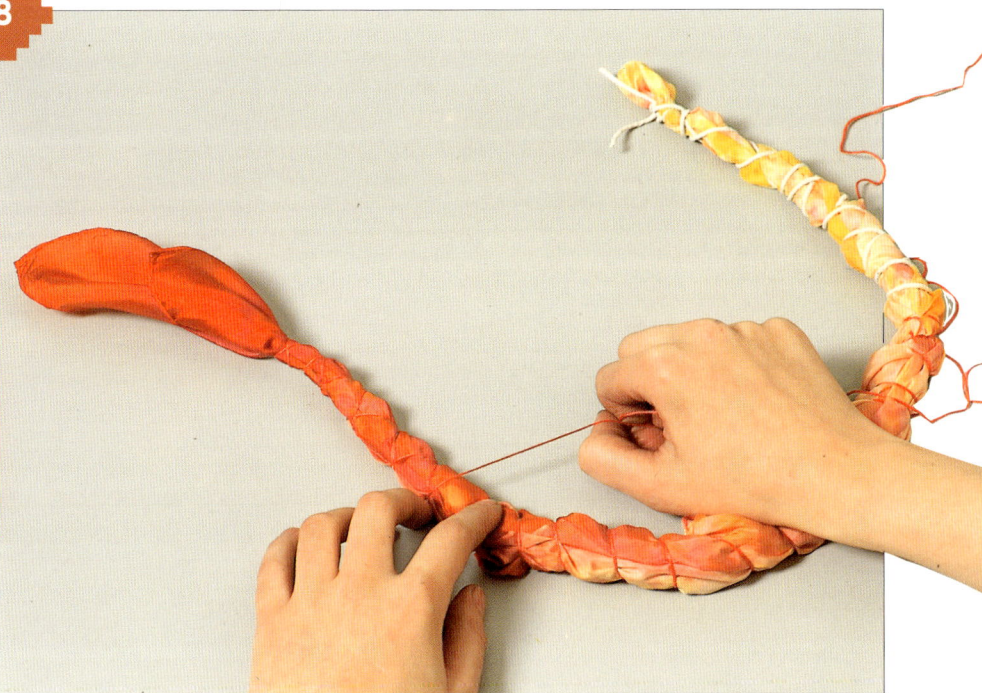

7 Rinse thoroughly, untie and dry before ironing to remove the creases.

8 Pinch and fold the silk as in step 5 and use twine to bind the top half. Bind the bottom half of the scarf more tightly with heavy thread so that more blue dye can reach the center of the scarf. Mix the blue dye as before and place the bound scarf in the bowl. You may wish to dilute the blue dye, because marine blue can be rather strong and may over-power the deep rose and yellow pattern.

9

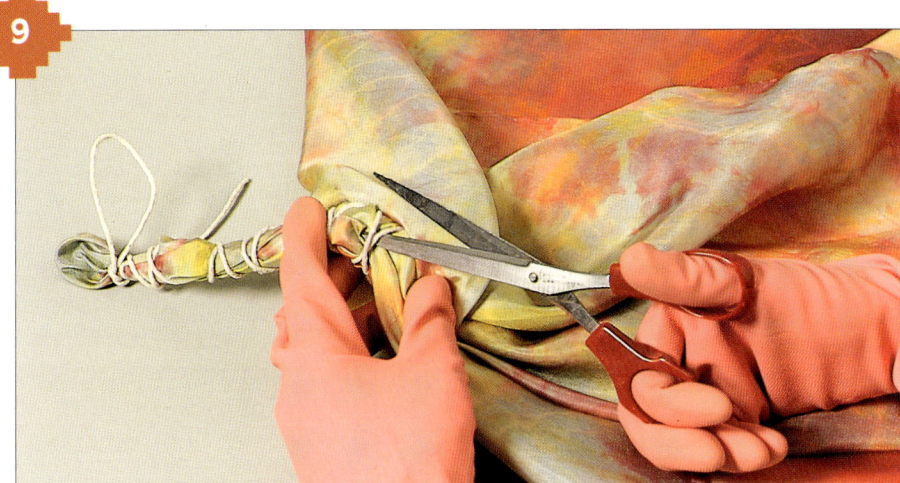

$\mathcal{9}$ Rinse the silk thoroughly before untying the scarf and allow it to dry.

COLOUR WHEEL

• Dyes behave differently from pigment-based colours – paints and inks, for example – because they rely on some form of chemical agent such as salt or vinegar to make them permanent. This attribute makes it difficult to judge accurately what the end result will be, and tie-dyeing coloured fabric or an already dyed item of clothing can add to this unpredictability. In general, however, you should be able to anticipate more or less what the end result will be, and you can use this wheel as a guide.

CUSHION COVERS

As you experiment with different kinds of fabric you will notice that different materials accept dyes in different ways. When they are bound and dyed, cotton and thicker fabrics, especially cotton lawn and cotton poplin, take on a softer, almost dusty pattern, which tends to be stronger on one side. This quality makes them acceptable for use in soft furnishings, where only one side of the fabric is visible. We have made two square cushion covers, which are easy to make and yet can bring an individual and highly personal accent to your home. The materials listed here are sufficient to make two double-sided cushion covers, each measuring 45 x 45cm (18 x 18in).

You will need
◇ 4 pieces of fabric, each 65 x 65cm (26 x 26in)
◇ Electric iron
◇ 4m (13ft) twine
◇ 1 packet of dye in each of golden yellow, marine blue and copper (or colours to suit your furnishing scheme)
◇ 1 bowl, large enough to hold 1.5 litres (3 pints)
◇ 2 cushion pads, each 45 x 45cm (18 x 18in)

TIP

• Some coloured twines – those that are sold for garden use, for example – may stain fabrics when they are dampened by the dye solution. Wooden clothes pegs may also retain traces of dye, and if you re-use them you may find that minute quantities of the original colour are transferred to your new pattern. These colours may enhance your design or they may ruin it – so take care.

1 Iron the squares of material to remove any creases, and for the first cover, fold the material in half then pleat it lengthways, making the pleats about 3cm (1¼in) wide. Iron again. Secure the pleats with clothes pegs, spacing the pegs at intervals of about 6cm (2⅜in). Bind the fabric with twine between each peg.

2 For the second cover, pinch the material in the centre and allow it to fall into drapes. Twist the fabric slightly, then tightly cross-bind it along its entire length with twine to limit the amount of dye that comes into contact with the material. This technique is especially useful for adding small splashes of colour.

MAKING A CUSHION

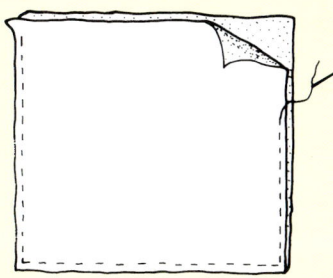

• Place two matching squares together, right sides facing, and stitch around three sides, leaving a seam allowance of about 3cm (1¼in), although the seam may vary if your material has shrunk slightly during the dyeing process.

• Fold down and iron a 2.5cm (1in) hem along both edges.

• Add a zip fastener, Velcro or press-studs to close the opening before turning to the right side and inserting the cushion pad.

TIP

• If you are making larger cushion covers, remember to increase the amounts of water and dye you mix and to use a large bowl so that the pieces of material can be completely submerged.

3 Mix the yellow dye, making sure that you use a bowl that is large enough to accommodate all the pieces of fabric. Add the salt to the dye bath if recommended by the manufacturer. Place both covers in the yellow dye and leave for 15–20 minutes, stirring occasionally. Remove the covers, rinse thoroughly and untie.

4 Dry the fabric and iron it. If the fabric is very creased, you may find it easier to use the steam setting on your iron or to dampen the material slightly to make ironing easier.

5 Take the first square and fold it in half, across the dyed lines then pleat it.

6 Iron and pleat the square, securing it with pegs and twine as before. Mix the blue dye and place the folded and tied material in it. Leave for 15–20 minutes, rinse thoroughly, untie and dry.

TIP

• If you make cushions that are backed with plain fabric, make sure that the material you choose for the backs shrinks at the same rate as the patterned square. If you do not, the cover will twist when it is laundered.

7 Take the second, ironed cover and pinch it in the centre to drape it in an umbrella shape. Cross-bind it half-way down its length with twine. Mix the copper dye and place the tied material in it. Leave for 15–20 minutes, rinse thoroughly, untie and dry.

LEGGINGS

Predicting how a pattern will turn out on a ready-made item of clothing is difficult because of such variable factors as the cut of the item and the weight and type of fabric that has been used. Most items of leisure-wear now contain a small percentage of lycra, which helps to keep them in shape but which, unfortunately, does not dye easily. The amount of lycra in the article may, therefore, result in the final colour being lighter than you had expected. We have chosen to dye a pair of cotton leggings.

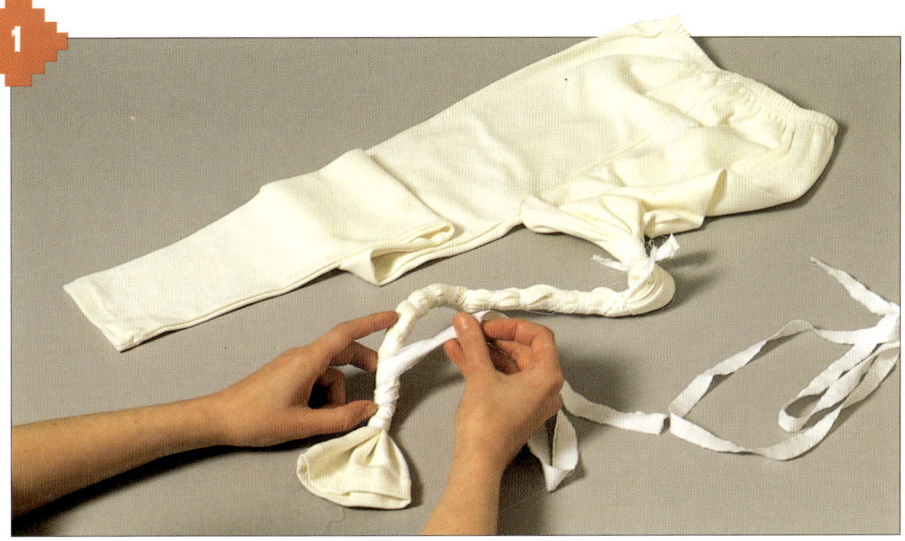

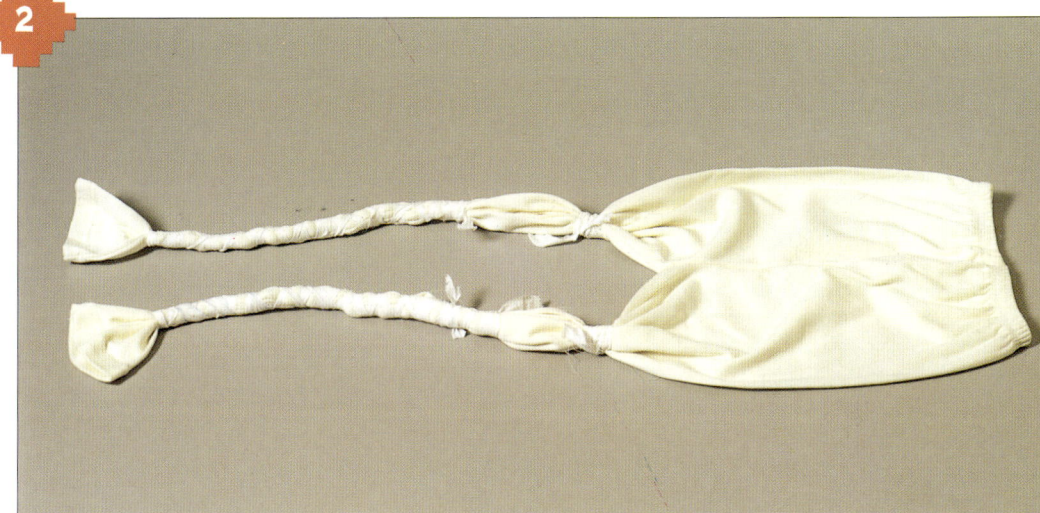

You will need
◇ 1 pair ecru leggings
◇ 2 strips of fabric, each
  25 x 2.5cm (10 x 1in)
◇ 4 strips of fabric, each
  1.5m x 2.5cm (5ft x 1in)
◇ 7.5g (1½ tsp) each of black
  and old gold dye
◇ 30g (2 tsp) salt
◇ 1 bowl, large enough to hold
  1.5 litres (3 pints)

1 Take the cotton leggings and bind each leg 7.5cm (3in) down from the gusset with short strips of fabric. Dyeing some tied items can lead to patterns appearing in inappropriate places, so some areas, such as the gusset and seat, should be left plain.

3 Mix the old gold dye in 1.5 litres (3 pints) of hot water and add 15g (1 tbsp) of salt or mix according to the manufacturer's instructions. Allow the water to cool before adding the leggings so that the garment does not stretch. Leave the leggings in the bowl for at least 20 minutes, remove and rinse thoroughly. When the water runs clear, wring the leggings out so that they no longer drip.

2 Leave a space of about 7.6cm (3in), then cross-bind down each length of 5cm (2in) from the foot. You will need two strips for each leg.

4 Mix the black dye as above or according to the manufacturer's instructions and place the top half of the leggings – that is, the unbound section – into the bowl, leaving the bound legs hanging over the edge of the bowl. Stand the bowl on plenty of old newspapers in case the leggings continue to drip dilute dye. Leave the leggings in the dye for at least 20 minutes.

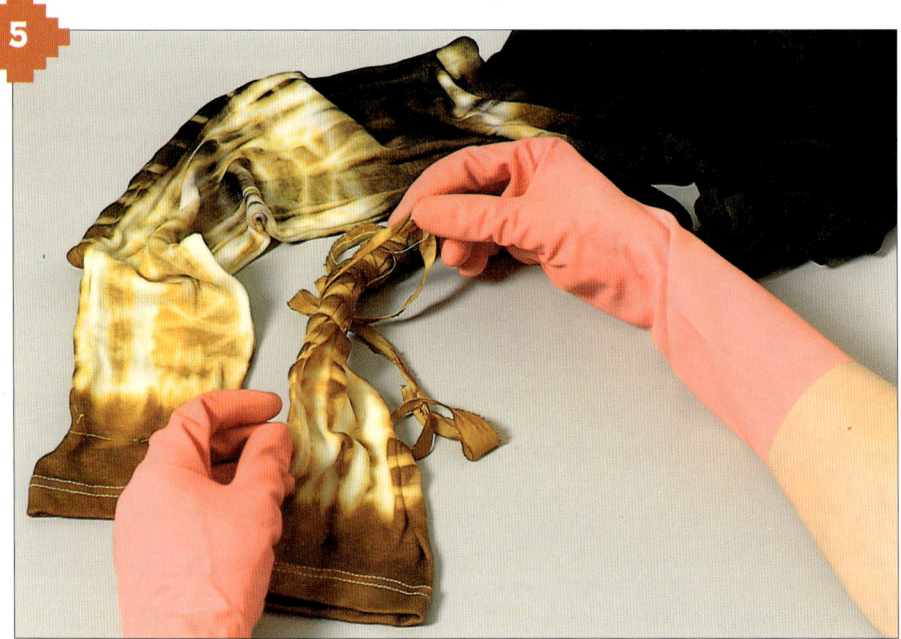

5 Rinse thoroughly in cold water before untying the legs. Because the fabric was still wet from the previous dyeing, the black dye will have crept along the legs to give a mottled, vignetted effect.

ALL-IN-ONE COTTON BODY

Combining several techniques in one item of clothing can produce fairly spectacular results. Although the final pattern can look complicated, the tie-dying process means that decorating in this way is relatively straightforward. Here, we have dyed a white all-in-one cotton body by using two colours and two different techniques to produce a three-colour pattern. This project also demonstrates how easy it is to isolate a pattern and colour on the same article.

You will need
◇ 1 white all-in-one cotton body
◇ 1 large marble or glass ball
◇ 60cm (24in) string
◇ 4 strips of fabric, each 1.5m x 2.5cm (5ft x 1in)
◇ 7.5g (1½ tsp) each of bright pink and violet dye
◇ 1 bowl, large enough to hold 3 litres (6 pints)
◇ 30g (2 tbsp) salt

1 Bind the large marble into the chest of the cotton body, making sure that you bind the string from the front of the garment, which will give slightly different circular patterns on the back and the front. Take each arm, twist it slightly and then tightly cross-bind each one with strips of fabric. You will need two strips for each arm. Twisting the fabric before binding stops the dye from saturating the whole of the sleeve.

2 Mix the pink dye in 0.5 litre (1 pint) of boiling water. Add the solution to a bowl containing 2.5 litres (5 pints) of warm water. Add the salt and allow to cool. Dye the whole garment, stirring it to help prevent patchy colouring and leaving it for a further 20–30 minutes. The longer you leave it, the brighter the colour will be. Rinse thoroughly in cold running water.

TIP

• Remember that the poorer the quality of the article you are dyeing, the cooler the dye solution should be before you place the item in it.

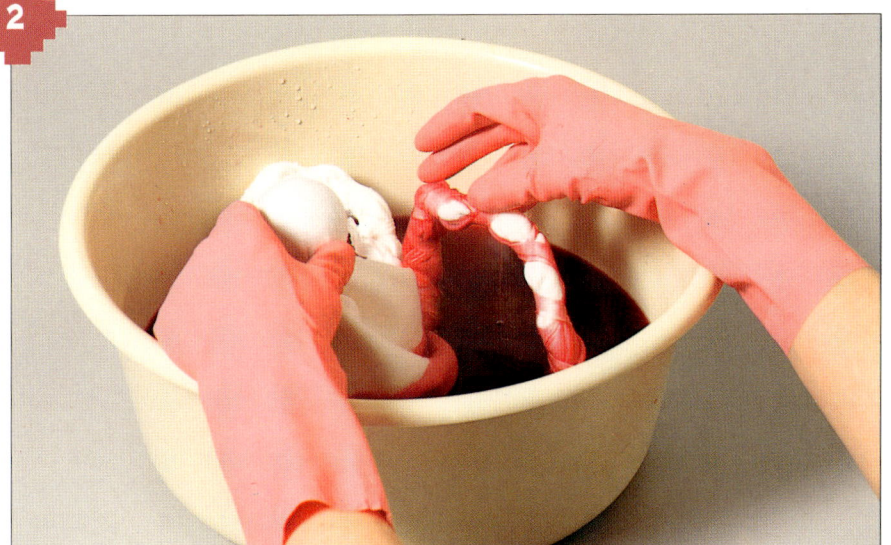

3 Wring the excess water from the garment and mix the violet dye. Place the gusset end of the body, up to the waist, and the bottom half of the sleeves into the dye. Leave for a further 20–30 minutes.

4 Remove from the dye, rinse thoroughly and untie. Tumble dry and iron to remove creases and any stretching that may have occurred.

SILK BOXER SHORTS

The softness and sheen of some types of silk make them ideal for underclothes, and the finish on silk also affects the way that the dyes take on the fabric. Dyeing flat woven or satin silk with acid tones, such as citrus yellow, fire red, bright green or hot orange, produces some dramatic results. We have used a pair of habutai silk boxer shorts for this project, dyeing them with citrus yellow and bright green to give a vibrant patterned effect.

You will need
◇ 1 pair white habutai silk boxer shorts
◇ 15–20 elastic bands
◇ 2.5g (⅛ tsp) each of citrus yellow and bright green dye
◇ 60ml (4 tbsp) vinegar (but check manufacturer's instructions)
◇ 1 bowl, large enough to hold 1.5 litres (3 pints)

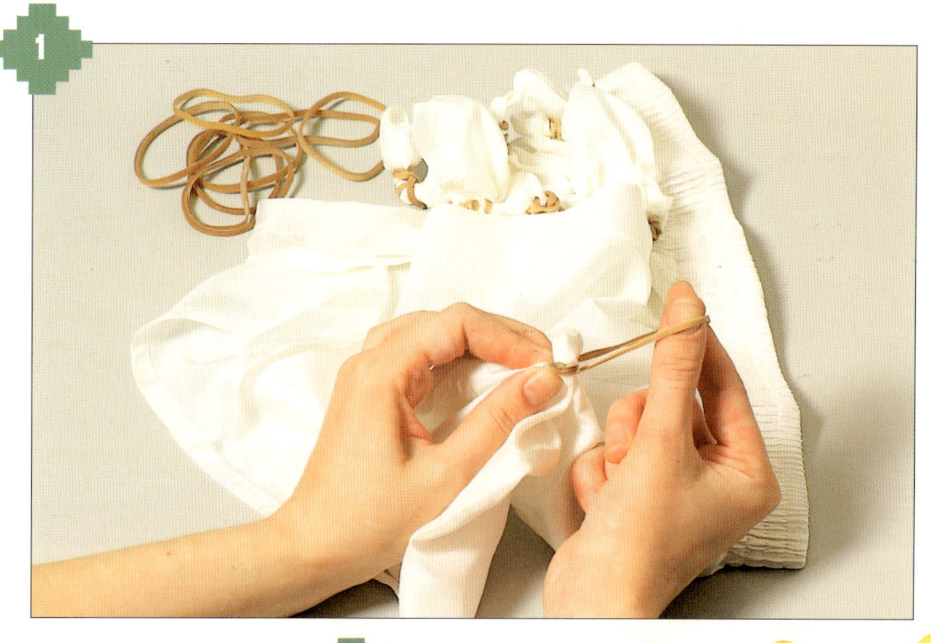

1 Lay the boxer shorts on your work surface and separate the front from the back. Randomly bunch small areas of both back and front and bind them with elastic bands.

2 Mix the yellow dye in 0.5 litre (1 pint) of boiling water and add 30ml (2 tbsp) of vinegar. Add the solution to a bowl containing a further 1 litre (2 pints) of hot water and allow it to cool to 50°C (about 120°F) before adding the shorts. Leave the shorts for 20–30 minutes, stirring occasionally.

3 Remove the shorts from the dye, rinse thoroughly, remove the elastic bands and allow to dry.

4 Repeat steps 1 and 2, but with the green dye. After 20–30 minutes, remove the shorts and rinse thoroughly.

5 When the water runs clear, remove the elastic bands and leave the shorts to dry flat.

SILK SARONG

The ruche method of tying makes it possible to create wonderfully vignetted patterns, which gradually fade along the length of the material. Using two or more colours allows you to build up multicoloured designs, in which bold motifs merge into subtler patterns. We have used a simple binding technique with a contrasting colour to decorate a simple cotton top and briefs to create an ideal compliment to the silk sarong for those hot sunny days on the beach.

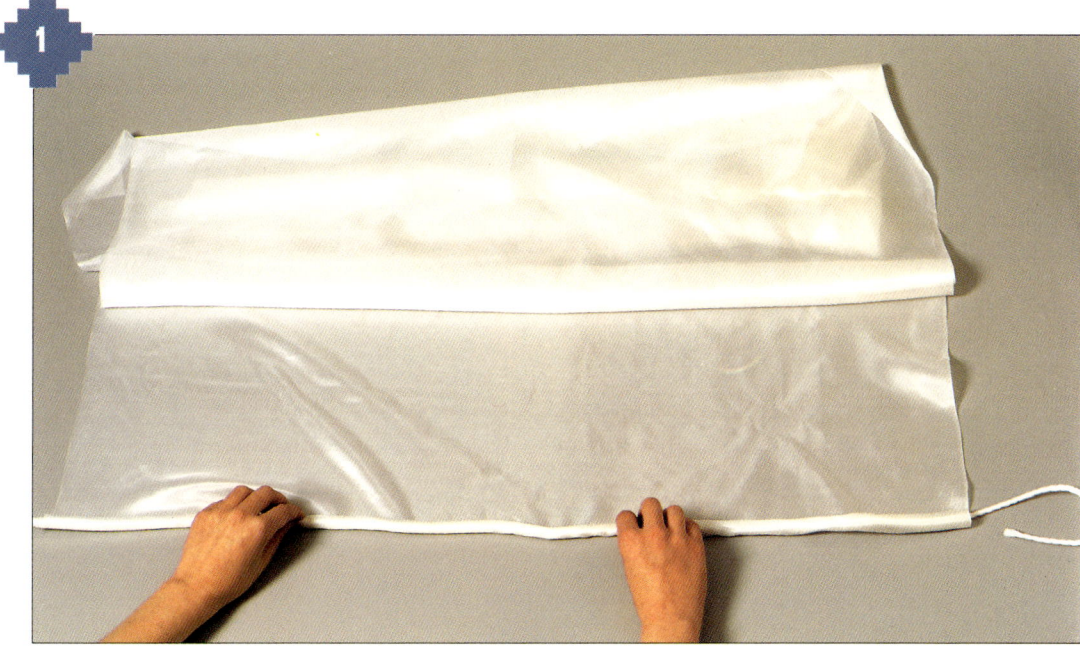

You will need
◇ 1 piece lightweight habutai or pongee silk, 2 x 0.9m (6 x 3ft)
◇ Electric iron
◇ 1m (3ft 3in) thick cord (plastic washing line, for example)
◇ 1 large marble and 2 medium sized marbles
◇ 2m (6ft) string
◇ 5g (1 tsp) each of bright red, bright blue and bright green dye
◇ 90ml (6 tbsp) vinegar (but check manufacturer's instructions)
◇ 1 bowl, large enough to hold at least 2 litres (4 pints)
◇ Top and briefs in 100 per cent white cotton
◇ 2 lengths of thick twine or string, each about 1m (3ft 3in)
◇ 30g (2 tbsp) salt

1 Iron the silk to remove the creases and lay it on your work surface with a short side towards you. Place the cord across the end nearest to you and roll the fabric around the cord until about 30cm (12in) remains unrolled.

2 Holding one end of the roll, push the fabric at the other end down the cord as far as it will go. Tie the ends of the cord tightly together with a double knot so that you have a circle of tightly ruched material with a flap.

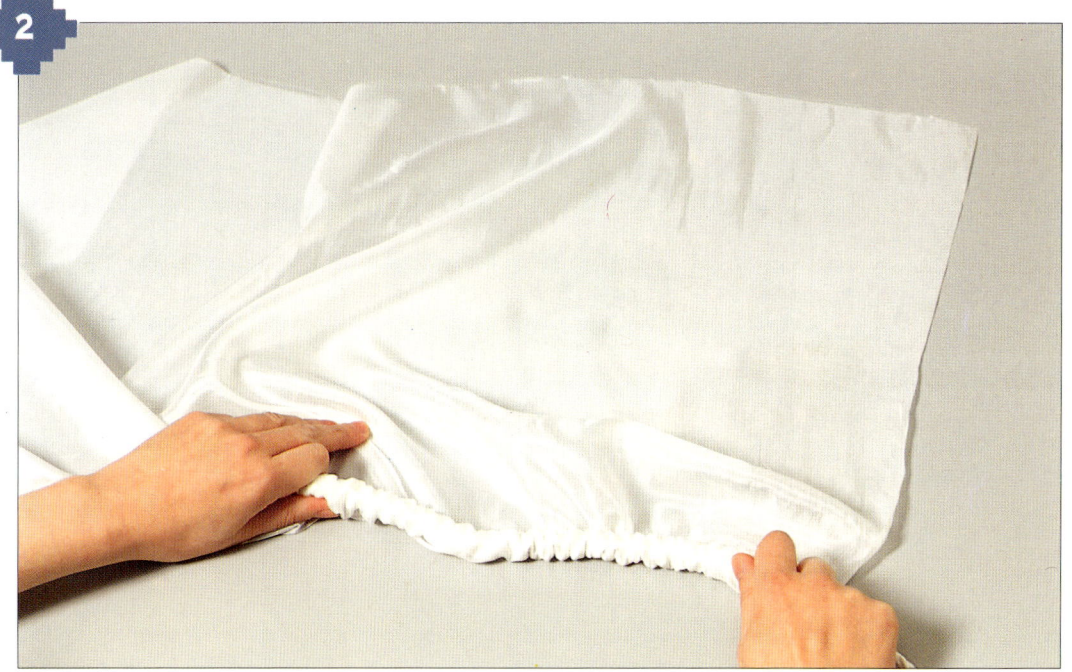

3 Use string to bind the large marble in the centre of this trailing piece of material. Bind the two smaller marbles at either side of the large marble.

4 Mix the blue dye in 1 litre (2 pints) boiling water, add 45ml (3 tbsp) of vinegar and add the solution to a bowl containing a further 1 litre (2 pints) of hot water. Allow to cool to 50°C (about 120°F) before adding the silk. Leave for 30 minutes. Remove the fabric from the dye, rinse thoroughly and untie. Leave the silk to dry and iron it.

5 Place the silk on your work surface with the section in which the marbles were tied nearest to you. Repeat steps 1–4, but use the red dye.

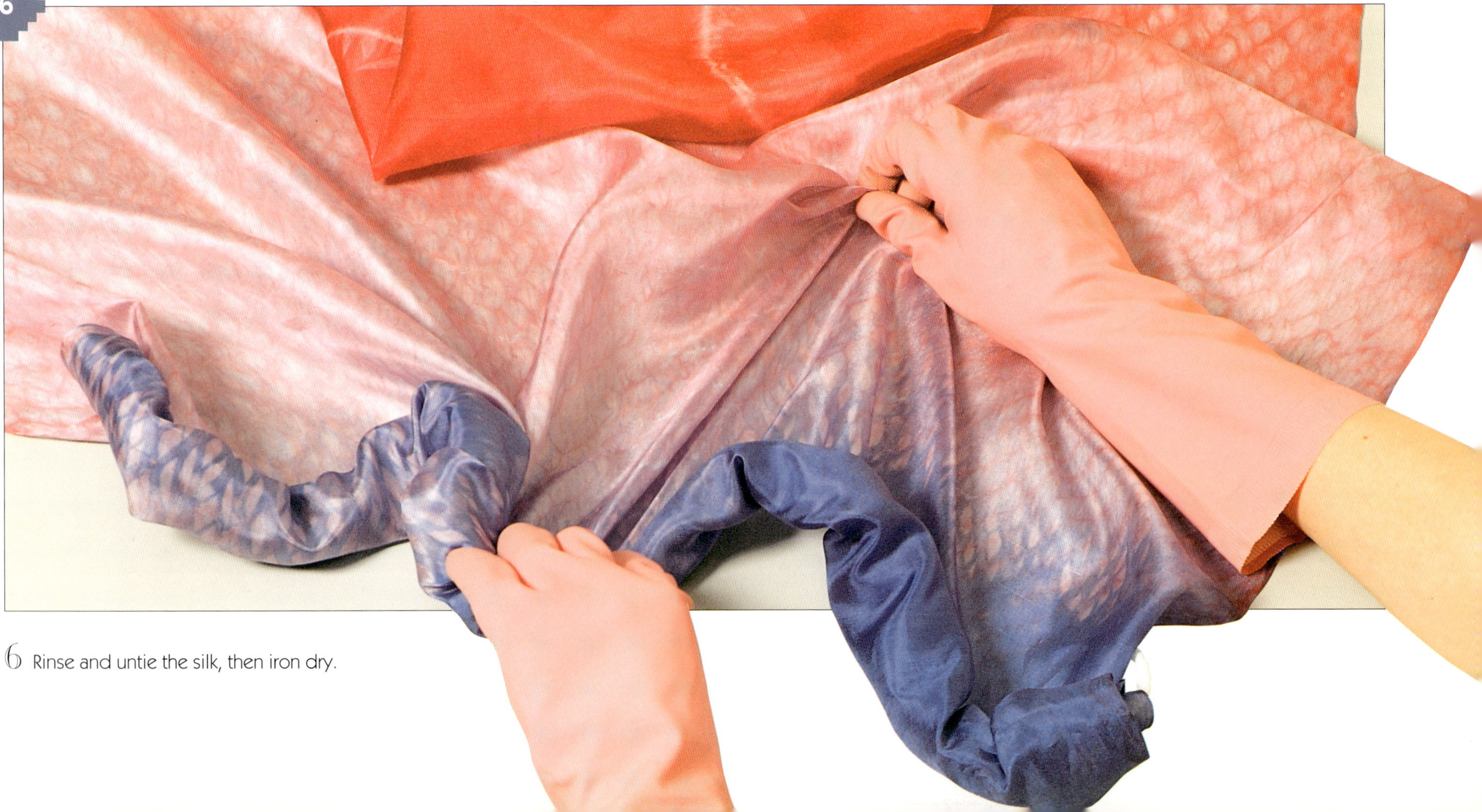

6 Rinse and untie the silk, then iron dry.

7 While the silk is dyeing you can prepare the cotton top and briefs for dyeing.

8 Use the two lengths of thick twine to bind around the width of the briefs just below the waistband and across the top of the chest. Mix the green dye in 1 litre (2 pints) of boiling water and add the salt. Add this solution to a bowl containing a further 1 litre (2 pints) of hot water. Allow to cool before adding the top and briefs. Leave them for 20–30 minutes before rinsing thoroughly, untying and drying.

SOFA THROW

So far we have dyed silk and cotton fabric or ready-made items, but most cold water dyes will also take well on wool, linen, rayon or viscose. A sofa throw needs to be fairly heavy, and this project uses wool lawn, which is sometimes known as nun's veiling. When you are dyeing wool, remember that it tends to stretch when it is wet and that new or virgin wool will still contain lanolin, the sheep's own waterproofing. You can either try to remove most of the lanolin by washing the wool before you begin or you can do as we have done here, which is to dye the wool straight from the roll, which adds a degree of unpredictability to the end result.

You will need

◇ 1 x 1m (3ft 3in x 3ft 3in) wool lawn (if the measure is narrow, you may need 2 lengths, stitched together)
◇ 3m (10ft) heavy string
◇ 10g (2 tsp) copper dye
◇ 150ml (10 tbsp) vinegar (but check manufacturer's instructions)
◇ 1 bowl, large enough to hold at least 3 litres (6 pints)
◇ 5g (1 tsp) black dye
◇ 1 bowl, large enough to hold at least 2 litres (4 pints)

1 Pinch the fabric in the centre and allow it to fall in drapes like a closed umbrella. If you are using a rectangle the fabric will not fall evenly, but this will not affect the end result. Working from the centre of the fabric, cross-bind it with heavy string to about 30cm (12in) from the bottom. At 7.5cm (3in) intervals bind around the shape several times.

2 Mix the copper dye in 1 litre (2 pints) of boiling water and add 90ml (6 tbsp) of vinegar. Add the solution to a bowl containing a further 2 litres (4 pints) of hot water. Allow the dye to cool to 50°C (about 120°F), then add the bound wool. If you have not pre-washed the wool you will find that the dye will take several minutes to penetrate the surface fibres.

3

4

5

3 Encourage the dyeing process by stirring the dye bath. Leave the wool in the dye for 30–45 minutes. If you have not pre-washed the wool, the shade will be several shades lighter than if you have, and for this reason the dye described here is fairly concentrated.

4 While the wool is in the copper dye, mix the black dye in 1 litre (2 pints) of boiling water and add 60ml (4 tbsp) of vinegar. Add this mixture to a further 1 litre (2 pints) of hot water. Allow this to cool. Remove the fabric from the copper dye, then place the tip of the bundle, the centre of the fabric, into the black dye, draping the rest of the fabric over the side of the bowl. Immerse about 20cm (8in) of the bundle in the black dye and leave for a further 40 minutes. Not rinsing out the copper dye before adding the black allows the wool to continue to absorb the copper dye. This stage can be messy, so if you cannot stand the bowl on a draining board, make sure that your work surface is covered with plenty of newspaper to absorb the drips.

5 After 40 minutes rinse the wool in cold running water and then untie. Do not wring out the wool, which will probably stretch it out of shape.

6 The naturally occurring lanolin will have acted as a kind of resist, and when you spread out the wool you will find small, irregular patches that have remained undyed.

6

SILK GEORGETTE SHIRT

◆

Different weights of fabric accept dyes in different ways. When they are tie-dyed, lighter weight materials and loosely woven fabrics tend to yield softer patterns, and it is worth considering the weight and density of the weave before you decide on your tying methods. For example, sharp, pleated designs are most effective on tightly woven, flat fabrics. Silk georgette, on the other hand, is a soft, open-weave silk, rather similar to chiffon or silk muslin, and you could use either of these materials or cotton cheesecloth or cotton muslin instead.

You will need

◇ 1 silk georgette shirt, either ready-made or one you have made yourself
◇ 3m (10ft) string
◇ 5g (1 tsp) each of dusky rose and dark grey dye
◇ 60ml (4 tbsp) vinegar (but check manufacturer's instructions and if you are using cotton remember to use salt instead)
◇ 1 bowl, large enough to hold at least 1.5 litres (3 pints)

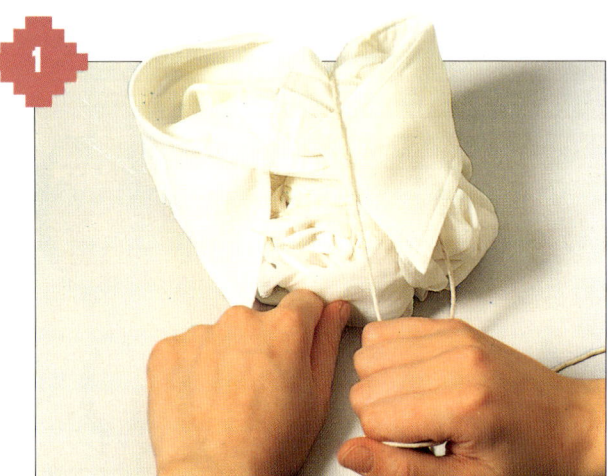

1 Bunch the shirt into a ball. Do not roll it, because this will limit the area exposed to the dye. Secure the bundle by wrapping string tightly around it. Mix the dusky rose dye in 1 litre (2 pints) of boiling water. Add 30ml (2 tbsp) of vinegar (salt if you are dyeing cotton) and add the mixture to a further 0.5 litre (1 pint) of hot water. Allow the solution to cool to 50°C (about 120°F) before adding the shirt. Leave in the dye for 20–30 minutes.

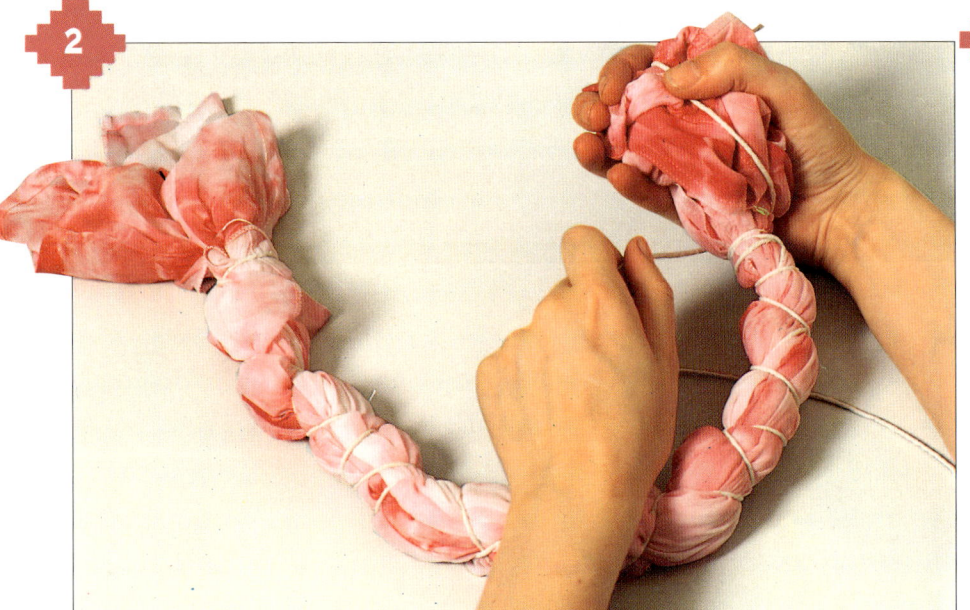

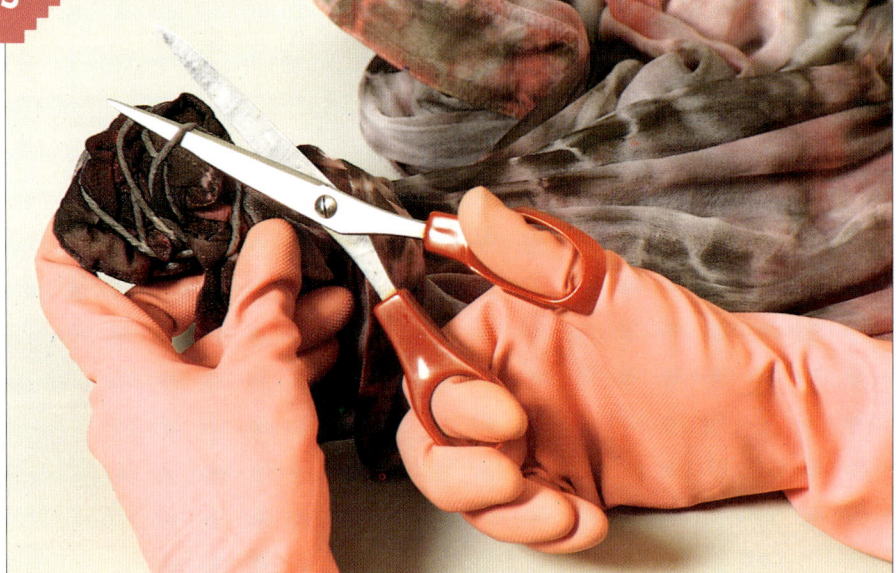

2 Remove the bundle from the dye, rinse thoroughly and untie. Dry the shirt flat to help avoid creasing and shrinking. When the shirt is dry, bunch the collar and neck into a ball and bind it with string. Loosely twist the body and sleeves together, and cross-bind the entire length of the garment with string.

3 Mix the dark grey dye as in step 1 and, when the dye has cooled, add the shirt to the bowl and leave it for a further 20–30 minutes. Remove the shirt from the bowl, rinse thoroughly, untie the string and leave the shirt to dry flat.

TIP

• Many open-weave silk and cotton garments contain a dressing or stiffener, and you will get better results if you wash the article before you attempt to dye it.

DUVET COVER AND PILLOWCASES

This duvet cover is built up in patterned panels, which are separated by plain panels of cotton lawn. Constructing large pieces in this way overcomes the problems of colour matching or under-dyeing that can occur with large quantities of fabric.

You will need

◇ 4 pieces white cotton, each 2m x 75cm (6ft 6in x 30in)
◇ 2 pieces white cotton, each 65 x 50cm (26 x 20in)
◇ Electric iron
◇ 52 clothes pegs
◇ 4m (13ft) string
◇ 15gm (3 tsp) dusky rose dye
◇ 5gm (1 tsp) cornflower blue dye
◇ 60g (4 tbsp salt)
◇ 1 bowl, large enough to hold at least 7 litres (4 pints)
◇ 2 pieces lightweight ecru cotton lawn, each 2m x 75cm (6ft 6in x 30in)
◇ 2 pieces lightweight ecru cotton lawn, each 65 x 50cm (26 x 20in)

TIP

• Working with large amounts of fabric poses certain problems, especially when it comes to binding the material effectively and achieving an even colour. When you are planning a project that requires a large amount of cloth you may find it easier to dye the fabric in panels and make the pieces into the item afterwards. Trying to colour-match panels that have been dyed in separate dye baths is, unfortunately, one of the drawbacks of attempting to apply a pattern to a large item in this way. However, even if you were able to fit the whole piece of fabric in one dye bath, you would probably find that the colour was unable to penetrate through to all areas of the fabric simply because of the mass of material.

ASSEMBLING THE DUVET

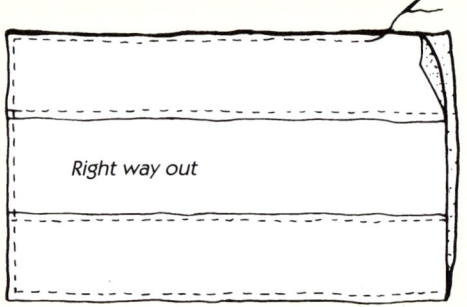

• When the pieces are dry, iron them flat. Assemble the duvet cover by stitching one piece of ecru cotton between two patterned panels for the front.

Right way out

• Repeat this for the back, then lay the two squares, wrong sides together, one on top of the other, and stitch three sides.

• We have allowed fairly generous seams in case the fabric shrinks during the dyeing process, but you have ample material to stitch French seams – that is, once you have stitched the three sides, turn the duvet cover so that the right sides are together and stitch around the same three sides to trap the raw edges in the hem.

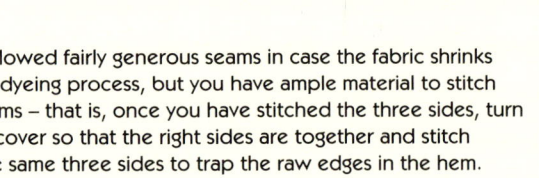

Inside out

• Turn in and hem the open edge and add fasteners.

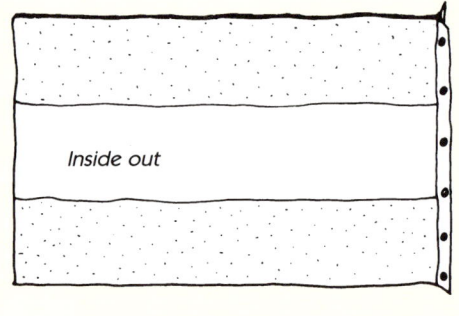

Inside out

• Make the pillowcases in the same way, stitching a patterned piece to a plain ecru piece and hemming the open seams.

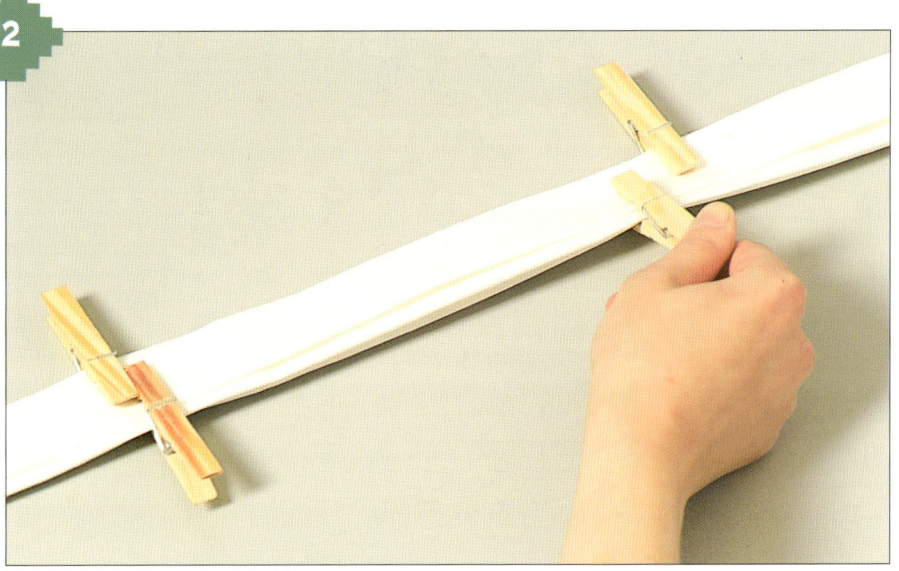

1 Iron the pieces of white cotton to remove any creases, then fold them, separately, in half lengthways and pleat them. Each pleat should be about 3cm (1¼in) wide.

2 Iron the pleats and secure them with clothes pegs on both sides of the pleat, spacing the pegs at intervals of about 30cm (12in).

3 Half-way between each peg, bind the fabric with pieces of string about 23cm (9in) long.

4 Mix the dusky rose dye in 1 litre (2 pints) of boiling water and add 30g (2 tbsp) of salt. Add this solution to a further 6 litres (12 pints) of hot water. You must use a bowl that is large enough to hold the fabric and the dye comfortably. Place all the bound white fabric in the bowl while the dye is still hot if you want a particularly vibrant colour. Leave it for 30–45 minutes. When the fabric is dyed, remove the bundles from the dye and rinse thoroughly but do not untie the bundles.

5 Mix the cornflower blue dye in 1 litre (2 pints) of boiling water and add the salt. Add this to a further 3 litres (6 pints) of hot water. Drape the pleated fabric over the bowl so that only the ends are in the dye – about 45cm (18in) each end for the duvet cover and 20cm (8in) each end for the pillowcases. Leave for a further 30 minutes. Remove the fabric from the dye, rinse thoroughly and untie the bundles. At this stage you can add an extra proprietary treatment to the fabric to make the dyes more permanent, but check the manufacturer's directions.

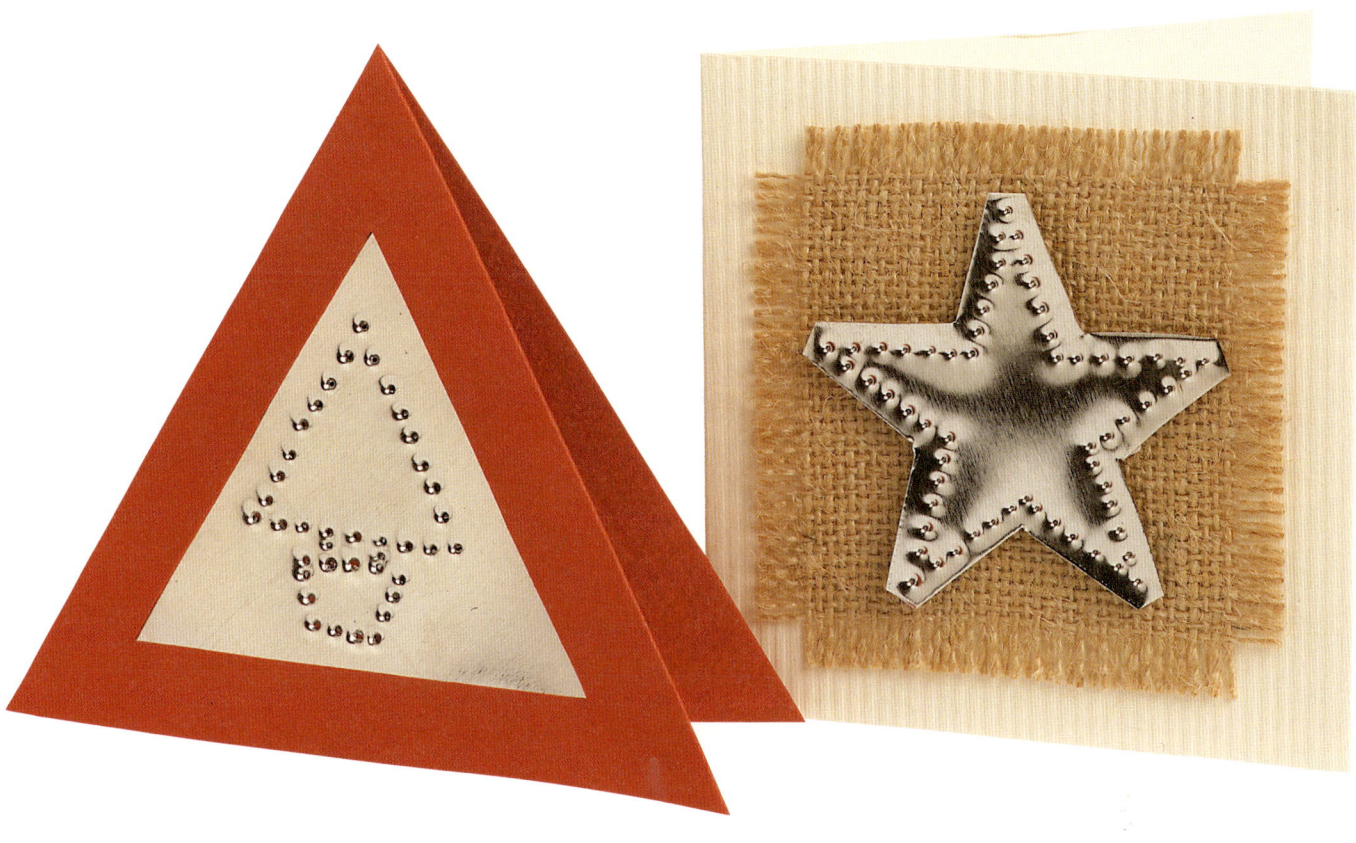

Christmas Crafts

Add a touch of originality to the festive season
by making your own decorations

BASIC EQUIPMENT AND MATERIALS

HARDWARE

SCISSORS. Have a selection of scissors ready for all your craft needs. Use small embroidery scissors for fine work, larger, general-purpose scissors for paper and card, large dressmakers' scissors for cutting out fabrics and finally pinking shears for making decorative zigzag cuts and neatening raw fabric edges.

TIN SNIP AND WIRE-CUTTER. These are tools used for cutting tougher materials, such as metal, wire or even twigs or plant materials that would damage the blades of your ordinary scissors.

CRAFT KNIFE. Scalpels and craft knives are used, with a metal ruler, for cutting straight lines and for cutting out tricky areas where scissors would not be suitable. A cannel knife can be used to cut grooves. A scalpel with a swivel blade is invaluable when cutting stencils. Have a blunt kitchen knife handy for scoring and cutting florists' oasis foam.

CENTRE PUNCH. A small metal gadget used for punching holes in metal or thick card.

PASTRY-CUTTER, CANAPÉ-CUTTER. Useful for cutting small shapes from dough or as a template.

HAMMER. Used with centre punch and for inserting eyelets.

LEATHER PUNCH. A useful tool for punching holes in paper, card and fabric. The star-shaped part revolves, enabling you to cut six different-sized holes.

RULER. A plastic ruler for general use and a metal one for using with a scalpel or craft knife.

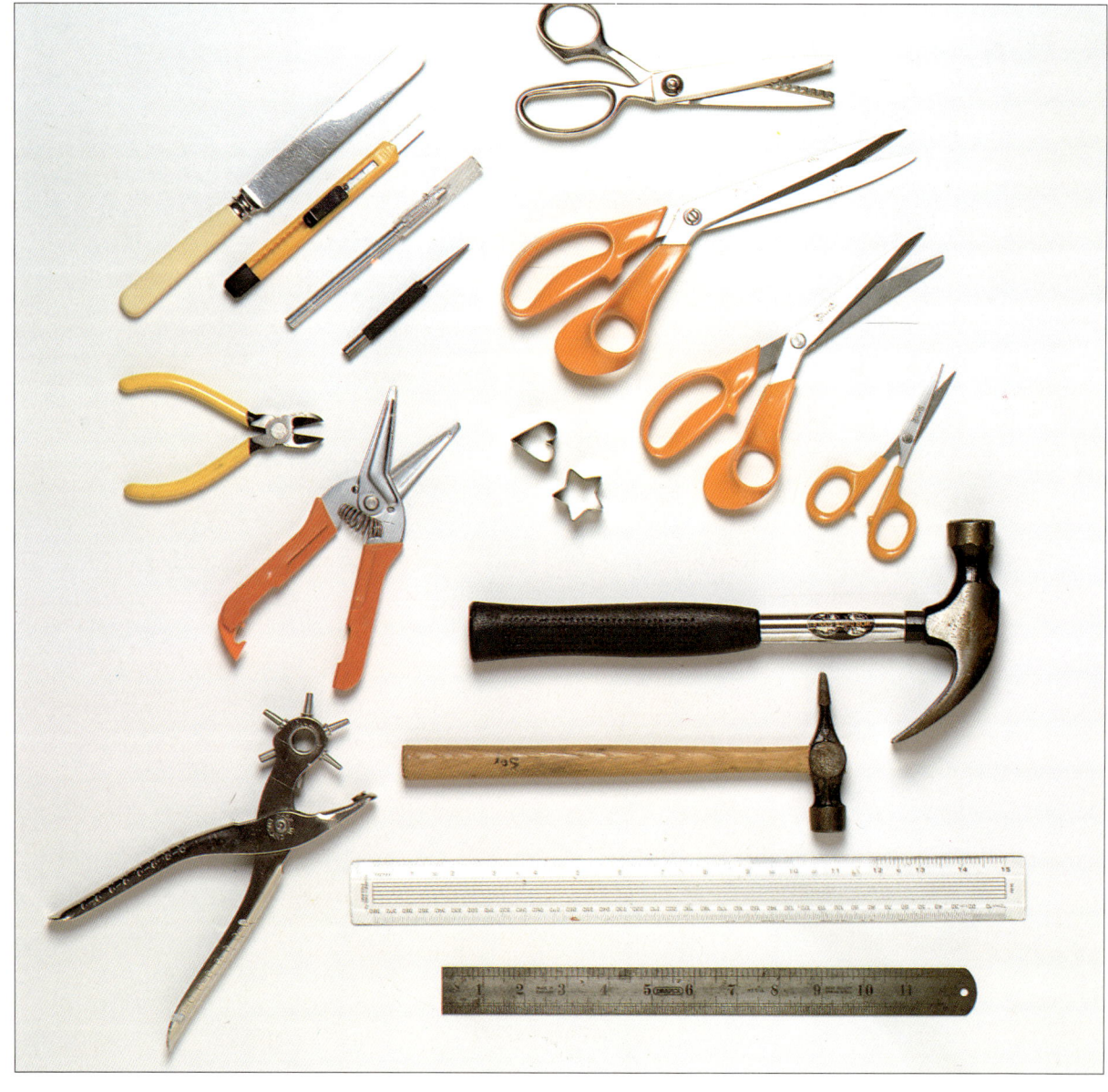

SAFETY FIRST

- Be careful when using sharp blades, scalpels, knives and scissors.
- Always use a thick card pad to protect your work surface when using scalpels or hammers.
- Use glues and spray paint in a well-ventilated room.
- Never leave candles unattended when lit. Always place them on a heatproof surface.
- Some of the projects in this book are simple enough for children to help with or to do by themselves, but children should be supervised when they are using scissors or craft knives.

PAPER

We are very lucky today to have a magnificent selection of paper and card to choose from for craft purposes. A variety of matt and metallic-finish papers and cards are readily available in craft shops, together with textured and corrugated materials and more unusual handmade papers. It's great fun to experiment with different colour and texture combinations. Remember to keep scraps for small projects such as greetings cards and gift tags.

HABERDASHERY

FABRIC. Build up a store of fabric pieces and scraps to use for sewing projects. Fabrics that do not fray easily are particularly useful.

RIBBONS. Ribbons are available in many different colours, patterns and widths. Use them as decorative trims or as functional ties and bows.

STRING AND RAFFIA. A more natural form of decorative trimming.

SEWING THREAD. Always have a supply of coloured thread at the ready. Sewing projects look much more professional when matching threads are used.

PINS AND NEEDLES. Use long, fine pins to hold your work in place. Have a selection of needles for use with ordinary sewing thread and thicker ones suitable for embroidery thread, string or raffia.

WIRE. Useful for wreathmaking and floral or dried arrangements.

BUTTONS, BEADS AND METAL TRIMMINGS. Use these small trimmings to add that special finishing touch to your projects.

TIP

- Don't throw anything away. It may be useful! Save scraps of fabric, ribbon, paper and card, odd buttons and beads, and use them to make your craft projects unique and interesting.

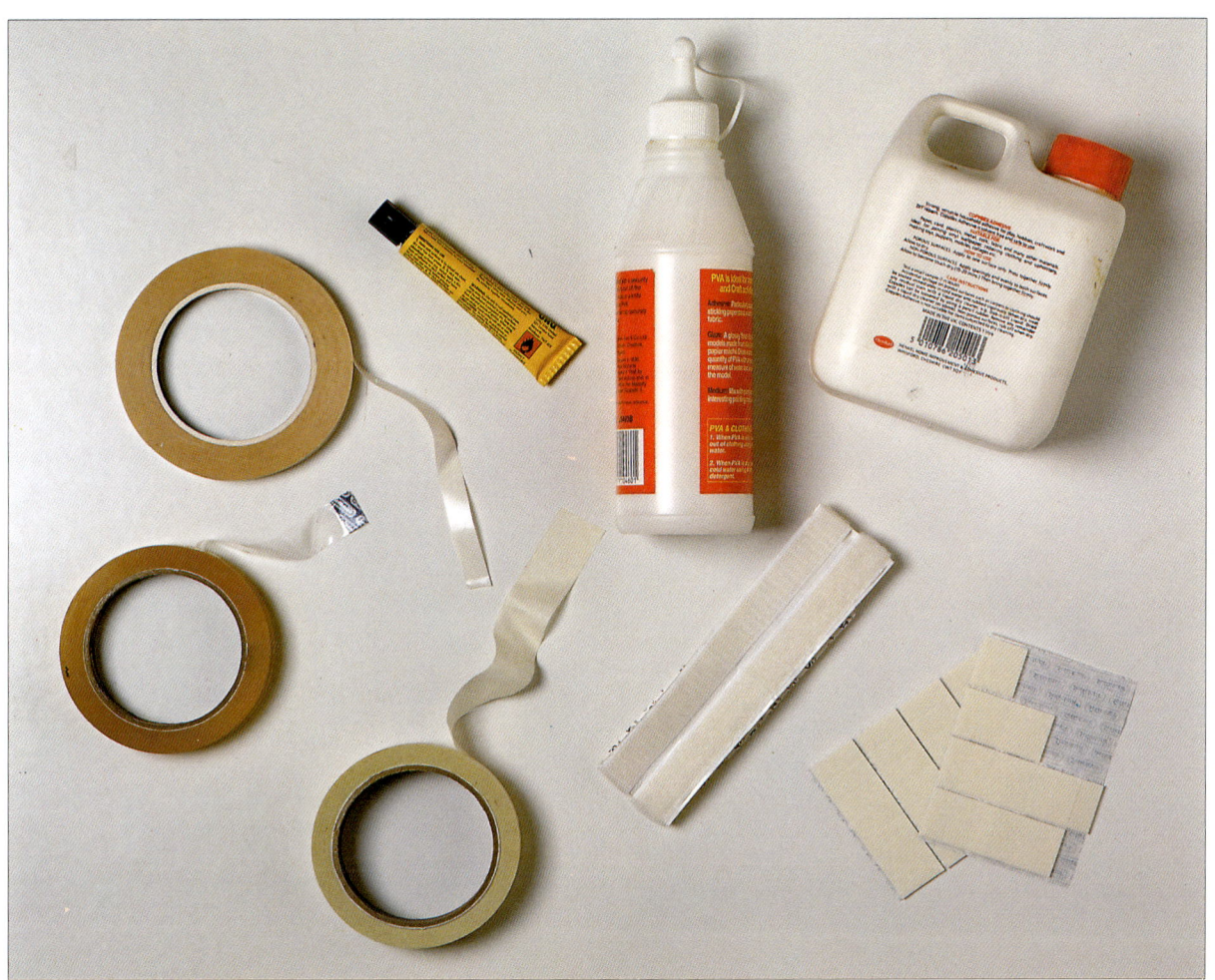

ADHESIVE TAPE AND GLUE

There are many different ways of fixing craft materials together. The success of your project often depends on choosing the correct one.

ADHESIVE TAPE. Double-sided tape is featured in many projects in this book. It is useful for fixing paper, card and fabric. Masking tape is low tack and is usually used for temporary fixing or for masking off areas. Clear tape can be used for paper or card but do not use it where the tape will be seen.

DOUBLE-SIDED ADHESIVE PADS. These are small foam pads with a strong adhesive on both sides, suitable for fixing most materials.

GLUE. Water-based glues are suitable for card and paper but you will need to use a stronger glue for fabric, beads or sequins. There are numerous specialist glues available for individual craft purposes, including those for metals and plastics.

VELCRO. This is a very clever form of fastening. The Velcro strip has lots of tiny loops on one side and hooks on the other; when pressed together, they hold quite firmly. Velcro is available in sew-in and self-adhesive form and a combination of both for use with paper, card and fabric.

PAINTING AND COLOURING EQUIPMENT

CRAFT PAINT. Acrylic paints are ideal for craft purposes, as they are quick drying and easily diluted. They can be cleaned up with water when wet but are permanent when dry.

SPRAY PAINT. Useful for painting delicate or intricate articles.

PENS AND PENCILS. Use soft pencils for sketching design lines or making tracings. Thick marker pens can be used for decorative purposes.

BRUSHES. Have a variety of brushes to apply both paint and glue. Always make sure to clean brushes thoroughly after use.

COCKTAIL STICKS AND SKEWERS. Useful for supporting craft items while they dry and for piercing holes, stirring paint and applying glue.

MIXING PALETTE. For mixing small quantities of paint or glue, though you can use an old saucer or dish for this.

CHRISTMAS WREATH

Nature has provided the basic materials for this delightful wreath. Holly, ivy and pine cones
are always in plentiful supply at this time of year. Hang the wreath on your front door or
use it as a table centrepiece with candles to celebrate the festive season.

You will need

◊ Long strands of variegated ivy
◊ Sprigs of holly
◊ Pine cones
◊ Small wire-cutters
◊ Florists' wire

1 Taking two long strands of ivy, wind them
loosely around each other to form a circle about
30 cm (12 in) in diameter.

2 Wind another three or four strands of ivy around
the base, tucking in the ends neatly as you go.

3 Trim the holly sprigs to about 18 cm (7 in) long.
Push the stems into the ivy base around the outside.
Fix the holly in place with short lengths of wire if this
seems to be necessary. Take care not to scratch your
hands: the holly prickles can be very sharp!

4 Finally, wind a short length of wire around the base of each pine cone, leaving two prongs protruding downwards. If the cones are open, this should be quite easy to do.

5 Fix each pine cone to the inside of the ivy base by pushing the wire prongs into the ivy base and twisting them together at the back, making them secure.

TIPS

• As this wreath is made from evergreen plants, it should last quite well for a week or more if kept in a cool place.
• When the foliage is past its best, dismantle the wreath and keep the pine cones for future projects.

STENCILLED INVITATIONS AND PLACE CARDS

Gold on ivory is a stylish colour combination for these matching invitations and place cards.
This project offers four different designs for you to choose from, each requiring a different skill level.

You will need

◊ Clear acetate stencil film
◊ Pencil
◊ Scalpel or swivel-blade craft knife
◊ Leather punch
◊ Textured paper, such as a heavyweight watercolour paper
◊ Gold stencil paint
◊ Sponge
◊ Ruler
◊ Scoring knife
◊ Sharp craft knife
◊ Metallic writing pen

STENCILS

1 Trace the stencil templates given on page 222. Place the traced design on a thick card sheet or a safe cutting surface and place a rectangle of acetate the same size on top. Use tabs of masking tape to keep the acetate in place. Carefully cut out the design, using your scalpel or swivel-blade craft knife. The star and heart are the easiest ones to start with. The holly involves more curved lines. The gift is a little more difficult. For the gift, cut out only the ribbon at this first stage.

2 Use the leather punch to cut the tiny dots on the gift stencil. These would be too difficult to cut with a blade.

TIPS

• Always use paints that are specially designed for stencilling as they are quick drying. This means that you are less likely to experience smudging. However, you will have to wash your brushes, sponges and mixing palettes quite quickly, before the paint becomes too hard.
• You could stencil some matching paper napkins, placemats or even a tablecloth for a totally coordinated look.
• Now you have mastered the art of stencilling in one colour, try two colours. The gift stencil would be ideal to start with. First cut out a stencil of the ribbon only. Then cut one with the dots only. Stencil the ribbon in one colour and the dots in another, but be careful to match the design. Try out your own designs when you become more confident.
• The invitations make pretty Christmas cards too.

INVITATION

1 Cut a rectangle of paper measuring 20 cm x 12 cm (8 in x 4¾ in) for each invitation. Mark the halfway point lightly with a pencil line. Place the stencil in the centre of the lefthand portion. Pour a little of the gold stencil paint onto a small saucer or mixing palette. Take a small piece of sponge and press the surface onto the paint. Do not overload the sponge with paint: only a small amount is needed. Now press the sponge lightly onto the stencil using a dabbing action. Stencilling is very easy when you get the hang of it, but practise on a sheet of spare paper if you are unsure. Allow the paint to dry a little and then remove the stencil carefully.

2 Beginning at the top of the stencilled pattern, halfway across the front portion of the paper, use the scalpel to cut carefully around the righthand side of the design. Stop when you reach the bottom, again about halfway across the front portion.

3 Using a ruler and a blunt knife, score along the halfway point. Then score halfway across the front portion, above and below the stencilled design, not across the design itself.

PLACE CARDS

Cut a square of paper measuring 12 cm x 12 cm (4¾ in x 4¾ in) for each place card. Mark the halfway point, then stencil the design as before but positioning the stencil slightly to the left of centre. Score across the halfway point, again avoiding the stencilled design itself. Write a name on the card with a metallic gold pen and then fold as shown.

4 Fold along the score lines as shown, so the stencilled design stands out of the folded front part. This gives a very simple 3D effect.

CHRISTMAS CARDS

Send your special Christmas greetings this year inside these unusual cards made from pieces of an old tin can! They're fun to make, and a card made by hand is always a joy to receive.

You will need

◊ Sheets of thin coloured card, some with surface texture
◊ Pencil
◊ Ruler
◊ Scoring knife
◊ Scalpel or sharp craft knife
◊ Pieces of tin
◊ Small hammer
◊ Centre punch
◊ Double-sided adhesive tape
◊ Masking tape
◊ Tin snip
◊ Protective gloves
◊ Hessian fabric
◊ Double-sided adhesive pads

The metal pieces we used came from the side of a large empty coffee tin. Use the tin snip to remove the top and base of the tin, then cut down the side and open up the tin to form a flat sheet.

FRAMED MOTIF CARD

1 Trace the card templates and motif outlines given on pages 223-224 (templates given for square, rectangular and triangular cards). Make sure to transfer all cutting lines and fold lines accurately. The dots on the motif outlines indicate the punch hole positions. Cut the basic card shape, then cut out the window, using a scalpel and a metal ruler. Score and fold where indicated.

2 Choose a motif for your card, then cut a piece of tin about 2 cm (1 in) larger than the motif all round. Place the metal piece on a thick card sheet, then place the traced motif on top. Hold the tracing in place with tabs of masking tape. Next, begin to punch along the dotted lines of the traced motif. Place the point of the centre punch on each dot and tap once or twice with the hammer. The aim is to make a clear dent in the surface of the metal, not to pierce a hole right through. Continue until the motif is complete, then remove the tracing.

3 Using the tin snip, trim the metal piece so it is 1 cm (⅛ in) larger than the window in the central portion of the card. Fix the metal face down behind the window, using double-sided adhesive tape.

4 Fold the lefthand portion of the card over the centre to cover the back of the metal piece. Fix it in place with double-sided adhesive tape.

CUT-OUT MOTIF-CARD

1 Cut out the basic card shape but do not cut out the window. Score and fold where indicated and make up the card as before. Cut a piece of hessian about 5 cm x 5 cm (2 in x 2 in) and fray the edges. Choose a motif and punch out the design as before, then trim around the edge of the design, using the tin snip.

2 Fix the hessian square to the front of the card with double-sided adhesive tape. Fix the metal cut-out motif to the centre with double-sided adhesive pads.

TIP

• If you cannot obtain suitable metal pieces, the same method can be used to punch design into metallic-finish card.

Stencilled Invitations and Place Cards
page 216

Heart

Star

Holly

Gift

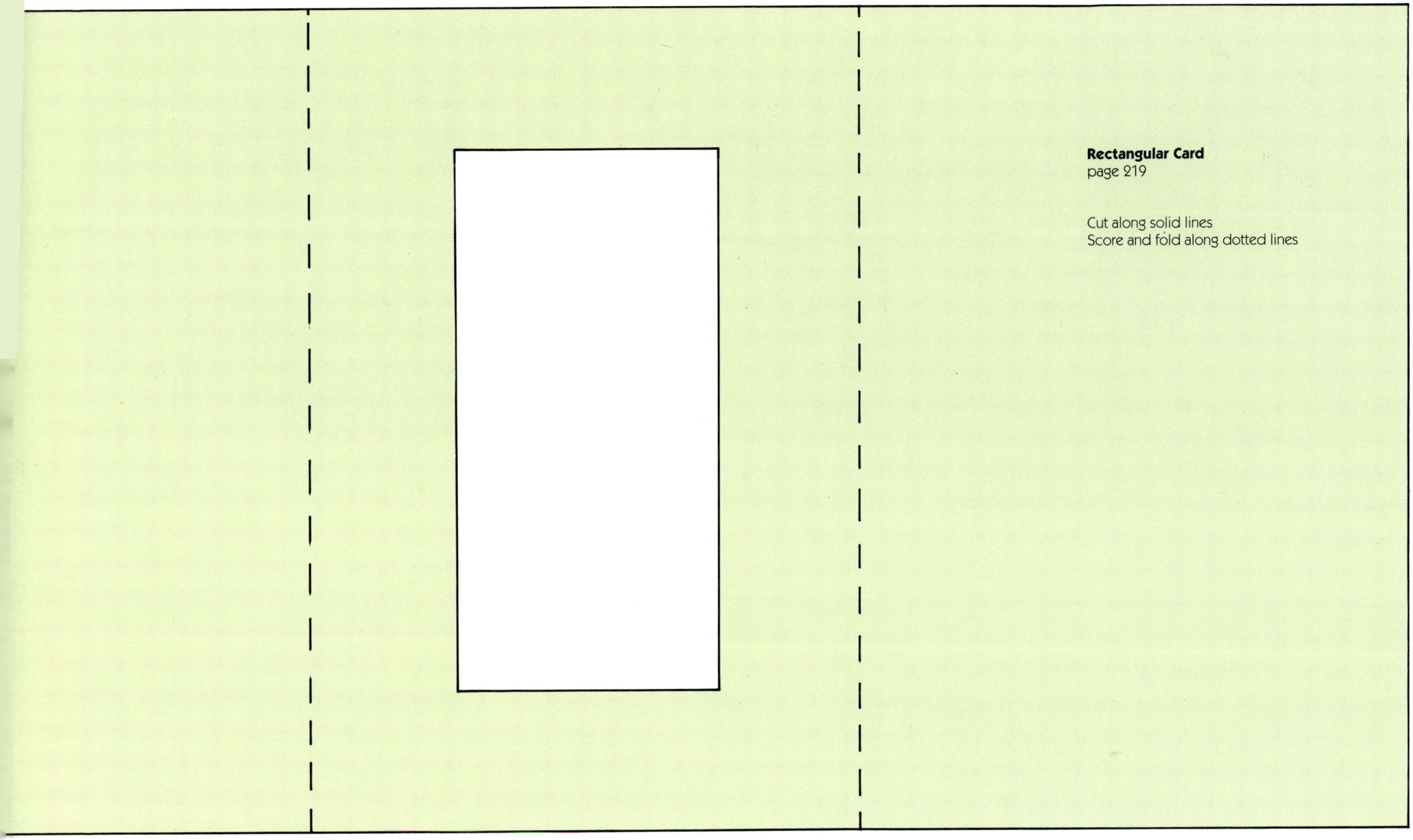

Rectangular Card
page 219

Cut along solid lines
Score and fold along dotted lines

**Christmas Cards
(Punched Tin Motifs)**
page 219

Dots show punch holes

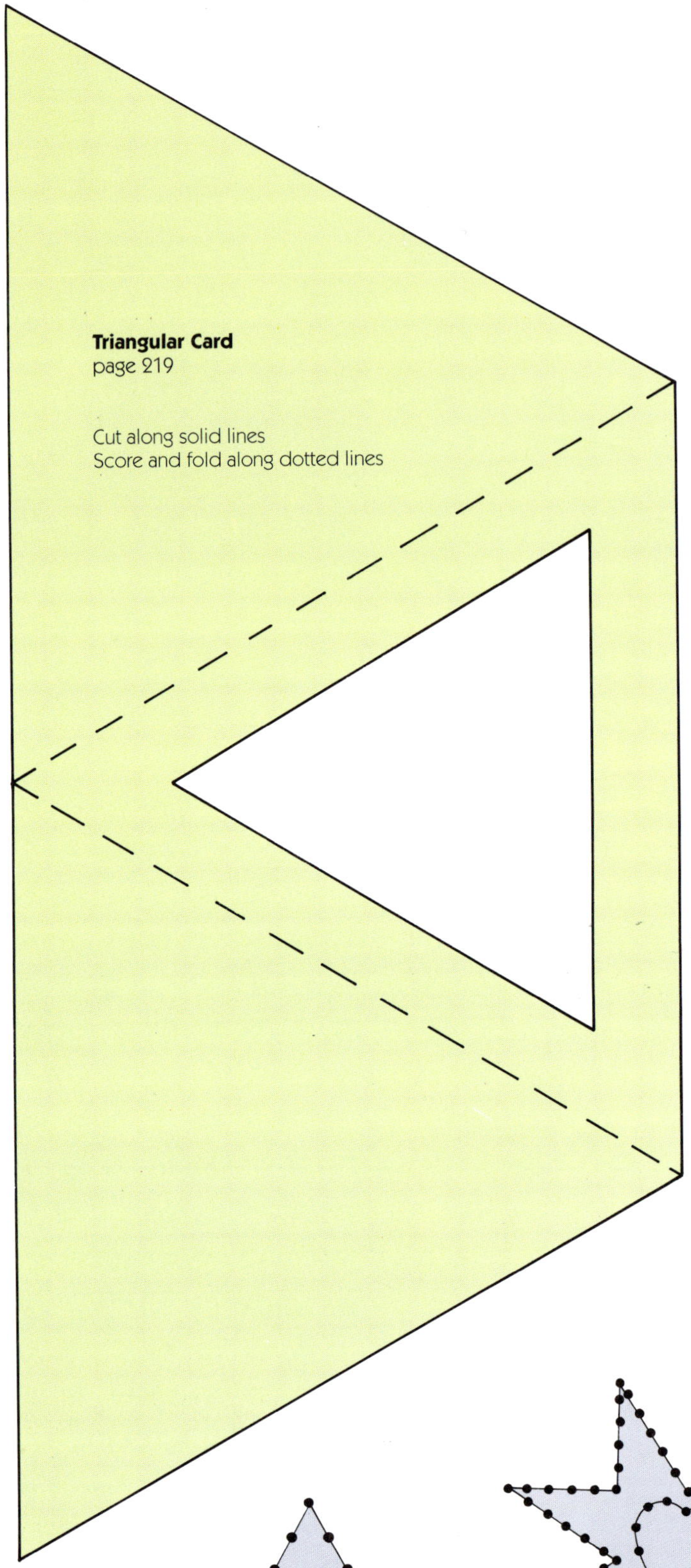

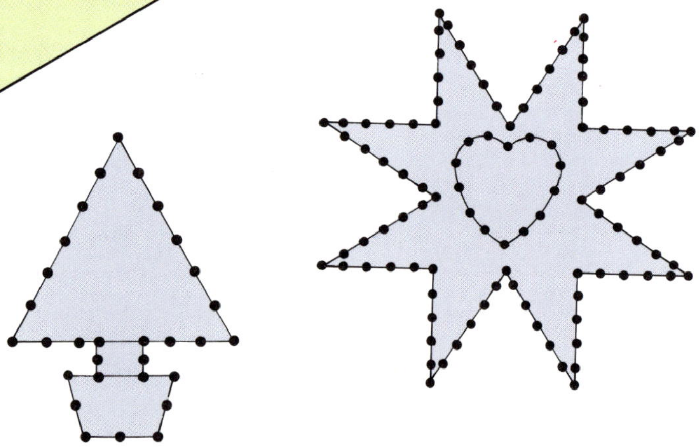

Triangular Card
page 219

Cut along solid lines
Score and fold along dotted lines

Square Card
page 219

Cut along solid lines
Score and fold along dotted lines

**Christmas Cards
(Punched Tin Motifs)**
page 219

Dots show punch holes